THE MINIMALIST VISION
OF TRANSCENDENCE

SUNY Series in Religious Studies
Harold Coward, Editor

THE MINIMALIST VISION OF TRANSCENDENCE

A NATURALIST PHILOSOPHY OF RELIGION

JEROME A. STONE

WITH A FOREWORD BY LANGDON GILKEY

STATE UNIVERSITY OF NEW YORK PRESS

Some of this material was originally published in *Truth and Method* by Hans-Georg Gadamer, English translation copyright © 1975 by Sheed and Ward Ltd. Reprinted by permission of The Continuum Publishing Company.

Published by
State University of New York Press, Albany

For information, address State University of New York
Press, State University Plaza, Albany, N.Y., 12246

Production by Diane Ganeles
Marketing by Bernadette LaManna

Library of Congress Cataloging-in-Publication Data

Stone, Jerome Arthur, 1935-
   The minimalist vision of transcendence : a naturalist philosophy
of religion / Jerome A. Stone ; with a foreword by Langdon Gilkey.
      p.   cm.—(SUNY series in religious studies)
   Includes bibliographical references and index.
   ISBN 0-7914-1159-1 (alk. paper).—ISBN 0-7914-1160-5 (pbk. :
alk. paper)
      1. Religion—Philosophy.   2. Transcendence (Philosophy)
   3. Ethics.   I. Title.   II. Series.
BL51.S6735   1992
211—dc20   91-33858
                                                         CIP

10 9 8 7 6 5 4 3 2 1

To Sue
whose love and friendship
have made it all worthwhile
and very real.
And to Debbie and Eric
of whom I am proud and delighted.

CONTENTS

FOREWORD

This volume is well worth reading. It is clear in what it wishes to say; it is fair, eminently fair, to alternative positions; and, perhaps most important, it is sensitive to the often clashing signals which both experience and philosophical reflection on experience give to us. Stone recognizes the deep and persevering presence of ambiguity in our existence—an ambiguity both in what happens to us and in what we do in response. In this he is "unmodern." (Compare him with the optimistic Humanists he discusses, perhaps too kindly.) Yet he is skeptical of large answers, be those traditionally religious and theological answers or metaphysical ones. He seeks to practice a "minimalism" that learns from both the theologians, whom he admires, and the wary naturalists, whose critical agnosticism he shares. While Stone is by no means alone—he is joined by a number of "younger" American neo-naturalists or pragmatists—nevertheless his particular synthesis of naturalistic caution with theological sensitivity and insight is to my knowledge unique and well deserving of attention.

Sobering events in the twentieth century even more than the weighty arguments of existentialist playwrights, novelists and theologians have for some decades blunted the now-incredible optimism of the early part of our century. A sense of the *ambiguity* even of critical intelligence and of liberal good will (note, *our* intelligence and *our* good will!) permeates our half-century; Stone shares this sense and seeks to incorporate it into his view.

What is perhaps more rare—among many existentialists as well as among academic rationalists—is his further accord with those theologians who have articulated a presence of *transcendence* in our common experience, first in the awareness of a 'shock of non-being' (Tillich), second in our consciousness of an 'unconditional' support and healing, and third in our experience of the lure, even the ultimate obligation, of the ideal possibility, of the moral *demand*. Hinted at with some embarrassment by both Dewey and Santayana, and scorned by Russell, this awareness of what one might call the 'objective value of being', an awareness echoed in our own values and valuing, has become more sure, more significant, and even more clearly objective in Stone's work. Hence his appreciation for and limited accord with the theological tradition in our century, an explicit alliance inconceivable to Dewey as to most twentieth century naturalists.

Still Stone remains a strict minimalist. Any religious, theological or metaphysical definition or ontological description of the ground of this transcendence or the ultimate source of these values is to him forbidden. He does not wish to talk either about God or Nothingness, however negatively or analogically this mystery may be delineated. This is, therefore, not theism but a frank recognition of the *plural*, perhaps the uncoordinated, sources of value in our widest 'natural' environment. Stone rightly calls this 'religious naturalism'; one might also term it an intelligent contemporary 'polytheism'. Hence despite his significant use of theological materials, he backs off as sharply from the limited process God, as he does from Tillich's unconditional Ground of Being and Meaning, or, of course, from the more traditional if revised deity of neo-orthodoxy or 'liberal' Catholicism. Whether one can on the one hand be consistently as 'existentially realist' as Stone is, recognizing the deep ambiguity of the human nature to its end, on the other as reticent about the extra-human grounds for confidence as he clearly intends, and *yet*, despite these two together, remain as serenely confident and doggedly hopeful as he wishes to be, is an unavoidable question for me.

Nonetheless, Stone's volume has given us what is to me a fascinating, original and well-articulated argument. He develops his position in relation to many of the most important contributors to twentieth century American philosophy as well as to a number of American theologians. Only wanting is a sustained engagement with scientific and linguistic positivism, unfortunately still the reigning if unarticulated self-understanding in academia generally. I am happy to recommend this volume to all those concerned for the status of value in our post-modern age and for all those who also enjoy a good philosophical argument.

LANGDON GILKEY

PREFACE

A friend of mine recently remarked that, "If anyone had talked to me about God a few years ago, I would have screamed. I thought you either had to accept the old idea of God or else nothing. There was no other alternative. And I sure wasn't going to accept the old idea. But now I realize that there are other ways of thinking about God." This book is an attempt to set forth one of these "other ideas." I hope my friend and others like her find something that they can get out of this book.

This book sketches a neo-naturalistic philosophy of religion combining a vision of this-worldly transcendence with an attitude of openness in inquiry and in action. At the center of this philosophy is a minimalist model of the divine.

In terms of its historical context this philosophy is located between the believers and the non-believers. Specifically it is situated between John Dewey and Henry Nelson Wieman, not as confident as the humanists in their anti-theism and not able to make the affirmations of most theologians.

I am joining with the recent revival of radical empiricism in religious thought as a viable third option to foundationalism and relativism. I believe I have drawn out some of the ethical implications of such a broader empiricism. I have also attempted to get clearer as to what we may mean by "God" or, as I prefer, the divine aspects of experience.

I debated about using the term "Minimalist" in the title. It seemed to connote lack of conviction. However, my wife pointed out that it conveyed a sense of strength, of getting down to the essentials, indeed, that the painter Georgia O'Keefe referred to herself as a minimalist. At that point the argument in favor of the word seemed irrefutable.

While autobiography does not determine validity, all thinking has concrete roots. It is reasonable for the reader to know something about the author in order to provide some context for the following ideas.

I was the pastor of three small churches over an eighteen-year period. I have also taught college courses in philosophy and religion for over twenty-five years. During this time as I have struggled to formulate my own beliefs, I have been in dialogue with my parishioners, students and colleagues as fellow companions in the attempt at understanding life and living it well. The following pages reflect these personal and professional concerns. These pages are written in a fairly detached and analytic manner, but the ideas have been forged in the midst of the confusions, despair, disappointments, joy and even boredom of life. These are, indeed, the truths that I live by. I, of course, reserve the right to change my mind at any point. As with any philosophy, it is a report on work in progress.

Since completing the work on this book I have read Charley Hardwick's *Events of Grace* in manuscript form and Emanuel Goldsmith has introduced me to Mordecai Kaplan. Hardwick's *Events of Grace: A Naturalist Theology of Creative Transformation* is one of the first major reconceptualizations of the idea of God to appear since the empirical theologies of Wieman, Meland, and Loomer and the process approaches of Hartshorne, Ogden and Cobb. Hardwick's physicalism and cognitivist "seeing as" represent a different way of doing philosophy of religion from a naturalist perspective. I believe that Hardwick's will set the agenda for discussion, at least among religious naturalists, for some time to come. Kaplan I find to be a kindred spirit, very akin to my minimal model, although a generation or two of global calamities make my view more tempered. His "revaluation"of the Jewish tradition, which reminds me so much of the revaluation of the Christian tradition by Shailer Mathews, has not only made Judaism come more alive for me but also has made me more acutely aware of the necessity to rethink the significance of the view of religious progress "from Old Testament to New Testament and thus from Judaism to Christianity" which informed so much of Protestant liberalism.

Personal thanks for their encouragement and thoughtful criticism go to Larry Axel, John Broyer, William Dean, Pete Gunter, Perry LeFevre, Langdon Gilkey, Leslie Muray, Bernard Meland, Marvin Shaw, Ed Towne, my niece Richilde Whalley, and, above all, to my friend and *Gesprach* partner, Harley Chapman. The community of inquiry which they have provided has a been constant exemplification of the inner-worldly transcendence spoken of here. Frissy Peden inspired the opening lines of this preface. Nancy Frankenberry read the entire manuscript and offered several stylistic and substantive improvements. For her support, encouragement, and helpful criticisms I am very grateful. My friend and colleague Judy Kaplow also helped with several stylistic and substantive issues and stimulated me with delightful philosophical conversation. I am only now beginning to guess at the challenge and grace from my family of origin: Walter and Hilda, William and Ernestine who gave me a deep sense of the realities spoken of herein and also the safety in which to ask questions. My wife Susan, my daughter Deborah, and my son Eric have been supportive and provided more creatively transcendent resources than they will ever know. In particular my wife has been most helpful in the struggle to give shape to these ideas. To the Board, administration, and sabbatical committee of William Rainey Harper College go my gratitude for a sabbatical to study John Dewey and Langdon Gilkey, the results of which are found in parts of chapters Four and Five. Special thanks to my Dean, Martin Ryan, who comes as close to exemplifying the virtues of an ideal academic administrator as I ever hope to find. The staff of the Library Services at Harper College, particularly Germaine Hesiak, has been very helpful and competent. And thanks to Lisa Larsen whose skill with a word processor is matched with her patience and personal graciousness and to Bobbye Levine, Betty Marscin, Pat Ciepley and Deanna Thiel, true professionals. Their competence has made my work easier.

Finally, my gratitude is expressed to Creighton Peden, Bill Dean and my well-remembered friend, Larry Axel, for their labors in nurturing a community of dialogue and mutually critical scholarship and to my friends in the Highlands Institute and the *American Journal of Theology and Philosophy,* which, for a time, will continue that mutual nurture and criticism. The philosophical community is in debt to the acuity of William Eastman and the many abilities of Diane Ganeles of SUNY Press.

INTRODUCTION

1. Closure to Judgment and Renewal

Our age is in the advanced stages of a process of secularization. Despite the continued vigor of traditional religions, the public life of much of humanity and the private life of several of us is essentially secular. This process has had some unfortunate consequences, including an impoverishment of the human spirit. Some aspects of this impoverishment are, hopefully, reversible.

One of the unfortunate results of secularization has been the loss of an experience of transcendence which provides a perspective, an Archimedean point, from which culture could be criticized and from which meaning could be given or restored to this world. Our Western secular life has become increasingly closed to resources of judgment and renewal because the criticism and healing of the Jewish and Christian traditions are largely lost through this lack of an experience of transcendence.

One method of ameliorating this impoverishment might be to reverse or check the trend of secularization by strengthening the forces of religion, by making the religious viewpoint more relevant, or by improving its communication. While these approaches may be legitimate or feasible, there is another avenue which bears study. This other way is to locate and nurture those resources within our secular life which tend toward the deepening of the human spirit by providing means for criticism and renewal. The present study is an attempt to work in this approach.

Modern culture is currently engaged in a desperate struggle against the forces of dehumanization. An important aspect of this struggle is the recovery of resources of criticism and renewal lost in the excesses of secularization. If these resources could be recovered

1

on a secular basis, an important gain would be made. I am not attempting to stand within the religious traditions and ask how they can be made more vital in the contemporary age. Rather I am attempting to stand outside these traditions and to ask about that in them which is worth appropriating today and also about that in them which can be appropriated from within a secular position.

Formerly Western culture had experiences of resources of criticism and renewal which the religious traditions helped to illumine and nurture with their transcendent perspective. As the secular spirit spread, the experience of these resources became less thematized and consequently weaker. It is probably neither possible nor desirable to recreate the full power of the religious myths which thematized these experiences, but it may be possible to use the insights of the religious traditions to analyze these aspects of our experience, in the hope that a more penetrating analysis will illumine these experiences within our secular life, remove unnecessary obstacles, and allow the creative potential within humanity to recapture these experiences.

Central to the religious understandings of these resources, indeed defining them, is the idea that they are indicators of or visitations from a transcendent realm or element, the loss or denial of which realm is characteristic of a secular orientation. It is my contention that even within our secular life there are unacknowledged experiences of resources of criticism and renewal which are in some way transcendent.

My purpose in this book is to develop a theory of this-worldly transcendence. It will be, in fact, a variety of religious naturalism. Such a theory will help us to apprehend and appropriate these resources of transcendent challenge and renewal. An appropriate descriptive term for this theory is a philosophy of openness.

Religion has provided some very important benefits for humanity, including resources of judgment and transformation, the loss of which is proving extremely dysfunctional for modern persons. Secular life generally lacks the attitude of openness to these resources of criticism and renewal which has characterized religious traditions at their best, although there are moments of openness within our secular life which could be articulated and nurtured. It is my concern to appropriate insights from the religious traditions, especially the Western, about transcendent resources of judgment and renewal which, if properly understood, might be available within our secular life. The clarification and nurture of these transcendent resources could provide the basis for a rehumanized secular existence through the recovery of openness to criticism and transformation.

2. *Two Moods of Secular Existence*

The loss of the experience of transcendence in our secular life has resulted in two quite different moods, the self-assured and the alienated. Given that the meaning of secularity is the loss of a transcendent source of meaning, secular existence will either find a source of meaning within this life or it will find this life essentially meaningless. Quite possibly there may be a vacillation or ambivalence between these two modes by an individual or culture, but these two represent the types of secular existence within which the ambiguities and dynamics of secular life are placed.

An analysis of these two types of secular existence is found in the writings of Paul Tillich.[1] For him the background of the modern mood is the spirit of self-sufficient finitude growing out of technology, science, and capitalism. This spirit of self-sufficient finitude is not our present spiritual situation. Rather Tillich finds the contemporary spiritual situation is one of anxiety and meaninglessness.

In Tillich's analysis both types of secular existence, the spirit of self-sufficient finitude and the spirit of growing anxiety are in agreement that there are no absolutes, epistemological, ontological, or axiological, that there is no transcendent grounding of knowing, existing, or valuing. The two types diverge, however, as to whether there is an immanent foundation within this life for knowledge, existence, and values. Having lost the transcendent source of meaning, secularity either tries to find an immanent source or finds no meaning at all. And having lost the transcendent source of judgment, self-assured secularity has no perspective from which to criticize its attachment to relative meanings. The secular world tends to be caught between a self-assurance tending to fanaticism and an alienation tending to despair. All too often "The best lack all conviction, while the worst are full of passionate intensity."[2]

The common character of both of these two types is, of course, that there is no transcendent source of criticism and renewal or help. A third type of secular existence may be possible, providing that a recovery of transcendence within the secular is possible. It is the purpose of this study to provide a new way of understanding and apprehending the appearance of transcendence within the secular, of this-worldly transcendence. It is hoped that such an understanding will help make possible this third type of secular existence, one which passes beyond both self-assurance and alienation, finding resources of criticism and meaning wherever the transcendent is experienced within the secular world.

One more concept should be introduced, the notion of openness. Openness is the orientation of an individual or group which is receptive to a transcendent source of criticism and renewal. The opposite of openness is closure. Let us note carefully that closure is neither identical with nor distinct from the secular. They are intersecting domains. Obviously much of the secular is closed to transcendence. Yet there are, as I hope to indicate, areas of openness within the secular. The religious world is, of course, open in principle to transcendent resources. However, as both H. Richard Niebuhr, in his discussion of henotheism within the official monotheism of the West, and Paul Tillich, in his discussion of heteronomy with the churches, have shown, there can be closure within the religious sphere.[3] There is this one difference between the religious and the secular concerning their relation to closure. The language and ritual which thematize the experience of the ultimate are present in the religious but absent in the secular. With the progress of secularization, the struggle against closure is now no longer within the religious alone or between the religious and the secular. This struggle now also takes place within both realms.[4]

3. Towards a Secularity of Openness

Both of the two types of secular existence result in serious dehumanization. The alienated type has lost the sense of the meaning to life, and in our time, has become almost synonymous with dehumanized existence. The self-assured type of existence leads often to a loss of humanity in two ways. In the first place, as Tillich points out, in our era it has been associated with a self-assertive spirit. Following Tillich, we can say that this spirit has reduced the knowable to the scientifically understandable, the real to the manipulable or manageable, and the good to the economically efficient. And those whom it does not incorporate into its system it subjugates into the exploited. In either case it unleashes forces tending to dehumanize those both within and without. I do not wish to argue either the extent or the intensity of this spirit. Rather I merely want to point out that the tendency towards dehumanization is at work in the world today, regardless of how far it has progressed. In the second place, when the immanent source of meaning fails, a disillusionment sets in, providing a transition from the self-assured type to the alienated. I do not claim that dehumanization is total, but that it is present.

One strategy in the face of this would be to achieve a recovery of the attitude of openness to transcendence. The renewal of the religious orientation alone is not enough, for closure to the transcendent can occur in both the religious and the secular worlds. The concept of God can be either a lid cutting off transcendence or the Archimedean point of transcendence. The effort should be made to recover openness to transcendence. Many people are engaged in this attempt within the religious sphere. However, since the secular orientation is becoming increasingly dominant, at least for a time, the writer has placed his effort in the task of attempting to recover the openness to transcendence within the secular.

If the secular experience of transcendence can be recovered, the resources of criticism and renewal necessary for a rehumanization of our existence may be at hand. If such a recovery is possible within the secular sphere, then a third type of secular existence, a secularity of openness, might be possible.

4. Plan of the Book

The following chapters will develop the theory of this-worldly transcendence as follows. Chapter One will develop a minimal model of transcendence. It will be, in effect, a tentative conceptualization of the immanent divine, of what can be affirmed of God (or in place of God) when we cannot make a full ontological affirmation of an ultimate reality. It will be a model which will at least give us a conceptual framework to explore the this-worldly experiences of transcendence. This is followed by a chapter exploring some of the historical context of this vision of transcendence. Chapter Three will develop some ethical implications of this theory. In Chapter Four various questions regarding language and experience will be discussed. In the final chapter I will try to show the merits of this approach by dialogue with a variety of contemporary thinkers: those representing a more theistic approach to life, those with a more clearly non-theistic outlook, and those representing a radical transformation of a theistic outlook.

5. Sources

In methodology and philosophy of language I have learned much from the radical empiricism of William James, John Dewey, Bernard Meland, Whitehead's *Modes of Thought* and (in today's intellectual climate dare I say?) from Henri Bergson. I have sought to balance this generous empiricism with an appreciation of the attempts of Henry Nelson Wieman and Bernard Loomer, formerly philosophers of religion of The University of Chicago Divinity School, to bring clarity to experience.

The metaphysics of naturalism involved in this approach owes much to John Dewey, Henry Nelson Wieman, and C. S. Pepper. This naturalism tries to articulate a sense of "depth," of this-worldly transcendence (in my more poetic moments, I like to speak of "the Divine"). In seeking to expand naturalism to include this sense of transcendence I have learned much from, even where disagreeing with, certain theologians.

The specific viewpoint in philosophy of religion I am trying to articulate is a minimalist position situated in between Religious Humanism on the one hand and Wieman on the other. This minimalism is akin to John Dewey, again with disagreements. The specific inspiration for this minimalism probably came in my early reading of Henry Nelson Wieman's *Religious Experience and Scientific Method.* According to Wieman, God

> would be those most important conditions which, taken collectively, constitute the Something which must have supreme value for all human living. The word God, taken with its very minimum meaning, is the name for this Something of supreme value. God may be much more than this, but he is certainly this by definition. In this sense, with this minimum meaning, God cannot be denied. His existence is absolutely certain.[5]

What I have done in these pages is to retain the sense of plurality in the phrase "collectively" and to soften the absolute certainty to a more appropriate tentativness.

A line of reflection upon the notion of a finite deity can be traced back from Edgar Sheffield Brightman through William James to John Stuart Mill, with a nod toward David Hume. However, the ontological reticence implicit in this reflection has not been carried through radically and completely by this line. It has been said that modern man is modest about what he claims to know but not about what he doesn't know. I attempt to speak to this charge of arrogant skepticism by acknowledging that the ontological reticence underlying the naturalism to be set forth in this book is a metaphysical position and needs whatever justification a metaphysical position can muster. Empiricism, radical or otherwise, cannot be itself defended on empirical grounds and I have attempted to be appropriately modest about my claims concerning the limits of our knowledge and as clear as possible about the type of justification possible for this position.

The theologians I have learned most from, despite my disagreement on the key essential of an ontologically supreme ultimate, include Bernard Meland, Bernard Loomer, Paul Tillich, the Niebuhr brothers and Langdon Gilkey. I have found it important to listen to these theologians. They have convictions without being dogmatic. They have a sophisticated knowledge of part of the history of ideas in our civilization and of the pragmatic function of religion in our lives. They are among the most profound observers of the modern world. They understand the competing symbol systems of the modern world better than many philosophers. Above all they are self-conscious and hard working practitioners of the art of disciplined reflection.

CHAPTER ONE

A MODEL OF DIVINE IMMANENCE

The question of the existence of God or of an ontologically superior reality or ground of being is far from settled for many people. Some claim to have proved the existence of God. But these proofs are far from convincing to many people who have examined the arguments carefully. There are serious difficulties with all of the major types of argument for the existence of God. Each makes a leap over a gap in the argument at a crucial point. We need not rehearse the standard criticisms of these approaches. We need merely say that these criticisms have never been decisively silenced. Their persistence suggests serious weaknesses in the philosophical arguments for the existence of God.

Appeal to revelation or religious authority is also open to objection. To accept a revelation or authority as genuine is already to affirm the reality of God. Why should we accept the claim of one revelation over that of another? The Qu'rān seems as self-authenticating as does the Bible. The Baha'u'llah has credentials at least as good as any other alleged bearer of revelation.

Still others claim that belief must be a matter of a leap of faith, a personal decision. But why leap into faith? Why not leap toward a denial of God or why leap at all? Granted that reasons can be given for belief, these reasons are open to dispute and are far from convincing to many people who have examined them.

If there is no God or analogous reality, is there anything left to believe in? It is the writer's contention that there is a third alternative to the dichotomy between theism and secular humanism. The purpose of this book is to explore the possibility of this alternative, to sketch a philosophy of religious naturalism with a minimal model of the immanent divine.

On the one hand some people make a bold assertion of the full ontological status of the Divine. This is based on one of a number of maximal models of divinity which underly both traditional theism

9

and many contemporary revisions of theism. On the other hand there is skeptical disbelief in such a bold assertion. In between these two positions, largely unnoticed save by a few thinkers, there is room for an affirmation of a minimal degree of transcendence. If a strong assertion is hard to defend, then perhaps a more cautious and more restrained model will be better able to answer the doubts of our age while providing some of the support and prophetic criticism which the traditions have offered. Perhaps a minimal model of transcendence can provide a genuine alternative to the choice between a doubtful maximal model and total secular humanism. If belief in God is abandoned, we are not left to our own resources. It is not true, as Nietzsche claimed, that if the absence of God is recognized we would be as if unhooked from our sun, condemned to plunge aimlessly in a meaningless universe.

1. The Model Elaborated

This minimal model is offered as a way of thinking about certain realities which provide resources of healing and criticism so badly needed today. The secular viewpoint tends to obscure these realities and renders us insensitive to them. The maximal models of divinity, on the other hand, expose these realities to the acids of disbelief and thus make an appropriation of their resources more difficult. This minimal model is an attempt to illuminate these resources without making excessive and counterproductive statements about them.

This minimal model may not provide a permanently satisfying standpoint for many people. Perhaps it takes a type of maturity to accept the fact that we see as if in a glass, darkly. However, for some of those who are laboring to recover or to keep from losing the sense of a transcendent dimension to life, this minimal model may provide at least a temporary campsite in the ascent of their spiritual mountain. For others, it may provide a more permanent, if restrained, way of thinking about the transcendent factors in our life.

At any rate, this model is an attempt at clarity as to what sort of reality there is corresponding to our thoughts about God. There is something deceptive, even dangerous, about this model. When we reach the limits of human understanding, the glass in which we see darkly puts a question mark over all of our attempts at conceptual clarity. Nevertheless, I feel at this point a greater affinity to

Augustine who said that we must speak, even while recognizing that we are in the area of mystery, than I do to Wittgenstein who urges us not to speak of that whereof nothing can be said.

Briefly put, the minimal model of transcendence can be formulated as follows: the transcendent is the collection of all situationally transcendent resources and continually challenging ideals we experience. The situationally superior resources can be called the *real aspect*, the challenging ideals the *ideal aspect* of the transcendent. This definition of transcendence is an attempt to state in the theoretical language of inquiry the meaning of what in the language of devotion we call "God."

There are five themes at work in the construction of this model.

1. This is a *minimal model*. Part of the problem with the maximal models of transcendence is that they assert too much. Their claims are too extravagant. For example, Anselm thought of God as "that than which nothing greater can be conceived." Aquinas conceived of God as *actus purus*. Tillich spoke of God as being-itself, the ground and abyss of being. All of these claims are extravagant in the sense of asserting a radical ontological distinction between God and all other beings. All of these are forms of maximal theism in that the difference in type of being between God and all other beings makes God to have the maximum of being and value and other things to have less. Often an attempt will be made by these maximal theists to use language which affirms this distinction in being and worth without bringing God into a comparative relationsip with beings and processes. Thus Tillich will assert that God is not a being, even the highest being. Nevertheless, maximal theism wishes to claim that there is a radical difference between God's being and value and that of everything else and that this difference amounts to God's superiority in a crucial sense in being and value to everything else. Such maximal claims are too extravagant in content and, often, in modality. However, if we define "God" or "the Divine" in a minimal sense, trying not to assert more than we legitimately can, we will gain in certainty. The less extravagant our claims about the transcendent, the more responsible our affirmations can be. The less we assert the more supportable our affirmations become. Thus the definition of God or the Divine is crucial and logically prior to making assertions about God. Therefore, in this presentation of minimalist religious naturalism we shall construct the minimal model of transcendence as an equivalent to a theoretical definition of God or the Divine.

From this minimalist theme four other themes follow. Each represents a minimalist alternative to a claim made by many maximal models of transcendence.

2. A *separation* is made between the *real* and *ideal* aspects of *transcendence,* between real creative processes within the world which are experienced as situationally superior transcendence and continuing challenging ideals. Most maximal models of transcendence affirm the unity of the real and the ideal aspects of the transcendent. However, from the minimalist perspective this unity is a claim which we do not have adequate ground for affirming. While I cannot definitively assert either the separation or the unity of the real and the ideal aspects, practically, to claim as I do that we do not have sufficient basis to affirm the unity results in a tentative and heuristic affirmation of the separation. The burden of proof, it seems to me, rests with the assertion of the unity.

Often religious naturalists assert one or the other side of this separation. One of the advantages of conceiving of the transcendent by means of the minimal model which we are proposing is that there is a clear assertion of both types of transcendence.

3. Since the unity of the transcendent cannot be affirmed, the minimalist approach remains with an affirmation of the *plurality* of the transcendent. In distinction from the affirmation of the unity of God, this minimalist model does not go beyond affirming the plurality of situationally transcendent resources and the plurality of continually challenging ideals.

4. This model also asserts this-worldly transcendence or *transcendence without ultimacy.* The model does affirm that there are real creative processes transcendent in a significant sense to our ordinary experience and that there are ideals which we may call transcendent. However, it follows from the minimalist intent of this model that it does not assert the ultimate efficacy of these processes nor the ultimate attainment of these ideals in the way which monotheistic believers normally affirm the ultimate efficacy of God's creative and redemptive process and the eschatological attainment of God's purpose.

5. As a corollary to these points, this model does *not affirm an intelligent purposiveness* to a transcendent Creator or Ruler, since presumably purposiveness presupposes a unity of individuality capable of entertaining such a purpose. As the theme of plurality indicates, such an affirmation of unity is not made by this model.

Each of these minimalist themes has an agnostic boundary. This model asserts that the transcendent is composed of at least the following characteristics which our experience reveals: real transcendent resources and continually challenging ideals. The transcendent in reality may have more than what our experience shows. There may be unity, ultimacy and intelligent purposiveness. However, there is not enough support for these affirmations for us to make them as publicly responsible assertions nor to take them as the basis for a personal faith. Hence our model makes the minimal assertion of a plurality of situationally transcendent resources and continually challenging ideals without ultimacy or intelligent purposiveness.

Conceived minimally, the transcendent has a real and an ideal part. These parts are the analogues in our minimal model of the polarities of blessing and challenge in the triadic schema of the religious experience which we discuss in the next section. There we hope to show that the three elements of our model: transcendence, the real, and the ideal, correspond to the three elements of religions experience: transcendence, blessing, and challenge. Thus our model will be a philosophical reconception of the object of religious experience. Furthermore, real and ideal transcendence will involve secular as well as traditionally religious life.

The Real Aspect of the Transcendent. The real part of the transcendent, defined minimally, is the *collection* of all situationally transcendent resources, that is, the *unexpected and uncontrolled* processes in the universe *in so far as* they are productive of good. These processes can be called "situationally transcendent resources." They are not totally transcendent but, as unexpected and unmanageable, they are relatively transcendent, that is, they are "situationally transcendent," or "situationally superior."

An example of a transcendent resource is the occurrence of unexpected healing. When the resources of a situation as perceived fail to heal the person but an unexpected healing agent enters the picture, then that agent is comparatively transcendent to that situation, provided that it is unexpected, unmanipulable, and superior in power and worth to the resources of the perceived situation. Traditional religious terms for such a transcendent resource are "miracle" and "the healing power of God." According to this model, however, the comparative or situational transcendent is the doctor, drug, healing power of the body or some interaction of these factors, provided that they are transcendent to the situation as perceived.

This paradigm illustrates the fact that situational superiority or transcendence is relative to a personal or temporal point of view. What is unexpected or uncontrollable for the patient may not be so for the doctor, and what is unexpected before the healing may become expected in a similar situation.

1. Defined minimally, the real aspect of the transcendent is a set or *collection*. It may have a greater degree of cohesiveness, enough to be called a unity or a unified system, but we don't have enough evidence to assert that. There is some degree of unity, of course, because the universe hangs together somewhat. Also this collection does have the common property of being productive of good. However, we cannot affirm that this collection has any more unity than that of a collection. The "real aspect of the transcendent" is a collective term used in the singular for the diverse creatively transcendent realities of the world considered together. It is a collective term in the sense that "wood" is singular collective term for diverse instances of wood. It is the sum of the forces of the world which are productive of good.

2. These processes are *superior* or *transcendent* insofar as they are unexpected and uncontrolled in relation to a perceived situation. This is the meaning of real transcendence within this minimalist perspective. Forces creative of good which are beyond our situation as perceived can enter the situation unexpectedly and hence are transcendent to the situation as perceived from within. Likewise, forces can be uncontrolled and unmanipulable. Such unexpected and uncontrollable processes are situationally transcendent.

Does this mean that such processes should not be studied empirically or that the attempt to control them should not be attempted? No, but insofar as such explanation and control succeeds these processes lose transcendence. They are no longer situationally transcendent. Does this mean that there is an overall process of gradual loss of transcendence? Probably not. Human understanding and control are inevitably limited and it is likely that there will frequently be situationally transcendent resources beyond our grasp. Since perception, understanding and technique never extend to the total system of all processes, the possibility of situationally transcendent resources is always present. This also means that we can combine the pursuit of scientific inquiry and technological movement with the attitudes of expectancy and receptivity to transcendent resources. Hope and openness are compatible with science and technology, although this does mean that the pursuit of truth is not the highest good and that the arrogance of manipulation in human and ecological affairs needs to be tempered. Science and technology need to be yoked with an attitude of openness to the real transcendent.

3. Many of the situationally transcendent processes which are creative in some amounts or situations may be destructive in other amounts or situations. Since we are seeking something analogous to the religious experience of transcendent benefit, we shall call the sum of these forces the real transcendent *only insofar as* they are creative of good.

Most situationally transcendent processes are ambiguous in worth. The "real aspect of the transcendent" is a collective substantive term with the function of an adjective, referring only to the worthy and valuable aspects of these resources.

To clarify the meaning of this model, let us show its application to two examples which are not normally considered part of the transcendent. First, are chemicals such as oxygen or glucose part of the transcendent? The definition is clear. Any chemical is part of the transcendent, in so far as it is situationally transcendent, that is, unexpected and uncontrolled, and also in so far as it is creative or supportive of good. In so far as these chemicals are understood scientifically or by pragmatic common sense they are not part of the transcendent. To the extent that they are controllable by technique they are not part of the transcendent. Further, whenever they are present in such amount or combination as to be harmful or destructive, they are not part of the transcendent. But when at birth or any other struggle for life their presence comes, hoped for perhaps, but beyond our control, they are transcendent resources. Within the minimal perspective, which is akin to naturalism, we do not say that the air and food are bearers of grace, but are gracious themselves. They are not signs of the divine but are part of whatever there is of the divine that we can know. In more poetic language, they are not signs or gifts from God, they are part of the real and visible presence of God.

To move to our second example of clarification, are we humans part of the real aspect of the transcendent? Yes, but again, only in so far as we are situationally transcendent resources, in so far as our graciousness is unmanipulated and is creative of good. Both of these examples seem analogous to what the monotheistic traditions deem idolatry, since the transcendent is our minimal analogue to God. However, we are not saying that either chemicals or people as such are part of the transcendent, but only in so far as they are both situationally transcendent and creative of good. The simple phrase "insofar as" is both the protection against the fanaticism which is analogous to idolatry and a harsh principle of criticism against the destructiveness of chemicals, people, and all other processes and forces of the world.

4. The situationally transcendent processes can give us security by keeping us in established ways, but they are also *potentially revolutionary* in relation to our established ways. They create, support and sometimes radically transform. This is the real aspect of the minimalist analogue to the frequently conservative but potentially radical nature of religion, so that the same religions which can support colonialism or a caste system also can produce such revolutionary figures as Martin Luther King or Mahatma Gandhi.

5. The real aspect of the transcendent calls for an attitude of *openness,* of willingness to grow and even, perhaps, be radically changed. This means that we should be open to resources of growth and transformation even when they are least expected.

The Ideal Aspect of the Transcendent. The ideal part of the transcendent, defined minimally, is the *set* of all continually challenging ideals *insofar as* they are worthy of pursuit. These ideals can be called "continually challenging ideals."

Let us take the pursuit of truth as a paradigm of the ideal aspect of the transcendent. No matter what level of understanding is achieved, truth continues to function as a goal in relation to which our theories are but approximations. The truth is an ideal, never fully attained, which functions as a continual demand that we push toward that goal. It calls for further disciplining of inquiry, refinement of concepts and deeper understanding. Thus truth functions as a continually challenging lure or demand.

1. Defined minimally, the ideal aspect of the transcendent is a *set* or *collection* of ideals. It may have a greater degree of cohesiveness, enough to be called a single goal or ultimate end, but we don't have enough experience or conceptual clarity to assert that. This set may not be capable of full mutual realization. Maximal realization of comfort and adventure, of liberty and security, full actualization of a person's potentials is probably impossible, given the inherent limitations of resources and the demands of survival and community needs. The "ideal aspect of the transcendent" is a collective term used in the singular for the diverse axiologically transcendent goals considered as a set.

2. These ideals are *transcendent* insofar as they continually challenge us to new attainment beyond our present level. This is the meaning of the ideal aspect of transcendence within this minimalist perspective and why they are called continuing ideals. Some ideals are not transcendent. They keep us in our routine or allow us to rest in self-complacency. However, when ideals challenge us, when they lure us to new attainment, forcing us to grow, we may speak of them

as part of the ideal aspect of transcendence. Thus any value which transcends in worth and claim any attempt to attain it is a part of the ideal aspect of the transcendent. In other words, a value or standard is an instance of ideal transcendence if it continues to call no matter what is achieved in pursuit of it.

3. Many ideals may be held in a destructive fashion. They become destructive whenever they are held fanatically, arrogantly or self-righteously. Generally speaking then, ideals are ambiguous. Since we are seeking something analogous to the religious experience of transcendent challenge, we shall call the sum of these ideals the Ideal Transcendent *only insofar as* they are held in a creative fashion. Since many of our ideals are ambiguous in this sense, our judgment of creativity and destructiveness will often be ambivalent.

4. Ideals can make us complacent or self-satisfied. On the other hand, continuing ideals are *revolutionary* in the relation to our established ways. They continually lure us to new levels, creating dissatisfaction with present levels of attainment and often promoting a sense of the worth of the pursuit. This is the ideal aspect of the minimalist analogue to the prophetic protest, to the potentially radical nature of religion.

5. The ideal aspect of the transcendent calls for an attitude of *openness,* of willingness to grow and even be radically changed, if necessary.

To summarize, the minimal model of the transcendent makes the following assertion: *the transcendent is the collection of situationally transcendent resources and continually challenging ideals in the universe.* In short, the transcendent is *the sum of the worthy and constructively challenging aspects of the world.* The central assertion of the minimalist approach to the philosophy of religion is that *the Divine (or God) is at least such as the minimal model asserts.* The Divine may be more than this, but it cannot be affirmed on a minimalist basis.

The distinction between openness to situationally transcendent resources and openness to continuing challenge finds a distinct parallel in Santayana's distinction between piety and spirituality. For Santayana piety is

man's reverent attachment to the sources of his being and the steadying of his life by that attachment. . . .

On the other hand, spirituality involves aspiration.

> A direction and an ideal have to be imposed . . . Religion has a second and a higher side, which looks to the end toward which we move as piety looks to the conditions and to the sources of life. This aspiring side of religion may be called Spirituality. . . . A man is spiritual when he lives in the presence of the ideal.[1]

An important parallel is that both piety and the minimal model's openness to transcendent resources refer to operative realities. The differences between Santayana's distinction and the minimalist model's distinction between openness to resource and openness to challenge is important, however. A major difference is that piety, in Santayana's conception, is retrospective, while the attitude of openness which we advocate is prospective. It is an awaiting, an expectation of resources of healing, of transformation. Further, these are not just any resources, but situationally transcendent resources. Without this note of transcendence, the key element in religion is lost.

This model is an attempt to articulate a concept of "this-worldly transcendence." It is an attempt to articulate what Bernard Loomer called "the transcendent qualities of the immanental relationships of this world."[2]

Is the transcendent the same as "God?" This is not a simple question to answer. It seems as if the question calls for a "yes" or "no" answer. But often such questions are inappropriate. Such questions may need to be revised to allow for a third answer. This one is such a question.

On the one hand this is a long, long way from most traditional (and revised) beliefs about God. On the other hand, the transcendent can function in a person's life much like the traditional God. It is real resource for living and a continual challenge for growth. This, I take it, is what the traditional notion of God does in a person's life.

My answer to this question is that whether or not one chooses to call the transcendent (as defined minimally) by the traditional name of God is a matter of personal choice and context. It is close enough to the traditional concept that one can extend the concept of God to cover the minimal transcendent.

The semantic decision made here is that the traditional term "God" can, whenever it is appropriate, be used to refer to the transcendent. When so used, the word "God" will be a complex term designating the collection of both transcendent real resources and the lures of continually transcendent values, imaginatively entertained in a unified fashion as an ontological and religious ultimate.

By "collection" I mean a set with a minimal degree of generic similarity, that is, the similarity of being situationally transcendent constructive forces or continually challenging values. To what extent the collection is merely a linguistic and imaginative convenience or convention we may never be able to decipher. However, the minimalist vision does not go as far as the maximalist tradition of Western monotheism in affirming a decisive ontological unity to this collection.

At this point I find myself in sympathy with Bernard Loomer's answer to this semantic issue. Having identified God as the "concrete, interconnected totality" of the world as a whole, of "this struggling, imperfect, unfinished, and evolving societal web," Loomer raises the question: "Why deify this interconnected web of existence by calling it 'God'? Why not simply refer to the world and to the processes of life?" Especially since on this view "God is not an enduring concrete individual with a sustained subjective life, what is gained by this perhaps confusing, semantic identification?"[3]

Loomer's identification of God with the interconnected, growing web of the world as a whole is a rather different view than the minimal model proposed here. However, his justification for using the term God is worth listening to.

> In our traditions the term 'God' is the symbol of ultimate values and meanings in all their dimensions. It connotes an absolute claim on our loyalty. It bespeaks a primacy of trust, and a priority within the ordering of our commitments. It points the direction of a greatness of fulfillment. It signifies a richness of resources for the living of life at its depths.[4]

My own approach to a functional justification for using religious language for plurality of situationally transcendent powers and norms differs in detail from Loomer. I tend to rely on a phenomenology of the transcendent, eliciting a triadic structure of transcendent blessing and judgment. But Loomer is fundamentally correct: "In our traditions the term 'God' is the symbol of ultimate values and meanings in all their dimensions."

In the language used here, the sum of the worthy and creatively challenging aspects of the world elicits a primacy of trust and a priority in our commitments. Thus it is appropriate to refer to the sum of these aspects as "God." However, since the real aspect of the transcendent is the sum of forces only in so far as they are creative of good and since there is no guarantee that the situationally transcendent resources will heal and rescue, this trust may not be requited. But this ambiguity and lack of guarantee is a continual possibility for the religious life anyway. I have been stimulated in my pluralistic understanding of the Divine by Harley Chapman's study of Jung. However, Jung has a sense of the divine ambiguity. For the minimal model while life is ambiguous, the divine is not.[5]

Many people tend to think in traditional religious symbols. Further, these traditional symbols are helpful in eliciting appropriate attitudes of openness and dedication and also in thinking conceptually of the objects of these attitudes. The term "God" has power.[6] By reason of its cultural and personal associations it (and its equivalents in other languages) has power to support and challenge as probably no other word in the Western languages. By showing the connection, however remote, between the terms "the transcendent," minimally understood, and "God," some of this power might be picked up by the term "the transcendent." This is a calculated risk.

It is a risk because the passion and familiarity of the traditional term can put an end to thinking, can lead to obscurantism, even fanaticism. On the other hand the term can repel people. It can lead to a fanatical and unthinking rejection of any viewpoint which uses the term.

In short, the proposal here is not that the transcendent is God. Rather, the proposal is that "the transcendent" and "God," minimally understood, share the same reference to transcendent resources and challenges. One term is more useful as an aid to careful reflection. The other term has more power which, like all power, is a two-edged sword. One term is in the language of inquiry, the other in the language of devotion.

If the reader finds the traditional term helpful, then she is encouraged to use it, but with the continual effort to keep the minimal meaning in mind. If the reader finds it a hindrance, then she should drop it. In any case, we should turn our attention to the concrete resources for growth and healing and to the relevant demands which can be discerned in our lives, to the experiences of the realities and challenges which constitute the real and ideal transcendent. That is where our attention should be focussed and is what this philosophy of openness seeks to further. We should use, carefully, whatever linguistic resources we have to thematize, celebrate, and nurture these experiences of this-worldly transcendence.

The key question, however, is not whether a person uses language about God. The key question is whether a person is open to transcendent resources and demands. Indeed, when properly understood, the first question resolves into the second. When the term

"God" is adequately understood, it will be found to refer to inner-worldly transcendent resources and demands.

II. The Triadic Structure of the Experience of the Transcendent

Even though the approach taken in this book renounces the full ontological affirmation of the transcendent which is normally contained in such religious notions as God or Brahman, the major religious traditions provide a clue to the notion of the transcendent which will be useful in our inquiry. This clue is found in the triadic structure of the experience of the transcendent as symbolized in these traditions. When this structure is abstracted and articulated, we are provided with a schema to help us explore our experience for clues to the minimal transcendent and also with the framework which helped us to construct our model of transcendence. In articulating this structure to use as a heuristic device, we will be bracketing for a moment the question as to whether there is any reality to which this concept refers and, if so, the nature of that reality.

1. The Triadic Schema

The apex of the triad is the sense of the otherness of the transcendent. The two base angles are formed by the polarity between the sense of blessing or salvific transformation on the one hand and the call to obedience or divine judgment on the other. In short the triadic schema is formed by the polar experience of blessing-renewal and demand-judgment and by the transcendent source of this experience forming the apex of the triad.

Following this schema we may say that the traditional monotheistic religious experience of the phenomena symbolized as "God" is an apprehension of a transcendent value-source. By "value-source" I indicate the source of meaning or value for a person or social group. (I do not mean to make a bifurcation between being and value, for a source gives being to value by way of creation.) By "transcendent" I mean that which is greater in power and worth, being and value, than things or events in the world as normally experienced by the person or group. There may be other value-sources in the world, such as food, sex, friendship, art, sleep, and so forth, but the transcendent value-source transcends these value-sources in power and worth.

The term "value-sources" has a dual implication. A value can either be factual or ideal as a goal. The transcendent value-source is thus both the transcendent fulfilment giving value to the person or group and the transcendent demand requiring value.

The polarity of the triadic schema is this sense of fulfilment and demand and the apex is the transcendent aspect of this polarity. As H. Richard Niebuhr has put it, the transcendent value-source is the object of both trust and loyalty.[7] As fulfilment it gives life and meaning. The fulfilment may be remembered as in the creation myths, be apprehended as present as in ecstasy or the presence of the Spirit, or be anticipated as in apocalypticism or nationalistic Messianism. The demand may be for performance of rite, the following of statutes, a return to God, a new heart, true worship, love of fellow man.

Normally the value-source is received as both fulfilment and demand. In Christian terms God gives both Law and Gospel. Conceivably there might be an apprehension of a value-source which involved only fulfilment or demand (a cosmic Santa Claus or god of wrath divested of mercy), but in view of the general presence of this dual reference, we can say that there is a triadic structure to religious experience: the element of transcendence plus the polarity of support and demand, of succor and obligation.

2. Illustration of the Schema

This triadic schema can be illustrated in a number of ways from the major religious traditions. If the schema is adequate it can be shown to cover major types of expression of the experience of the transcendent. A brief sketch of such a demonstration of adequacy could cover the following items.

The element of transcendence is included, as just indicated, in the experiences of the phenomena symbolized by the concept of God. The polarity of gift and obligation also runs through the major types of expression of these experiences. In the covenant-faith of early Israel it is the polarity of God's election and covenant love (*chen* and *chesed*) and the demand that Israel be faithful. In the priestly tradition it is the polarity between the observances and the temple as expressions of God's presence and as demands for observance and purity. In the prophetic tradition it is the polarity between God's deliverance and the call to return. In the rabbinical tradition it is the polarity between *Torah* as the sign of God's favour and as the demand of obedience. In the apocalyptic tradition it is the polarity between the final triumph of God's eschatological deliverer and the call to persevere to the end. In Jesus' parables it is the polarity between the coming of the Kingdom and the call to enter it, between God's mercy and the call to be merciful. In Paul and the later history of the Christian tradition it is the polarity between Law and Gospel, or between grace and good works. In Islam Allah is both the All-Merciful and the Judge who calls for belief and obedience.

This same triadic structure is present in the phenomena thematized by the other main religious symbols of the monotheistic traditions. The "soul" is the locus within the self where transcendent demand and succor are apprehended and responded to. "Creation" is a transcendent act of the giving of being, so that it primarily refers to the pole of gift. However, the Creator is the Lord, and creation bestows an obligation to the Creator. "Life after death" refers to a transcendent mode of existence on the other end of the time line. The polarity is present there in the dualism between heaven and hell, although hell represents not obligation so much as the mode of being for those who do not fulfil the obligation or reject the offer of succor. Finally the Torah, Christ, and the Qu'rān exhibit the same structure. They come from God, that is, are transcendent. Also, while they primarily are gifts, they contain the demand to remain faithful to their demands.

This triadic schema is also exemplified in the Hindu and Buddhist traditions. Both traditions are concerned with a transformation of the empirical self. Such a transformation exhibits the polarity of challenge and blessing. Even if the transformation is through "self-power" or self-discovery, its disclosure is salvific. Furthermore, the state of liberation or enlightenment is transcendent to the present state. In the Vedānta of Shankara, Brahman is the transcendent reality. The recognition of the identity of one's true self with Brahman is salvific, while the contrast between this identity and our present misery constitutes a challenge to move towards recognition.

3. Other Scholars

Among researchers who come closest to my triadic structure are Otto, H. H. Farmer and H. Richard Niebuhr. In Rudolf Otto the apex of this triad appears as the *mysterium* while the polarity of demand and blessing appears as the experiential polarity of the *tremendum* and *fascinans*. Herbert Farmer spoke of the polarity with the terms of "claim and succor" and indicated the transcendent apex as "absolute claim and final succor." Similarly Niebuhr described this schema as radical trust and loyalty.[8]

A more extended comparison with William James' articulation of the structure of religion is in order. In *The Varieties of Religious Experience* James asserts that there are three common beliefs to man's religious life: 1) "that the visible world is part of a more spiritual universe from which it draws its chief significance," 2) "that union or harmonious relation with that higher universe is our true end," and 3) "that prayer or inner communion with the spirit thereof—be that spirit 'God' or 'law'—is a process wherein work is really done, and spiritual energy flows in and produces effects, psychological or material, within the phenomenal world." Furthermore religion includes the following psychological characteristics: 4) "a new zest which . . . takes the form either of lyrical enchantment or of appeal to earnestness and heroism" and 5) "an assurance of safety and a temper of peace, and in relation to others, a preponderance of loving affection."[9]

This five-part common structure of religion is congruent with the triadic schema we have articulated. The "more spiritual universe" (1) is roughly equivalent to the transcendent apex of the triad. The effects produced by communion with this world (3) and the psychological characteristics (4 and 5) correspond to the salvific pole of the schema, while the relation to the higher universe which is our true end represents the challenge pole.

It is not always clear in dealing with James as to whether we are dealing with religious experience or the expressions of experience in myth, scripture, ritual or other forms. If we are looking for a common structure of religion our data will be these expressions of religion and it will help if we remember this.

Furthermore James comes to the common characteristics a bit too easily. This is most obvious in his assertion that the conduct of a Christian, a Stoic, and a Buddhist saint are essentially the same.[10] I suggest that, while there are some generic resemblances, they are not identical, however similar they may look to a distant perspective that has just been contemplating libertines or conquerors. In short, the common structure of religion will be generic in character.

A number of scholars have come up with a scheme with a soteriological emphasis. For example, John E. Smith articulates a three-fold structure common to all religions: an Ideal, a Need and a Deliverer. This is somewhat analogous to the three central ideas of Christianity delineated by Josiah Royce: "The Spiritual Community in union with which man is to win salvation," "the hopeless and guilty burden of the individual when unaided by divine grace," and

"Atonement." William James, in *A Pluralistic Universe,* has a similar scheme. Here he analyzes specific religious experiences which
he feels are particularly helpful clues to the nature of the universe.
Taking Luther (and perhaps Paul) as a paradigm, James refers to
feelings of renewal and transformation from experiences of failure
and despair to a new range of life. These feelings refer to a transcendent factor which James calls an experience of continuity with a
wider spiritual environment.[11]

Another soteriological approach is made in T. Patrick Burke's
thoughtful *The Fragile Universe.* Burke finds five elements in all religions: 1) a sense of the unsatisfactoriness of ordinary experience,
2) a contrasting ideal, 3) a path from the former to the latter, 4) a
hidden reality making salvation possible, and 5) the disclosure of
this reality. In terms of our schema, the first three represent demand, the fourth is the apex, and the fifth (and the third in one aspect) is blessing. Perhaps the most concise of these soteriological
views is that of Frederick Streng: "Religion is a means of ultimate
transformation."[12]

There is some question as to whether the soteriological views
have captured the common structure of religion. For example, does
the scrupulous conscience of the legalist fall under it? In any event
the soteriological approaches fall under the triadic schema which
we have articulated. Taking Streng's view that "religion is a means
of ultimate transformation" as typical of the soteriological views,
we find that the element of ultimacy parallels the transcendent
apex of our triad. At the same time the process of transformation
constitutes both the pole of blessing and at the same time a demand
to be transformed.

4. Methodological Comments

The triadic schema is an empirical generalization, as is any
similar articulation of a structure found in a field of data. As such,
it is hypothetical and vulnerable. Its empirical fit is testable by: 1)
its exemplification in the major types of religion, 2) its congruence
with other generally recognized statements by competent scholars,
and 3) recognition by competent researchers in the field. I have attempted a sketch of a demonstration of the first two of these means
of testing. Furthermore, it is corrigible in the light of criticism and
of fuller explication of the data.

An interesting methodological problem is whether we start
with a delimited field, such as religion (or art or disease or whatever) and then perceive and articulate the structure of the field or

whether we articulate a structure based on a few paradigms and then delimit the field by means of the extent of the instantiation of this structure. This is, of course, similar to the problem of definition in logic or semantics.

I suspect that what happens is that there is a reciprocal determination of structure by a field and of field by structure as the process of inquiry unfolds. An approach which naively follows Aristotelian assumptions (unlike Aristotle himself) tends to assume that fields of inquiry are clearly articulated. Wittgenstein's challenge to conceptual clarity with his discussion of family resemblance is surely a needed corrective to the former approach. But if the former approach can suffer from premature closure, a refusal to delimit a field can likewise result in never attempting closure. Talk of family resemblances may result in giving up the search for the common structure by declaring too soon that it has none.

Given the methodological stance of the reciprocal determination of field and structure, attention needs to be spent on the main boundary disputes. In terms of the present inquiry, do Theravāda Buddhism, the Way of Confucius, and such secular analogues of religion as Marxist-Leninism or Maoism qualify as religions? Such cases as Theravāda and Confucius need not detain us. The fine points of scholarship and interpretation are matters of controversy. Clearly the polarity of demand and benefit is present in both. As to whether transcendence can be said to be genuinely present in these cases depends in part on how transcendence is defined.

The secular analogues to religion, what Tillich called "quasi-religions," are a different matter. In general we can define a religion as a cultural system with an explicit reference to a transcendent direction, while the quasi-religions do not make such explicit reference.

Our triadic structure is not the only structure that could be articulated from the field of religion. The schemas of William James, John E. Smith, T. P. Burke and Frederick Streng are examples of alternative schemas. My claim here is not that my schema is superior to the others, but rather that it is as adequate to the facts as the alternative structures. The reason why I employ it is that it provided the foundation for the minimal model and thus is basic to the rest of this philosophical approach to religion. Any structure will be articulated in reference to the data of the field and in view of the function of the schema in furthering inquiry. (Smith is quite clear about the function of his schema in understanding religious phenomena.) In other words, purpose helps shape (but does not dictate) the articulation of the structure. Therefore, a schema is to be tested not only for clarity and empirical fit but also for its pragmatic adequacy in further inquiry.

The triadic schema was shaped to provide: 1) a framework to help us construct our minimal model of transcendence, 2) a direction for exploring our experience for clues to transcendence, and 3) a foundation for the criticism and renewal of secular life, both cultural/social and personal.

We have now completed our minimal model of transcendence and its basis in the structure of the experience of transcendence in religion. The problem before us now is to provide a case for the minimal model.

III. A Case for the Model

A rigorous proof for the adequacy of this or any model of transcendence cannot be given. Nevertheless, a case for it can be made, even though the argument will not be conclusive. In the end we will be left with a wager, but it will be a reasoned and weighted wager with a presumption that one side is more likely to be true.

This model is the outgrowth of an ontological commitment in regard to the reality of God considered as an ontological ultimate, a stance of ontological modesty. This ontological stance must be argued for the same as any ontological position must be argued for, that is, on the grounds that it seems, at least to the writer, to be the most adequate of available outlooks.

Ontological reasonings do not rest on a simple empirical basis, although empirical evidence may have some relevance to them. The type of empirical epistemology which rejects ontological reasoning as non-empirical seems to beg the question. On the other hand, our position of ontological restraint is itself an ontological position and cannot be simply argued for on the basis of empiricism without some attempt at justification.

An ontological position cannot be proved, but it can be argued for. It cannot be proved, for one thing, because it is a fundamental position in terms of which criteria of proof themselves are based. But a case for an ontological position can be made, although such an argument will be controversial and not conclusive. Chapman and Robert Neville, for example, are vigorous contemporary defenders of an ontologically supreme ultimate.[13]

1. The Negative Argument

One important, albeit negative, argument for the position of ontological restraint is that none of the major arguments for the reality of God considered maximally as an ontological ultimate make their case. While the following list does not exhaust all possible justification procedures, it probably covers the major types. A full refutation of these arguments is not possible here. However, a sketch of the weaknesses of these arguments will help indicate the objections which can be raised against them.

1) Empirical justification will not work. Although I do advocate a type of radical empiricism in religion, as I discuss in chapter four, the outcome is minimal. It is not pursued to a God or other ontologically supreme reality. D. C. Macintosh and H. N. Wieman may be taken as representatives of this approach. Macintosh starts by defining God as the Object of religious dependence and the Source of salvation. However, he extends the character of this Object and Source beyond what experience yields. For example, he defines God's absoluteness as "meaning absolute satisfactoriness as Object of religious dependence, absolute sufficiency for man's religious needs."[14]

Wieman also goes beyond an empirical justification. As he puts it, the creative good is the absolute good, that is, "what is good under all conditions and circumstances." Further, the creative event is "a single, total event continuously recurrent in human existence." A careful analysis would show that the singularity of this event is also not capable of empirical justification.[15] (See below in chapter four.)

2) The history of ontological argumentation for the reality of God considered maximally also offers slim hope for a firm basis for justification. Three common types of reasoning for God as an ontological ultimate are the ontological, the cosmological, and the argument that God is the necessary presupposition of an inescapable human endeavor. I shall indicate difficulties in examples from each type.

Hartshorne's Modal Arguments are typical of the ontological arguments. The core of the weakness of these arguments lies in the ambiguity of the meaning of "necessity." Hartshorne argues correctly that the modal arguments assume that the existence of a perfect being is in the mode of necessity, not contingency. However, logical or modal necessity is not the same as real necessity. The second weakness is that, even if the modal arguments were valid, they would only give us a necessarily existing being, not the object of religious devotion. I do not see how we can go from a necessarily existent being to the "fellow-sufferer who understands."[16] (See below in chapter five.)

Aquinas gives us a classic expression of the cosmological arguments. In them he makes three unwarrantable assumptions. The first is that all finite beings are dependent on other finite beings for motion, efficient causation, or existence. The second is that an infinite regress in the chain of dependence is an untenable idea. The third is that the anchor of this chain, the first cause or necessary being, is the proper object of religious devotion.[17]

Royce provides an example of the epistemic variety of the argument to a necessary presupposition. Royce asserts that the possibility of truth and error depends on a higher thought which includes both a particular thought and the object of this thought in its thinking. This higher thought compares the particular thought and its object and makes the necessary judgment of truth or falsity on the particular thought. Ultimately, the possibility of truth and error presupposes an Infinite Thought capable of holding all other thoughts and their objects within itself. This argument is not cogent. The assignment of the values of truth and falsity may be made by any particular mind, and the significance of the distinction between truth and error does not depend on a correct assignment of these values nor on the notion of the simultaneous presence of all moments of time to a mind capable of such an absolute judgment. [18]

3) There is no experience of the Unconditioned that yields an idea of God that is sufficiently specifiable and beyond reasonable question. Schleiermacher is the classic representative in modern times of this approach. He refers to "the immediate consciousness of the universal existence of all finite things, in and through the Infinite, and of all temporal things in and through the Eternal." He later referred to piety as the consciousness of being absolutely dependent. The absoluteness of this dependence separates it from dependence within the world which is the realm of reciprocal dependence and freedom.[19] However, it is just such a feeling of absolute dependence which many, perhaps most, people do not have, if we can believe their lack of reports concerning it. People do have feelings of radical contingency, but this is an awareness of dependence on beings in the world, not an awareness of a foundation of the world.

Tillich is also in this tradition, for he talks of an immediate awareness of the unconditional. Sometimes this is an awareness of the Power of being giving courage to face the threat of nonbeing. I have experienced courage to face this anxiety of finitude and I know to what extent it is situationally transcendent as a gift. But I do not know of a ground of all being which is the source of this courage. Tillich asserts that the immediate awareness of the unconditional should not be called an experience, since that word applies to the observed presence of one reality to another, while the Unconditioned is not a matter of observation of a finite object. I agree that the unconditioned is not a matter of experiential observation. Then what is this putative immediate awareness? There is no immediate awareness of the unconditioned. What we have here is Tillich's own mediated experiences of courage and meaning designated, incorrectly, as immediate awareness of the unconditional by the exigencies of his system. [20]

4) Justification by revelation or religious authority is also open to objection. To accept a revelation as genuine is already to affirm the reality of God. Also appeals to historical revelation involve a matter of historical contingency. Why should I, on the basis of an accident of birth or communication, accept the claim of one revelation over that of another?

I have been attempting to show the inadequacy of specific attempts to justify belief in God. Now I wish to affirm that the assertion of the reality of God, conceived maximally, cannot in principle possibly receive any valid justification. I cannot prove this assertion, but offer it as clarifying what I think is probably the case. "God," understood maximally as the ontological ultimate, is a limiting concept, a regulative rather than a constitutive notion of thought. In the usual maximal conception, God is supreme in being and worth and the ultimate source of being and worth. The concepts of supremacy and of ultimate source are both limiting concepts, defining the boundaries of reason. As such, affirmations about entities corresponding to these concepts are probably incapable of justification.[21]

It should go without saying, but may need some comment, that these attacks on a variety of argumentations and justifications of a maximally conceived deity are not attacks on the person, intellectual competence, or style of living of those making these arguments. I have respect, and in some cases affection, for those with whom I differ on these matters. Besides, personal rancour would belie the stance of restraint and modesty as well as seriously interfere with creative interchange. This needs to be said because discussions about such personal and often passionately held convictions can degenerate into acrimonious quarrels or else strained silences. There is some sense in the myth of the old Adam, which I take it puts an emphasis on our personal responsibility for our cussed dispositions.

2. The Positive Argument

The negative defense of the minimal model which we have just rehearsed by trying to find the weakness of the justifications for a maximally conceived deity, needs to be supplemented in two senses. First, a positive case for the model must be attempted. The next few pages are devoted to this. Second, a sense of how life can be lived by this model needs to be sketched in contrast to a maximally conceived theistic orientation on the one hand and to an orientation which rejects all explicit reference to transcendence, whether maximally or minimally conceived, on the other hand. Such a contrast will be given in our last chapter. We now proceed to the next task, a presentation of the positive case for the minimal model.

On the one hand this model does not exceed proper ontological tentativeness. This model rests on a stance of ontological reticence, of caution in making affirmations about reality. It is a minimal model. Two considerations urge this caution.

The first is the fertility of our mythological and ontological imagination. The fertility of human imagination, coupled with our propensity for wish-fulfillment, urges constant caution against the unrestrained affirmation of the truth of our ideas concerning transcendence. This need for caution implies restraint upon our metaphysical impulses. The second is that we lack a consensus concerning the ontological nature of the transcendent, even conerning the type of method appropriate to use in justifying religious or metaphysical assertions about the transcendent. These two reasons, the need for ontological restraint coupled with the weakness of the reasons for affirming belief in God or any other full-fledged, maximally conceived Transcendent, shifts the burden of proof against the full affirmation of Transcendence in favor of our minimal approach.

On the one hand, while this model does not exceed proper ontological caution, it does retain a notion of the transcendent. This model explicates and so helps to nurture the experiences of the transcendent without going too far in making assertions about it. In our time we need to nurture our sensitivity to transcendent resources of renewal and to cultivate our openness to continuing criticism and the lure of unattained value.

A further advantage of this model is that it thematizes secular experiences of the transcendent, as will be shown next. The paradigms used to explicate this model are chosen from our secular life, examples from healing and the search for truth. By the conceptualization of secular experiences of transcendence this model helps to uncover and symbolize experiences of transcendence which could wither and die without explicit articulation. The struggle for rehumanization in our time can be greatly aided by the exploration of secular experiences of the transcendent.

The traditional models of divinity make such bold claims as to expose the very real transcendent realities and values to the acids of modernity, making it difficult to be open to their power to criticize and heal. The present model makes a smaller claim, thus protecting and nurturing the experiences of transcendence so badly needed today.

Pascal says that we have everything to lose by not wagering on the existence of God. I suggest that everything would not be lost, given an attitude of openness to the resources of renewal and to the continually transcendent ideals which are pointed to by this model. We do not need to lose the baby when we empty the tub. We do need to understand just what the baby is.[22]

This argument against affirming maximal conceptions of Transcendence seems to be more persuasive than the opposing arguments. We must make a judgment on partial but persuasive reasons, a weighted ontological wager. The fecundity of human imagination, whether mythological, occult or metaphysical, coupled with the propensity for wish-fulfilment, urges constant caution against the unrestrained affirmation of the truth of our ideas. This need for caution urges restraint upon our metaphysical impulses. Since there appears to be no cogent reason for affirming the reality of God or any other full conception of Transcendence and since caution is in order, I advocate an attitude of ontological restraint resulting in an agnosticism about the reality of maximal transcendence as classically conceived. Nevertheless, we can affirm that there are real instances of situationally transcendent resources and challenge in the world. Inner-worldly transcendence is real.

Our culture gives mixed signals concerning fundamental notions. Some strands of our culture encourage intellectual honesty and the examination of ideas. Other strands discourage these and emphasize accepting what you are taught. Many people as they develop adopt one or the other of these approaches as the dominant motif in their orientation to life. Others, with various amounts of comfort, live compartmentalized lives, examining beliefs in some areas and accepting inherited or current views in other areas.

For those who operate in the critical mode, the minimalist approach offers much. It encourages careful examination of opinions. It attempts to make cautious and minimal affirmations. It utilizes tentative language. In these ways the minimalist approach attempts to be credible to a critical orientation. However, this approach also challenges some of the basic themes of our culture. It specifically challenges the reductionism of much current intellectual life and tries to thematize and thus hold open the possibility of experiences of transcendence and their nurture.

IV. Experiences of Transcendence

Let us spend some time exploring experience with the aid of this model of transcendence. My purposes are twofold. I shall delineate various experiences in order to exemplify the model and shall also use the model as a guide to further discovery of transcendence in experience. Thus there shall be a reciprocal interplay between the model and experience. Drawing from experience will provide concreteness to the abstract model, while the model will function as a guide to the exploration of experience.

We shall follow the two aspects of our model and consequently shall search for situationally superior or transcendent resources and then for the call of continually challenging values. This will not be an exhaustive exploration of possible experiences of transcendence, but it should give an indication of how the minimalist approach is derived from and verified by experience.

1. Situationally Transcendent Resources of Renewal

Situational transcendence has been defined above as referring to resources of growth and renewal which are transcendent, that is, unexpected, uncontrollable, and superior in power and worth to the antecedent ingredients of the situation as perceived by an individual or group. The occasions of renewal, which occur when these resources are operative, are intermittent, spontaneous, unexpected and uncontrollable. The experiences of such transcendence are moments in which people are open to such resources. Although these experiences all have this basic character, it is possible to divide situational transcendence into some fairly common types.

A. Openness in Extremity

Moments of extremity are moments of defeat and despair or victory and joy. In such moments the limits of normally perceived resources are met. Such moments can be closed in despair or a complacent jubilation. However, such moments can also involve an openness through a longing for transcendent resources in defeat or an awareness of them in joy. I have been influenced here by Bernard Meland and, recently, by Marvin Shaw, although Shaw's naturalism is not explicit.[23]

The main characteristic of these occasions is that they are occasions of extremity, when we reach an awareness of our limits, either through a sense of defeat and despair or through a sense of a goodness not our own. Experiences of the limits of the self are of two kinds, experiences of defeat or of joy. An experience of defeat is clearly an experience of the limits of the self. An experience of joy is also, for in the "capacity to be joyous, even in affliction . . . one rises above the demands of the ego to recognize the reality of goodness in our very midst when it does not happen to meet the demands of the self at that very moment."[24]

This awareness of the limits of the self can be coupled with an awareness of resources beyond the self. In experiences of defeat there may be an awareness of healing, renewal or forgiveness. In experiences of joy there is the sense of a blessing from beyond the limits of the self. Such experiences of resources from beyond the self in moments of defeat or joy I call experiences of situationally transcendent resources.

Often in these moments the good which comes to the self comes through some form of personal meeting. Often there is an unexpected and powerful good which moves in acts of love or forgiveness. The caring touch, a negotiated resolution of conflict by parties with mutual respect, the appreciation of the preciousness of another human can at any time be vehicles of transcendent renewal and resource. Sometimes it seems as if grace comes from the other. At other times the transcendent blessing comes when one reaches out in beneficent acts or sacrificial love. These may be brief moments or life-long friendships. They may be moments of passion or of a steady covenant.

These interhuman relationships need not be on a one-to-one basis. A community can sustain the individual through a nexus of living relations. A situation of renewal can come from working together to establish communication and rapport. Such rapport waits for growth of mutual appreciation and results in a widening orbit of meaning which goes beyond an individual's good to include a larger family of loyalty.

Both joy and suffering can be occasions of transcendent renewal. A deepened sensitivity increases the possibility of both enjoyment and anguish. Joy and suffering are not opposites, but are concomitant experiences. The true opposite of joy is cynicism, callousness the opposite of sorrow.

Joy and sorrow are both grounded in appreciative awareness. In the words of Bernard Meland:

> The capacity to praise life, like the capacity to lament, reveals both deliverance from the tyranny of self and a mature adjustment to the exigencies of life itself. . . . Where there is a genuine acceptance of tragedy and loss, the clinging to existence, which intensifies greed and self-love, is relaxed. . . . Thus the good that is present, operative, and real is not obscured by self-attentiveness. [25]

Joy is not egoistic satisfaction. In the capacity to be joyous one rises "above the demands of the ego to recognize the reality of goodness in our very midst when it does not happen to meet the demands of the self at that very moment."[26] The capacity for joy in the midst of defeat depends on restraining egoistic demands.

Particularly important are experiences of repentance and forgiveness. To quote again from Meland:

> In this very act of reaching our extremity and of acknowledging to ourselves that it is our extremity, a curious transformation of the human psyche occurs. It is not just that one feels purged of a sense of guilt; the action upon the psyche is more healing. It is as if one is forgiven in a decisive way such that one can accept himself and be accepted by others, even by the one toward whom wrong might have been done. [27]

B. COURAGE IN SPITE OF FINITUDE

The recognition of finitude can arise from the contemplation of many aspects of life, but especially from reflection upon birth and death. The recognition of finitude may appear as an intense personal experience and it may be symbolized in individual or cultural forms of expression. It may be a recognition of the givenness of one's own existence or of the threat to that existence. The stubborn

givenness of existence includes the relative and unavoidable facts of
my somatic and social inheritance, the fact that I am, that I am I,
and that I am here now.[28] This givenness that I am up against leads
to a recognition of the other side of contingency, that I am continually threatened by non-being, that I am self-aware finitude. This
contingency provides me with the twin experiences of the irremov-
able hardness of my givenness and the yawning abyss of nothingness ready to swallow up this existence.

H. Richard Niebuhr refers to the radical deed by which "I am"
and "I am I", by which I have the so-ness and the thus-ness of my
life.[29] This existence of mine is completely contingent, inexplicably
present, absolutely dependent. The words "I am" and "I am I" seem
to refer to selfhood and to the particularity of elements which go
into the self without exhausting it.

> The radical action by which I am and by which I am present with
> this body, this mind, this emotional equipment, this religion, is not
> identifiable with any of the finite actions that constitute the par-
> ticular elements in physical, mental, personal existence.[30]

I am contingent. I did not elect to be born, I do not maintain my
existence by my own power, and, in a sense, I cannot choose to die,
if the radical act whereby I am continues me in existence.

One may attempt to hide from this fact of contingency by ignoring it. Or one may acknowledge this contingency with despair, with
an aggressive clutching at life defending oneself against the threat,
or by resolutely facing the threat with stoic courage. However, one
might also accept the givenness of life with gratitude as a gift and
an opportunity. This is a recognition of life as a gift and as a demand
to realize one's own potential and the optimum of good in an on-
going context. Regardless of the ontological conceptualization of the
source of this gift, upon reflection it becomes apparent that this
givenness of life comes to one from a source outside of oneself, that
is, from a source transcendent to oneself. Such a recognition enables
one to accept and overcome the anxiety of finitude. Whenever the
response of acceptance occurs, together with the reflection that
there is a *whence* from which our life comes that is situationally
transcendent, we experience transcendence.[31]

c. The Courage to Act in the Opportune Moment

The self in interaction with other selves and objects forms part
of a system. Now it is characteristic of both natural and social

systems generally that they oscillate between periods of relative equilibrium and disequilibrium. Periods of disequilibrium are frought with danger and opportunity, danger because of the possibility of the disintegration of the system, opportunity because of the possibility of the formation of more significant systems. My thinking here tries to reshape Tillich's concept of *kairos* using the language of systems analysis.

The activity of the self in such situations is important, without precedent, and ambiguous, in short, fraught with risk. It is important because new habitual patterns of behavior for the system are being formed and there is increased potential for good and evil. It is without precedent because norms of accepted behavior concerning interaction within the system are challenged or deteriorating. It is ambiguous because the complexities or speed of change within the system make the value of any new move often inclusive of both good and evil.

To act in such moments requires courage. Now sometimes such courage is habitual or arises from trusted resources. Often, however, in such times of crisis courage comes from unexpected resources outside of the perceived situation. This is situationally transcendent resource.

Filled as they are with such opportunity, these moments of crisis are pregnant with the demand to act. Because the demand often calls for new modes of behavior, we can speak of situationally transcendent obligation.

2. Continually Challenging Goals

We shall call a goal continually challenging if it continues to beckon or challenge no matter what level of attainment is achieved or when the goal is a demand which differs from the accepted norms in such a way as to call these norms into question. Let us take the pursuit of truth as a paradigm of continuing transcendence. No matter what level of understanding of the world is achieved, the goal of truth continues to function as a lure in relation to which our theories are but approximations. The truth is an ideal, never fully attained, which yet functions as a continually transcendent challenge that we push towards that goal. Thus the truth functions as a continually transcendent value.

It is convenient to speak of four types of the pursuit of value. I am dependent upon Paul Tillich in this classification, although I differ in detail and do not claim that this classification is exhaustive.[32] The four types of value pursuit are reflective inquiry, art, the moral life, and social responsibility. Reflective inquiry includes any disciplined attempt at understanding, including science, mathematics, philosophy, and some forms of practical sense. Art includes the generally recognized arts and also all attempts to produce or maintain significant perceptual forms. The moral life includes the making of choices in one's personal and interpersonal life which involves responsibility to oneself and other selves. Social responsibility includes one's activity to form, preserve, and reform social, political, and economic institutions and systems.

Thus we can say that these pursuits of value sometimes involve the recognition of a demand to realize meaning. Thus these pursuits, particularly in their creative as distinct from their preservative phases, often involve openness to a continually transcendent albeit naturalistically conceived goal. This transcendent dimension of our search for meaning, when recognized, aids in the avoidance both of a cynical rejection of the possibility of significant realization of value and also of a fanatic assertion that the most superior value has already been achieved.

Continuing transcendence of goal and presupposition is not always present in the humane pursuits, but it often is. For example one locus of such continuing transcendence sometimes occurs in science, which is a major type of reflective inquiry. It occurs in science when there is a commitment to the search for truth, that is, for a systematic and coherent understanding, universal in scope, precisely stated and experimentally tested. Commitment to each of these goals, system, coherence, universality, precision, and verification, is the pursuit of a continually transcendent yet ever relevant goal. When this is recognized it is held that not merely the present hypothesis under consideration is subject to testing, but that the entire scientific enterprise inevitably results in conclusions with the quality of tentativeness, that all theories are continually open to question in principle no matter how well established. This is a clear case of continuing transcendence of goal. Continuing transcendence of the presupposition of inquiry is manifested wherever there is confidence in the viability of the quest for truth or confidence that all things are potentially meaningful.

A second locus is art, where continuing transcendence is found whenever any particular creation of significant form is felt to be, while complete in itself, yet also not a full manifestation of the possibilities of that style, tradition, or medium, but a lure to further creation.

The third locus, the moral life, involves responsibility to persons, including oneself. To be responsible to a person involves both understanding that self and acting for its benefit. Since a person is both highly complex and also continually changing, such understanding and acting or listening and giving, when seriously pursued, are continually transcendent tasks.

A fourth locus of continuing transcendence is social responsibility. We often recognize that social responsibility involves the continuing questioning of both established and proposed structures. No society or institution is without the need of correction. When this is recognized it is held that not merely the present situation is in need of reform, but that all social structures need improvement, that there must be continuing reform and perpetual accountability. In short, continuing transcendence in social responsibility manifests itself in the attempt to be responsible to the universal society or in the struggle to build a truly democratic, just, or self-correcting social system.

These are examples of continuing transcendence of goal, the making of the principle of self-correction a permanent feature of the enterprise. And lest the burden of continuing demand becomes impossible to bear as the presupposition of the enterprise there is the feeling that this perpetual quest for and questioning of the goal of the pursuit is worthwhile and that significant attainment is possible, not merely in this situation, but in principle.

Let us recall that we have spoken of the concepts of openness and closure to transcendence, of presupposition and goal. I have been influenced here by Tillich's concept of the dialectic between openness or transparency to the ground of being and turning from it. Openness is that attitude of recognition and receptivity to the challenge of continually transcendent goal and presupposition. Closure is the self-contained attitude of ignoring or shutting one's self off from such challenge. Openness is the personal or cultural attitude which responds to transcendence. Openness in the pursuit of value is a self-critical attitude, an attitude which refuses to remain satisfied with any concrete achievement of value. At the same time it is an eager attitude, a hopeful attitude which trusts in the possibility of significant attainment. Openness is the way beyond fanaticism and cynicism.

Openness to continuing transcendence in the search for the realization of value is an important alternative to the fanatic assumption that the absolute has been achieved and the cynical assumption that the search is fruitless. Continuing transcendence is a lure to the pursuit of meaning at the same time providing a prod against complacent self-satisfaction when any meaning has been realized. The continually transcendent is, in short, an unattainable but ever-attracting goal, a demand for value pursuit, the corrective to fanaticism and cynicism. One of the things which naturalism can learn from Tillich is to make explicit the continuing transcendence of presupposition and goal, thus making explicit the antidote to fanaticism and despair and, by pointing to it, helping us to keep open to it.

Within our minimalist framework what can we assert in regard to the reality, the ontological status of the unconditioned goal of the search for meaning? We can affirm that the continually transcendent goals are lures of attainable and attractive ideals, acting as continually effective lures toward significant attainment.

But within our naturalistic framework we cannot speak of an ontologically ultimate correlate to these pursuits or even speak of the unity of these goals. To do this would be an illegitimate move beyond the available evidence. Of such an ontologically unified ultimate we must be reticent. The continually transcendent goal of the pursuit of meaning is akin to Kant's notion of a regulative, as distinct from a constitutive, concept.[33] It is a placemarker, standing for the yet-to-be attained in axiological discourse. The continually transcendent presupposition of the pursuit of meaning is our sense of the worthwhileness of the pursuit of meaning.

Those who dismiss the ultimate as an illusion have missed an important point. There is at least something going on in the belief in the ontological or religious ultimate that is usually lost when it is dismissed as an illusion. This something is the function which the ultimate plays in our pursuit of value. Given our modest model, what we can legitimately affirm is not an ontological or religious ultimate but rather the continually transcendent presupposition and goal of the pursuit of value.

CHAPTER TWO

HISTORICAL CONTEXT

This minimal model emerges within a tradition of philosophical and theological thinking and seeks to develop creative fidelity to this tradition. This tradition has sought to reflect seriously on the real aspect of the Transcendent. This is a fairly well defined stream of American thought. Its philosophical phase, often called radical empiricism, includes William James and an aspect of Whitehead's thought. Its theological phase includes the so-called Chicago School of theology. In addition I include within my understanding of this tradition some other thinkers not always included, particularly some British thinkers and some American religious empiricists.

In addition there are certain continental thinkers who are either influential in the development of certain parts of the thinking in this book or who should be considered to clarify by contrast the positions developed herein. The former include Kant, Tillich and Ricoeur, the latter, Feuerbach.

I. Philosophical Background

1. David Hume

One historical inspiration for the minimalist principle is Hume's *Dialogues Concerning Natural Religion*. In criticizing Cleanthes' argument from design, Philo challenges the attempt to base infinite attributes of the Deity on an experiential starting point. "The cause ought only to be proportioned to the effect."[1] Starting from this principle of the proportionality of the cause to the effect—which is a classic statement of minimalist thinking—Philo suggests that there is no way to curb "the utmost license of fancy" in framing the hypotheses concerning the causes of order in the world. The Deity could be an infant pondering his first work, an inferior deity, or

41

the result of dotage in a superannuated deity.[2] Or the ultimate principle could be vegetation or generation. The choice is entirely arbitrary.[3] Arguing from the world to God, Philo continues, is like arguing from a very badly planned house whose design is "the source of noise, confusion, fatigue, darkness, and extremes of heat and cold."[4]

The reasoning of Philo could be interpreted as a *reductio ad absurdum* of all arguments from the nature of the world to the nature of God. The response taken in this study is to turn this into a *reductio ad minima*. Instead of showing that arguments from the character of the world can lead to preposterous conclusions, the minimalist approach seeks to show that they can lead, provisionally and with proper safeguards, to some minimal claims about the nature of transcendence within the world.

Negatively we must say that with proper ontological reticence Hume's characterization of the choice as entirely arbitrary is incorrect. A truly minimal approach would not give a deity in infancy or dotage. It would not give a deity at all. It would give fragmentary and ambiguous divine qualities of experience. As for vegetative or generative principles, these terms are left undeveloped by Hume. Similar ontological caution would also lead us to dismiss them unless they were understood in so minimalist a sense as to lose all the absurdity that Philo seems to imply by these terms.

Positively we can say that Hume is correct that it is as if we are arguing from a very badly planned house. However, as do many who take the approach of a limited deity, our approach agrees with the ambiguous nature of the world but clearly argues from this to a limited cause (in our case to a somewhat attenuated religious response to the abstracted unity of finite causes), not, as Philo seems to leave open, to a bungling, confused, or cruel designer. We have, rather, no designer at all. Instead the minimalist approach takes seriously the conception of design as arising from the immanent play of forces working out mutual adaptation. This is the alternative which John Stuart Mill considered, although he thought it as less probable than his limited (but not minimal) deity. In between Hume and Mill, of course, was Charles Darwin.

2. John Stuart Mill

The key fountainhead for the minimalist approach, as William James, Edgar Sheffield Brightman, Edward Scribner Ames and Douglas Clyde Macintosh affirm, was John Stuart Mill's essay on Theism.[5] I wish to isolate three key ideas of this essay.

1) The most important idea is Mill's own minimalism. The crucial section is Part II of the essay, entitled "Attributes." Mill starts with an examination of the power properly to be assigned to God.

> What attributes are we warranted, by the evidence which Nature affords of a creative mind, in assigning to that mind? It needs no showing that the power if not the intelligence, must be so far superior to that of Man, as to surpass all human estimate. But from this to Omnipotence and Omniscience there is a wide interval.[6]

Mill carries this argument through next with God's knowledge, particularly God's foreknowledge.

> The knowledge of the powers and properties of things necessary for planning and executing the arrangements of the Kosmos, is no doubt as much in excess of human knowledge as the power implied in creation is in excess of human power. And the skill . . . is often marvellous. But nothing obliges us to suppose that either the knowledge or the skill is infinite. We are not even compelled to suppose that the contrivances are always the best possible. If we venture to judge them as we judge the works of human artificers, we find abundant defects.[7]

Clearly the minimalism developed in this book goes beyond Mill to reject affirmations of God's knowledge or designing, especially if either requires unity, purpose and consciousness.

After his treatment of God's knowledge, Mill turns to God's benevolence towards his creatures. Here Mill carries his minimalism through slightly more tentatively.

> If the motive of the Deity for creating sentient beings was the happiness of the beings he created, his purpose, in our corner of the universe at least, must be pronounced, taking past ages and all countries and races into account, to have been thus far an ignominious failure.[8]

Mill carries this minimalist approach through in his discussion of the divine justice.

> There is no evidence whatever in Nature for divine justice, whatever standard of justice our ethical opinions may lead us to recognize. There is no shadow of justice in the general arrangements of

Nature; and what imperfect realization it obtains in any society (a most imperfect realization as yet) is the work of man himself.[9]

This minimalism allows Mill to escape the necessity of attempting to reconcile God's power and benevolence.

> We now pass to the moral attributes to the Deity, so far as indicated in the Creation; or (stating the problem in the broadest manner) to the question, what indications Nature gives of the purposes of its author. This question bears a very different aspect to us from what it bears to those teachers of Natural Theology who are encumbered with the necessity of admitting the omnipotence of the Creator. We have not to attempt the impossible problem of reconciling infinite benevolence and justice with infinite power in the Creator of such a world as this.[10]

This is the way Mill avoids Hume's *reductio ad absurdum* of natural theology with his dichotomy of omnipotence and goodness. Mill clearly opts for the limitation of power (and possibly benevolence and justice) and claims it is a reduction to the more probable and more certain.

Mill's conclusion is a classic statement of the minimalist approach, although the present book attempts to carry it through more radically.

> These, then, are the net results of Natural Theology on the question of the divine attributes. A Being of great but limited power, how or by what limited we cannot even conjecture; of great, and perhaps unlimited intelligence, but perhaps, also, more narrowly limited than his power: who desires, and pays some regard to, the happiness of his creatures, but who seems to have other motives of action which he cares more for, and who can hardly be supposed to have created the universe for that purpose alone. Such is the Deity whom Natural Religion points to; and any idea of God more captivating than this comes only from human wishes, or from the teaching of either real or imaginary Revelation.[11]

2) The second key idea which I wish to isolate from Mill's essay is found in the Introduction to the First Part. This notion is that religion should be tested by scientific methods and the canons of scientific evidence. This ties in with the dominance of empirical methodology in the rest of his philosophical approach.

It is indispensable that the subject of religion should from time to time be reviewed as a strictly scientific question, and that its evidences should be tested by the same scientific methods, and on the same principles as those of any of the speculative conclusions drawn by physical science. It being granted then that the legitimate conclusions of science are entitled to prevail over all opinions, however widely held, which conflict with them, and that the canons of scientific evidence . . . are applicable to all subjects on which knowledge is attainable, let us proceed to consider what place there is for religious beliefs on the platform of science; what evidences they can appeal to, such as science can recognize, and what foundation there is for the doctrines of religion, considered as scientific theorems.[12]

The minimalist approach elaborated in this book is in accord with Mill that the subject of religion should be reviewed and tested from time to time. However, his extension of "the canons of scientific evidence" from the various fields of strictly scientific investigation into the areas of religious inquiry is too broad an expansion of scientific procedures, based on too simplistic a conception of scientific methodology. We shall examine this topic in greater detail in chapter four.

3) The third key idea from Mill is his probablism, his recognition that adaptations in nature provide no more than a probable ground for a claim of creation by an intelligence.

I think it must be allowed that, in the present state of our knowledge, the adaptations in Nature afford a large balance of probability in favour of creation by intelligence. It is equally certain that this is no more than a probability; and that the various other arguments of Natural Theology which we have considered, add nothing to its force.[13]

The significance of this for our minimalist approach is not of course the notion of an intelligent creator, but that there is a probable ground for a religious claim. The attempt is made in this book to carry this temper of probability through not only to the premises or grounds but also to the claims of philosophy of religion.

3. William James

William James was a major pioneer of minimalist thinking. He elaborates a notion of a finite, temporal, and pluralistic deity and, above all, the tentativeness of our knowledge of God. James makes the point emphatically that any characterization which we make concerning the nature of the reality to which the vector character of the experience points must be made tentatively and with a clear understanding of its hypothetical nature, even though this hypothesis can be made with conviction. The data, says James, "establish, when taken together, a decidedly *formidable* probability.... The outlines of the superhuman consciousness thus made probable must remain, however, very vague."[14]

James is also quite clear that all sorts of wild beliefs will tag along once hypotheses are allowed to be attached to the data.

> It is true that superstitions and wild-growing over-beliefs of all sorts will undoubtedly begin to abound if the notion of higher consciousness enveloping ours... grows orthodox and fashionable.... But ought one seriously to allow such a timid consideration as that to deter one from following the evident path of greatest religious promise?[15]

James describes his notion of the superhuman consciousness with which we seem to be in relation as "an hypothesis trying to make itself probable on analogical and inductive grounds, a speculative assumption based on the analogy of our own minds as compounded of conscious parts."[16]

James uses the illustration of a pet in a library, surrounded by books and conversations, the meanings of which surpass the ken of the animal and in which he participates only to the extent appropriate to the level of his awareness.

> We may be in the universe as dogs and cats are in our libraries, seeing the books and hearing the conversation, but having no inkling of the meaning of it all.[17]

The tentativeness and meagerness of our apprehension of the encompassing spiritual environment makes it appropriate for James to use the phrase, "the More." This is a sign indicative of intellectual humility. Also it indicates that the issues of the infinite or finite character and the plurality or unity of the wider environment are not to be prejudged through the use of a definitive appellation. Both the tentativeness of our apprehension of the divine and the possibility of a plurality in the divine are key steps on the road to a minimalist understanding of religion.

James returns briefly to this notion of possible polytheism in *A Pluralistic Universe.*

> The outlines of the superhuman consciousness must remain, however, very vague, and the number of functionally distinct 'selves' it comports and carries has to be left entirely problematic. It may be polytheistically or it may be monotheistically conceived of. Fechner, with his distinct earth-soul functioning as our guardian angel, seems to me clearly polytheistic; but the word 'polytheism' usually gives offence, so perhaps it is better not to use it. Only one thing is certain, and that is the result of our criticism of the absolute: the only way to escape from the paradoxes and perplexities that a consistently thought-out monistic universe suffers from . . . is to be frankly pluralistic and assume that the superhuman consciousness, however vast it may be, has itself an external environment, and consequently is finite.[18]

James argues that this larger spiritual self need not be finite, nor need it even be a unity, in order to account for the facts of regeneration.

> All that the facts require is that the power should be both other and larger than our conscious selves. Anything larger will do, if only it be large enough to trust for the next step. It need not be infinite, it need not be solitary. It might conceivably even be only a larger and more godlike self, of which the present self would then be but the mutilated expression, and the universe might conceivably be a collection of such selves, of different degrees of inclusiveness, with no absolute unity realized in it at all. Thus would a sort of polytheism return upon us—a polytheism which I do not on this occasion defend.[19]

Thus while James hesitates to assert that the spiritual environment must be conceived polytheistically, both because of the tentativeness of our knowledge and possibly because of anticipated dismay, he is willing to assert that:

> there is a God, but that he is finite, either in power or in knowledge, or in both at once.[20]

> We are indeed internal parts of God and not external creations, on any possible reading of the panpsychic system. Yet because God is not the absolute, but is himself a part when the system is conceived pluralistically, his functions can be taken as not wholly

dissimilar to those of the other smaller parts—as similar to our
functions consequently.

Since the universe is best conceived pluralistically, everything
real will have an environment and exist in time, including God.

> Everything you can think of, however vast, or inclusive, has on the
> pluralistic view a genuinely 'external' environment of some sort or
> amount. Things are 'with' one another in many ways, but nothing
> includes everything, or dominates over everything.[21]

> Having an environment, being in time, and working out a history
> just like ourselves, he escapes from the foreignness from all that is
> human, of the static timeless perfect absolute.[22]

James approaches this conception of a pluralistic universe with
a finite, temporal deity in a way characteristic of his style of pragmatism.

> It *might* be true. . . . for it is not self-contradictory.

> It *may* be true . . . even here and now.

> It is *fit* to be true, it would be *well if it were true,* it *ought* to be
> true . . .

> It *must* be true, something persuasive in you whispers . . .

> It shall be *held for true,* you decide; it *shall be* as if true, for you.

> And your acting thus may in certain special cases be means of
> making it securely true in the end.

Not one step in this process is logical, yet it is the way in which
monists and pluralists alike espouse and hold fast to their visions. It
is life exceeding logic, it is the practical reason for which the theo-
retic reason finds arguments after the conclusion is once there.[23]

4. Alfred North Whitehead

Whitehead has been a chief philosophical source for many
American religious thinkers. Two important themes stemming from
Whitehead are: (1) the view that the world has the character of a
temporal passage with the occurrence of novelty, that is, that genuine novelty occurs during the passage of time, and, (2) the view

that events which occur in the temporal process tend to form wholes or societies, the parts of which have internal relations, that is, there are social units within the world that are not analyzable into their elements without the destruction of the whole.

The possibility of novelty has merged in the background of this book with similar notions from James, Bergson, Alexander, and Jan Christian Smuts, to form a readiness to speak of situationally transcendent factors which are not reducible to the past factors in the situation. Clearly, however, the viewpoint elaborated in this book does not commit one to Whitehead's notion of the atomicity of becoming. Nor can the conceptualization of situationally transcendent factors be derived simply from Whitehead or any of these thinkers.

1) The notion of the organic interrelatedness of events is a fairly common notion today. Smuts, Dewey, early twentieth century physics, even Hegel have merged into the worldview of complex situations. Probably most significant are the related notions of the situation and the transactional interrelatedness of self and situation.

According to Whitehead's principle of relativity, the entire world is involved in the concrescence of each actual occasion. This is meant perspectivally. The world of each occasion is relative to the occasion, making up its past. And to retain the pluralistic emphasis, Whitehead asserts that there are degrees of relevance in the prehension of the entire world. Our conception of a situation has taken this Whiteheadian notion and given emphasis to relevance. The entire past of the entire world may indeed be involved in the becoming of each occasion, but only significant relevance delineates a situation.

2) The notion of situational transcendence recognizes the interaction, indeed, the mutual formation of self and situation. When speaking of situational transcendence, the factor(s) transcendent to the situation may be from within the organism or its subconscious depths. Even though this is from "inside" the organism, it could still be considered as outside the situation as perceived and hence as situationally transcendent. Furthermore, factors within the skin and without the skin must be in some degree of reinforcement. Hence, situationally transcendent resources inevitably involve at least the harmony and cooperation of factors within the organism and the subconscious. Furthermore, we are creatures of language, and it is impossible to separate language as internal and external. We are social beings, and there is a mutual formation and transformation of self and situation.

All of this is to say that factors "within" the self will probably always be involved whenever there is situational transcendence. This does not make the transcendent illusory or arbitrary.

In a related point, our minimalist model has stressed the role of the imagination in abstracting and unifying the situationally transcendent resources and axiologically transcendent challenges into a concept of God or the divine. This discussion of the mutual formation of self and situation should help dispel the notion that an imaginative construct is purely imaginary. Our models, images, symbols, doctrines and philosophies are corrigible, provisional, and hypothetical. They need not be arbitrary. Our concepts are like the checks we use to pay our bills. Although they bear our private signatures, we claim that they hold good in circulation and that they can be used to purchase in the world. A promissory note has both subjective and objective elements. Our notions also. A note or a notion may depreciate, may become worthless. Neither, however, can be dismissed immediately as worthless.

Whitehead, along with Dewey and Wieman, has been a major source for the notion of mutual formation of self and situation. Whitehead, as indicated by the term "philosophy of organism," is a major affirmer of the significance of sociality as a key descriptive category. To assert this without succumbing to monism, Whitehead also stressed the ultimate significance of the individual occasion. Hence, neither individuals nor their societies are more basic. The fundamental emphasis must be, in the pregnant phrase of *Religion in the Making,* the individual in community. Whitehead decomposed the world into individual occasions in order the better to recompose the world. Whitehead made society a derivative notion from the more basic fact of prehension, thus escaping the trap of assuming that there is one basic species in which each individual belongs and also helping to preserve the integrity of the individual against the whole.

3) Most important for our philosophical approach is the theme of Whitehead (shared with divergent nuances by Bergson, James, Alexander, Smuts, Wieman and Meland) that there is a richness or complexity to events which cannot be exhaustively captured in conceptual thought. That is, the intellectual factor is selective and yields an abstraction from the fullness of the world of events. Conceptual thought is to be given its due, but at best it gives us only a limited grasp of the moving complex richness of the data. The concreteness of reality overflows conceptual precision and the process of reasoning inevitably abstracts from this concreteness.

Clearly, for Whitehead, consciousness is abstractive. He continually protests against resting philosophic thought on clear and distinct factors in experience.[24] One related theme in Whitehead is that feelings are prior to intellectualization and that there is a major role for the body in our knowledge of the world. A second related theme, very important for our approach, is the tentativeness of all human thought, above all of philosophic reflection.[25]

Whitehead, along with Charles Hartshorne, has been the fountainhead of a number of religious thinkers in contemporary America, including Schubert Ogden, John Cobb, David Griffin and Lewis Ford. But there is an alternative stream coming from Whitehead and James, including Meland, William Dean, and Nancy Frankenberry, which draws heavily on this theme that the concreteness of reality as experienced overflows conceptual precision.[26]

A brief quotation from Hartshorne and one from Meland can perhaps focus this divergence between the two streams. First, from Hartshorne:

> One may admit the impenetrable divine mystery but believe also in the unrivalled lucidity of the divine essence as an abstract aspect of the mystery.[27]

Now from Meland:

> Where depth and complexity are taken seriously . . . something other than appeal to logic, or even to the claim of observation, is involved. The appeals to logic and observation are important to sustain. They represent our most disciplined forms of utterance in dealing with the realities of experience. But they stand under the judgment of the very realities to which they attend. They appeal to these realities as metaphors to recall Whitehead's memorable statement, speaking of the words and phrases which philosophers use: 'they remain metaphors mutely appealing for an imaginative leap.' As such they are as words listening for a truth that is given, not as one defining or describing that truth.[28]

It will be obvious that the minimalist approach departs totally from Whitehead's conception of God. The stance of ontological caution advocated here appreciates Whitehead's notion of concreteness and tentativeness, but urges that his conception of God moves far beyond proper metaphysical modesty.

II. The Chicago School

There are a number of scholars of religion who are often spoken of as the "Chicago School." The religious naturalism developed in this book draws very heavily on this school, including especially the conceptual theism of Shailer Mathews, and the work of Henry Nelson Wieman and Bernard Meland and, to a lesser extent, Edward Scribner Ames. For the purposes of our study Shailer Mathews, E. S. Ames, Gerald Birney Smith and Bernard Meland have been selected for discussion.

1. Shailer Mathews

The work of Shailer Mathews, who taught at The University of Chicago Divinity School from 1895 to 1933, first helped me to formulate my minimal model of transcendence. His later writings have a number of similar statements of his conception of God.

> *For God is our conception, born of social experience, of the personality-evolving and personally responsive elements of our cosmic environment with which we are organically related.*[29]

Two aspects of this definition demand note. First, this is both pluralistic and unitary. The conception is singular, although the elements in the environment are plural. Second, this is both subjective ("our conception") and objective ("of . . . elements of our cosmic environment"). Both of these emphases have influenced the theoretical model of transcendence in the first chapter.

Mathews' formulation needs to be used with caution. It lacks a sense of a prophetic stance. There is a potential for self-satisfaction here ("thank God we are persons!") which does not provide the sense of transcendence needed to overcome modernism's implication in a sense of Western (and thus white), Christian, Protestant superiority.[30] I have added the radical and continuing demand of the ideal aspect of transcendence to the real aspect of transcendence (which parallels the formula of Mathews) in part in order to correct this lack of prophetic judgment.

Furthermore, Mathews' emphasis on personality is too narrow. He dichotomizes the personal and the mechanical and tends to gloss over the subpersonal and organic levels of selfhood.

2. Edward Scribner Ames

Edward Scribner Ames, a "fellow-traveller" of the Chicago School of theology, taught in the University of Chicago's department of philosophy from 1901 to 1935 and was Dean of Disciples House, and thus influential in the Disciples of Christ denomination, from 1928 to 1945.

Ames thought that just as the ideas of soul or mind are being reconceived, so also should the notion of God. When this reconception takes place, God will be understood as "the reality of the world in certain aspects and functions." These functions are listed as orderliness, love, and intelligence and then again as order, beauty and expansion.[31] Note that for Ames God is not a "mere projection of human ideals," but refers to real aspects or functions of the world.

There is another way of thinking of God for Ames.

> God is used as the standard of reference for the adequacy of specific ideals. When a line of conduct is considered, the question arises for the religious man as to whether such conduct is consistent with loyalty to God.[32]

God is the standard of reference for our ideals as well as the world in certain aspects. To use the language of our theoretical model of transcendence, there is both a real and an ideal aspect to the divine.

Such a framework of reference is found in "any type of thinking or practical interest."

> In reasoning, men seek a procedure which validates their arguments. They appeal at last to the nature of reason, to the law of contradiction, or to the sufficient law of reason. . . . The scientist assumes the orderliness of nature . . . and regards his experiments as having general validity.[33]

A similar framework of reference is found in our moral life. For example,

> Kant's dictum, 'So act that the maxim of our deed may become a universal law,' expresses this craving for the substantiation of individual conduct by a law or principle. . . . This is the way the religious man uses God. God is the judge, the umpire, the referee.[34]

Many questions are raised by Ames' discussion. First, it is not clear how a God free from anthropomorphic crudities, as Ames desires in the process of reconception, would function as a framework of reference. What would a judge, umpire, or referee be that is purged of anthropomorphisms? I have tried to answer this in my notion of the ideal aspect of transcendence. A second question concerns how God as the framework of reference of the religious man relates to the framework of reference of reasoning, of science and of morals. How does God relate to the principle of non-contradiction, to the orderliness of nature, and to the categorical imperative? In the model of transcendence I propose that the ideal aspect of God is explicitly the set of all of these frameworks in their function of providing continuing challenge.

Finally, when Ames specifies aspects of reality (e.g., order, intelligence, love) which make up God, we are left with questions as to whether the list of aspects is complete (should sublimity be included?) and whether these aspects are compatible. By defining the real aspect of transcendence as the set of situationally transcendent creative processes, the model of transcendence in chapter One is logically more general, so that while it is open to the exploration of specific types of experience, it by-passes the questions of completeness and compatibility.

3. G. B. Smith

One of the themes involved in the minimalist orientation affirms the tentativeness of all human thinking and discourse about the divine. One of the strongest proponents of this emphasis was Gerald Birney Smith, teacher of theology at the University of Chicago in the first three decades of the twentieth century. A brief statement of his view can be found in his article "Is Theism Essential to Religion?"[35]

1. This article is a sustained attack on the concept of theism. However, it is important to see precisely the concept of theism Smith is attacking here. Smith has in mind a concept of God who exercises creatorship and control as creator and governor of the world. In more detail, he has in mind a concept which provides a theological foundation for nature, society, and personal life elaborated into a consistent and intellectually satisfying philosophy. Citing Robert Flint, he elaborates the theistic view:

> there is, in the first place, the theological explanation of the physical universe; in the second place, a theological theory of political authority; and in the third place a theological interpretation of religious and moral experience. . . . This theological interpretation of the three realms of nature, society, and personal life can be readily elaborated into a consistent and intellectually satisfactory philosophy. All problems find their solution in the appeal to the perfect rational and moral character of God.

The first part of this article is a sketch of the dissolution of this three-fold theory through the secularization of these three realms.

Smith's complaint against this view is that it is too complete to face all the facts and likewise too definite.

> Philosophical theism is unconvincing to many people because of its very completeness. Has it not usually been more eager to give a theoretically complete definition of God than to face frankly all the facts?

Among the facts which theism seems not to face are, first, that modern science shows us that the evolutionary process seems to be a series of experiments without a clearly defined goal and, second, and even more important, the presence of evil.

> If we take the facts as we find them, we are compelled to recognize that the cosmic process seems to be largely indifferent to moral values.

Theism, in Smith's views, is not only too complete to face all the facts, it is too definite.

> The theistic hypothesis suffers from being too definite to suit our rapidly enlarging knowledge of the nature of the cosmos. It is too thoroughly rationalized. One of the common experiences of today is the sense of unutterable wonder as the incalculable spaces disclosed by astronomy and the unimaginable stretches of time suggested by the doctrine of evolution and the almost incredible marvels of atomic structure and action are apprehended. What we know suggests powerfully the mysteries which we do not, and perhaps cannot, know.

It is interesting to note that the sense of mystery for Smith comes from science. It is when religion has hooked up with philosophy that we pretend to have all the answers.

2. G. B. Smith, however, is not just a critic of theism. The truth lies somewhere between theism and antitheism, although the theist is "doubtless nearer right." Although the consistent minimalist might not put it this way, this is close to the spirit of our minimalism. (Part II of the article is a treatment of "proposals to organize religious values without resort to theism," specifically the attempts of Max Otto and E. S. Ames.)

Smith's attack on antitheism (and on religious humanism) is contained in his notion that man is not enough, that we must be related to the non-human environment. "Important as is the emphasis on human achievement, ultimately we are thrown back on the non-human forces of nature." Clearly, for Smith, religion involves a relationship to this non-human world.

> In religions man brings his highest ideals and his more precious values into the presence of that vast cosmic mystery which has produced him and which holds him in its power. He seeks to obtain from this cosmic power some kind of a blessing on these values and ideals. Thus far interpreters of religion would probably agree.

The question then becomes whether a notion can be formed which can speak to this belief in a cosmic power without falling into either theism or antitheism.

> If the theistic hypothesis becomes too difficult to maintain, may we not abandon it for some more suitable conception without thereby abandoning our belief in *some* kind of cosmic reality capable of stimulating in us the experience which we call religion?

> Humanity finds its values and ideals so precious that it dares to bring these in religious aspiration into relationship with the great cosmic mystery, believing that through such relationship cosmic support may be found, not merely within the circle of human society, but also in the non-human environment on which we are dependent, a *quality* of the cosmic process akin to the quality of our own spiritual life.

Surely here is a clear anticipation of our minimalist orientation. Note the vagueness of the language: "*some* kind of cosmic reality." Note also that this conception is held to support a religious stance. Finally, Smith's use of the word "quality" is an interesting anticipation of Dewey's reference to the religious quality of experience.

The sense that we are dealing with "reality which supports" is of paramount importance. The minimal model seeks to focus on this in its reference to the real aspect of transcendence, however immanent. Religion is not an illusion, however full of error its interpretations may be. We are in touch with reality or realities, although we usually misconceive them.

However, Smith probably does not display the needed ontological reticence in his talk of the cosmic power, although his language is self-consciously tentative. The idea of a cosmic power still sounds too much like an ontologically supreme being. There is a superlative and unitary sense to such a phrase which oversteps the bounds of what we may legitimately affirm.

Also, Smith seems to place less emphasis on the human factors, except in an epistemological regard, than he needs. Since all experience involves a transaction between person and situation (as Dewey and Wieman constantly remind us), our "cosmic" support will always involve the interaction of our selves. To use our paradigm of unexpected and uncontrolled, situationally transcendent healing, the body (and often mind) must interact with the healing factors. A holistic view is a transactional view. That does not preclude a sense that the healing may be transcendent to the situation as perceived and manipulated.

Smith affirms a strong sense of the worshiper's relationship with this cosmic power and mystery, often using personalistic language.

> The belief in God means that there may be found, not merely within the circle of human society, but also in the non-human environment on which we are dependent, a *quality* of the cosmic process akin to the quality of our own spiritual life. Through communion with this qualitative aspect of the cosmic process human life attains an experience of dignity, and a reinforcement of spiritual power. The quality of this reinforcement can be adequately expressed only by the conception of a Divine Presence in the cosmic order.

> The mind which has discovered the marvels of the incalculably vast and complicated universe . . . will demand some kind of spiritual fellowship with the non-human. . . . Just what conception of God will emerge from the great experiment we cannot yet tell. But it will express the experience of kinship between man and that quality in the environment which supports and enriches humanity in its spiritual quest. God will be very real to the religious man, but his reality will be interpreted in terms of social reciprocity with an as yet inadequately defined cosmic support of human values, rather than in terms of theistic creatorship and control. The experience of God will take the form of comradeship with that aspect our non-human environment which is found to reinforce and to enrich our life. Anthropomorphic symbols will frankly be used to promote that experience, but they will not be pressed into exact theological descriptions.

Smith is more committed to the use of personalist language than our minimalist approach is, though its value is clearly a matter of debate. He is definite that these "anthropomorphic symbols," although used frankly, should not be pressed into exact description. However, he does not seem to be quite so cautious about the personal language (such as "fellowship" or "social reciprocity") used to describe the interrelationship between man and the cosmic power. Note the deliciously ambiguous term "environment," a term with environmentalist and functionalist connotations, which can easily be interpreted in an immanental or ontologically transcendent sense. (This is one reason why the approach here set forth tends to favor the term "situation" or, rather, "forces transcendent to a situation.")

4. Bernard Meland

Bernard Meland, culminating in his teaching at the University of Chicago from 1945–1964, developed and persistently urged consideration of a type of empirical realism in religion which is an alternative both to the process thought inspired by Hartshorne and to the empirical approach of Wieman. In this regard Meland offers a number of themes important for our reflection. 1) He explores occasions of awareness of a supervening goodness, occasions of extremity which show the limits of selfhood and also resources beyond these limits. 2) He urges upon us that we broaden our empirical orientation to include a sense of wonder and appreciative awareness. 3) He teaches us to anchor our empirical inquiry within the structure of experience of our culture. 4) Meland cautions us to be mindful of the fallibility and abstract nature of all human formulations. Each of these four themes calls for careful reflection and we shall return to them in later chapters. However, at this point in our sketch of the roots of the minimalist approach to the divine we shall focus on one of these themes, the tentativeness of all human formulations of our apprehension of the divine.

Referring to a "discontinuity between manageable and unmanageable aspects of events," Meland asserts that

> the realities of any experience are to be accounted deeper than, or in some aspects resistant to, man's powers of observation and description. . . . The structures of reason which we are able to formulate and employ are but tentative ventures in apprehending the meaning of those realities.[36]

Meland sees this as a necessary corrective to the one-sided Cartesian emphasis on clarity and precision of language which permeates so much of our academic and technical life.

Meland uses the term "depth" to indicate three characteristics of reality which make up this provisional quality of our language. The first characteristic is the complexity of events. Experience is thick, it is made up of complex tangles of relationships. Reality is concrete, while our rational processes abstract and thereby oversimplify reality. There is a penumbra around the clear area of the rationally apprehended. The second characteristic is that the world has a dynamic character, that novel things happen. Consequently our rational formulations often lag behind the changes of events. Third, there is a mystery which surrounds us, a presence of ultimacy in the concrete. Ultimacy refers to reality beyond the immediate data of empirical observation or to concerns reaching beyond immediate satisfactions and practical problems. "Ultimacy" or "ultimate" is applied to those concerns, meanings, values, truths, and hopes which are grounded in a reality beyond one's own being.[37]

> Every concrete situation bears witness to an ultimacy peculiar to the interplay of circumstances and the limitations of resources that attend its witness.[38]

In physics this stance of tentativeness is required by the notions of relativity, the evidence of discontinuities in nature given by quantum mechanics, and the principle of indeterminacy. In metaphysics this tentativeness is expressed by Whitehead's characterization of metaphysical first principles as "metaphors mutely appealing for an imaginative leap."[39]

Meland is clear that this call for the recognition of tentativeness is not a call to irrationalism, but rather a caution against "the enclosure of the concrete event within pre-established universal categories," and against a dogmatic, "rigid empiricism."[40]

Meland has been the most persistent voice among all of the roots of the philosophy of openness urging an awareness of the tentativeness and provisional nature of our thinking and language about the world, especially about the ultimate reaches of thought and experience. His contribution to the minimalist approach is not so much to the minimal model of transcendence as to the recognition of the provisional character of all models, theories, and concepts of the divine. His recognition of the complexity and novelty of events is salutary. Surely there is a depth to things, a penumbra beyond the clarity of perception and thought.

Meland's language about ultimacy is slightly problematic for the naturalism espoused here. In the first place, the minimalistic approach finds the very term "ultimacy" to be questionable. It tends to refer to a basic ontological superiority between the ultimate and the less-than-ultimate, a distinction which minimalism does not make, although his use of the term "ultimacy" might be a deliberate attempt to avoid this distinction. The problematic nature of Meland's language about ultimacy is reflected in two of his key statements about God. The first is his reference to God as "a sensitive nature within nature." The second is to God as

> a matrix of sensitivity and meaning of sublte and vast dimensions, transcending our own, in fact all human structures, which serves as the ultimate ground of our meaning and the source and center of all that we are and of whatever else we might become in the mystery of creation and recreation. God is a structure of infinite goodness and incalculable power.[41]

Both of these statements reflect an ontological distinctness, unity and superiority which seem to be too close to the maximalism of classical or revisionary theism. Meland's language is somewhat unclear about the minimal or maximal implications of his statements, possibly because he did not think in these categories. Also, on principle, he wished to be tentative about the formulations which he always recognized as fallible. He was unhappy with precision of language. Nevertheless, the maximalist possibilities here are problematic from a minimalistic position. Despite this, surely there is an affinity between our concept of transcendence within immanence and his sense of ultimacy and immediacy trafficking together. Meland would no doubt be restive with the restrictiveness of our minimalism. Yet we both seek to move beyond the luminous core of the immediately observed and the presently practical.

In general I share in Meland's appropriation of the radical empirical tradition of James, Bergson, and Whitehead. Like Meland I wish to be selective in this appropriation. All three are to be used cautiously. Furthermore I agree with Meland that post-Newtonian physics reinforces this sense of the provisional character of all of our thinking. While too much can be made of finding one's philosophical or theological programme buttressed by the latest in physics, it is helpful to know that the science which is often taken as the paradigm of human certainty (together with mathematics, which is having its own reexamination of its foundations) is having a tussle with uncertainty. If this does not prove our contention about the tentativeness of all human thinking, it does provide some corroboration. This is nicely put in one of the quotations which Meland frequently made from Whitehead:

> When I went up to Cambridge early in the 1880's . . . nearly everything was supposed to be known about physics that could be known—except for a few spots, such as electromagnetic phenomena, which remained (or so it was thought) to be coordinated with the Newtonian principles. But, for the rest, physics was supposed to be nearly a closed subject. . . . By 1900 Newtonian physics were demolished, done for! Speaking personally, it had a profound effect on me; I have been fooled once, and I'll be damned if I'll be fooled again! Einstein is supposed to have made an epochal discovery. I am respectful and interested, but also skeptical. There is no more reason to suppose that Einstein's relativity is anything final, than Newton's *Principia*. The danger is dogmatic thought; it plays the devil with religion, and science is not immune from it.[42]

Obviously, Meland wrote before Thomas Kuhn and Richard Rorty. While this is not the place here to enter into this discussion, recent trends in philosophy would seem in general to support Meland's contention about the need to grant provisional status to philosophical claims to certainty or foundational first principles.[43]

III. Other American Theologians

1. Douglas Clyde Macintosh

The goal of D. C. Macintosh, writing at Yale from the 'teens through the 1930s, was to make theology a scientific discipline. More specifically, "whatever discoverable laws of empirical theology there may be will be general or universal statements of what in human experience God can be depended for," when the correct human adjustment is made. "We shall learn what God's character and power must be, in order to account for what experience shows he can be depended upon to produce in the life of man, when the human adjustment to God is made what it ought to be."[44] This dependence of our knowledge of God on human experience is the basis for the degree of tentativeness implicit in the very notion of empirical theology and also the basis for the degree of minimalism contained in Macintosh's notion of the sufficiency of God.

> The religious Object, whatever else it may be, must be absolutely sufficient to produce, in response to the right religious adjustment on man's part, the experience of adequate salvation. . . . In other words, God must be great enough and favorable enough to man to enable the person who finds the right religious adjustment to meet without moral failure or any absolute disaster whatever he may be called upon to face.[45]

This notion of sufficiency is spelled out in discussion of the traditional attributes of God. For example, "there must be change enough in the divine Being for the divine activity." Likewise, God "is able to do all that man needs to have done for him by the divine power." Likewise, "He can forecast the future sufficiently for all his purposes as God—i.e., sufficiently to enable him to work in the best way for the realization of his purposes. But this does not necessarily mean that he knows before the time, as certain, what in the nature of the case is uncertain until the moment of decision."[46]

This notion of "sufficiency" can be thought of as on the road to current minimalist thinking. Whatever else God is, God is *at least* sufficient for man's salvation. This suggests positively what minimal thinking states negatively. God may be less than superlative, but God is at minimum sufficient for man's salvation (Macintosh) or sufficient as a description of situationally transcendent resources (minimalism).

One differentiation between the contemporary philosophy of inner-worldly transcendence and the earlier orientation of Macintosh is that his experiential root is specifically religious, more narrowly a liberalized version of American revivalism. The minimal model, on the other hand, tries to draw from a much wider variety of experiences, secular and religious, provided that they have a dimension of transcendence.

A second point of difference is that Macintosh is far less minimalist than the present writer. In part this is a difference between "sufficient" and "minimal." But it goes further. I am not asserting that God is sufficient for all of our needs or even our religious living, but only that God is sufficient for some of our needs sometimes (namely, those of our needs that are met in an unexpected and unmanageable fashion).

2. Edgar Sheffield Brightman

Another historical root of minimalist thinking is found in the writings of the personalist, E. S. Brightman, who was active in the department of philosophy at Boston University from 1919 to

1951. For the minimalist what is significant is Brightman's notion that God is finite and limited. The limitation for Brightman is primarily internal, an element in God which Brightman calls The Given in God.

> This Given, then, is a limitation within the divine nature, a problem for the divine will and reason additional to that which is constituted by the existence of finite selves.
>
> The conception of a God limited by The Given within his own nature, yet wrestling meaning from it by the achievements of his rational will, seems to account more adequately than other ideas of God for the paradoxical assertion of religious experience that its object is both a Mighty God and a Suffering Servant. It places the Cross in the eternal nature of God.
>
> If we suppose that God is eternally both matter and form, then from eternity to eternity the divine will has The Given as a stimulus to activity and a source of problems to solve.[47]

Although Brightman's approach is rather different from the naturalism which is presented here, a brief analysis and evaluation of the Boston personalist should help further clarify the issues.

1. We should be very appreciative of the courage and imagination of Brightman and other American philosophers of religion to radically rethink the theistic tradition.

2. The notion of a finite God functioned historically as one of the suggestions and inspirations to minimalist thinking (which is how Brightman himself referred to William James).[48]

3. Brightman has a deep sense of struggle, suffering and evil. Although the impact of this sense affects this minimal model differently than Brightman's idea of God, this sense is very important and must be confronted in any theoretical or practical musing on the divine. If not a theodicy, we must have a sense of how the divine relates to the dark side of life.

4. There are a number of differences between the concepts of Brightman and that set forth in our minimal model. First and most obvious, Brightman's idea of God is that of a personal, conscious creator.[49] This concept is far removed from the quasi-pluralistic model which can employ oxygen, food, and medicine as paradigms for at least some situationally transcendent forces.

5. A major distinction between Edgar Sheffield Brightman's ontology and that on which this minimal model floats is that Brightman has a version of personalistic idealism while our conception is

based on a type of naturalism (although it need not be incompatible with other world views).

> Belief in God is the belief that personality is not really caused by body, but that divine personality is the supreme and ultimate cause of all bodies that there are: human bodies being only the expressions of divine will, the concrete form which that will assumes in acting on human persons.

> Theism . . . holds that all so-called neutral entities are forms of the divine thought or will.[50]

His particular variant of idealism is fused with an evolutionary approach.

> This history of the cosmos and the history of God may be different aspects of one and the same striving of rational form to shape and control a content which is not in itself rational but is capable of producing rational results.[51]

6. A third distinction between Brightman's finite God and our minimal model of transcendence is that the limitations to the personality of God in Brightman's view are to a major extent internal, a sort of principle of inertia which Brightman calls The Given. While the very notion of minimalist thinking implies limits, our model does not speak of these limits as internal to the divine, especially not as recalcitrant matter slow to be formed by reason.

However, if we are careful of our statement, there are a couple of faint echoes of The Given in our notion of the plurality of divine forces. The first echo is that a plurality of forces and goals is not fully rational. The second echo is that there is somewhat of a hope that these forces and goals may turn out or even grow to become compatible and even mutually reinforcing, thus partially paralleling Brightman's rational forming of the material. However, this hope of a growth towards an inclusive complexity we do *not* affirm as either metaphysically founded nor as having any degree of certainty.

7. There are some further instructive points of comparison. E. S. Brightman chooses goodness over power. God is limited in power so that God's goodness may be expanded. This is the same choice which Wieman makes. Loomer, however, in his later writings, thinks of God as the concrete totality of the world and, as such, ambiguous. Thus Loomer, in effect, reverses the choice of God's goodness over power which Brightman and Wieman make. In our

minimal model we side with Brightman and Wieman. The divine is minimal (very minimal) in power, yet unambiguously good, because the good has been selected out of the ambiguous forces of our experience.

8. There is a key and illuminating difference in methodology between Brightman and the model presented here. Brightman's concept is presented as an explanatory hypothesis. Its truth is established only in part by its ability to meet religious needs and to explain evils. These count as evidence for it and should not cause it to be dismissed as a rationalization. The hypothesis is a "coherent whole and any proposed idea of God must be tested by its comprehensive adequacy to explain experience as a whole."

> The conception of a God limited by The Given . . . yet wrestling meaning from it . . . seems to account more adequately than other ideas of God for the paradoxical assertion of religious experience that its object is both a Mighty God and a Suffering Servant.

> The Given would account for natural evils and the "mistakes" of evolution, would give God an eternal reason for activity, would render him more sympathetic with the limitations of man, would give more significance to the temporal process, and yet would not unduly impair the divine dignity, and would maintain God's transcendence and, by providing for the mysterious and irrational along with the moral and the rational in his nature, make him a more worthy object of numinous worship.[52]

In distinction from Brightman I am not presenting the minimalist model of transcendence as an explanatory hypothesis, either empirical or metaphysical. Apart from the fact that I don't need to explain cosmic drag, I find metaphysical explanations generally to be suspect. 1) They tend to assert too much. They go beyond proper ontological reticence. 2) They do not function adequately as explanations. They are really rather trivial in their cognitive content. 3) They tend to be apodictic in modality although Brightman does tone this down by speaking of his explanation as "most adequate" rather than as necessary.

Instead of an explanatory hypothesis what I offer here is a descriptive hypothesis, a sketch of what the transcendent appears to be.

9. Brightman has a keen sense of the divine sympathy with our suffering, a sense that God "shares as a comrade in the struggles and sufferings of humanity."[53] This sense parallels Whitehead's

"fellow sufferer who understands" and is a constant theme of Hartshorne's writings.

The minimal model proposed here is closer to the approach of Wieman which does not assume the personality of God and awareness on the part of God. Reading Wieman on prayer and forgiveness offers some illuminating contrast with Brightman here. I believe with Freud that we must learn to be mature and to survive the loss of the Ultimate Companion. (See *The Future of an Illusion*. Of course, saying this does not commit me to all of Freud's psychoanalytic theory nor to his crude psychoanthropology.)

10. Brightman has a keen sense of the religious experience of the irrational.[54] (He refers to Rudolph Otto and Jacob Boehme.) The following brief remarks hardly do justice to this very important topic.

Our minimal model clearly does not focus on what Tillich called the "personal elements" of God. To that extent it is very open to those aspects of our experience of the divine which draw on the "transpersonal" elements of the divine. I gladly admit that Paul Tillich and the Upanishads (as well as a cursory reading in the Western mystics) have helped overcome a Kantian, even Ritschlian, version of Calvinism in my background. Liberal New England and later mid-Western urban Congregationalism played a parallel role in both Dewey's and my own travels towards religious naturalism.

While the minimal model is rooted in a desire for a minimal clarity, it never rejects ecstasy or dark experiences, even though it strives for a conceptually clear model and, at the analytic level, would probably relate some of these experiences to unconscious emotional forces, possibly even archetypal experiences, and to naturalistically conceived experiences of the sublime, the powerful, or the uncanny. In short, the minimal model is not an attempt to domesticate irrational forces and mystery. It is an attempt to achieve a measure of understanding of them.

3. Philip Phenix

Another exponent of the minimalist approach to the philosophy of religion is Philip Phenix. An educational theorist who taught philosophy at Teachers College, Columbia University during the decades of the 1960s and 1970s, he wrote a thoughtful sketch of a philosophy of religion called *Intelligible Religion*.

Phenix's approach seems determined by his goal, which is to achieve clarity and universal intelligibility for religious ideas. The foundation of intelligibility he finds to be in that aspect or type of human experience which has the twin characteristics of being specifiable and shareable.

Phenix explores five common human experiences which he claims have these two properties of potentiality for being specified and potentiality for being shared. These are the experiences of change, dependence, order, value, and imperfection.

Each of these experiences generates a family of attitudes. While space does not permit a detailed discussion of these attitudes, they include such attitudes as generosity, hope, confidence, humility and zest. The approach of Phenix bears similarity to mine, chiefly in terms of his concern for describing an objective correlate to these attitudes which is easily intelligible in secular terms and yet which will not encourage the typical secular attitudes of technological optimism and existential despair. In short, the recommendations of Philip Phenix bear a strong similarity to the attitude of openness urged in our approach. This is particularly true in his discussion of the experience of imperfection and its correlative attitudes of hope, humility, and tolerance. This seems very close to the attitude of openness to ideal transcendence advocated here. Indeed, there may be a common rootage of both Phenix and our minimal model in Tillich at this point. This is suggested not only by Phenix's reference to the Protestant Principle, but also to his assertion that knowledge, love, organization or society, and artistic creation or appreciation is always imperfect, an assertion seeming to reflect Tillich's four functions of culture.[55]

Most relevant for our purpose, Phenix explores a "minimum view" of these experiences. For example, given the experience of change, on a minimum view this is a world full of surprises. Note that the minimalist position of Phenix is analogous to that elaborated here, in that the minimalist strategy is an attempt to say more than the elimination of the minimum asserted by reductive positivism. The minimum implication will be minimal, but as an implication it will go beyond the bare description of the experience. "The *minimum* implications of the fact of change ... should be intelligible to all who cannot rest content merely with a description of the changing order of things."[56]

The minimalist approach of Phenix is explicitly seen in his treatment of infinity. "The infinite," he says, is a way of signifying the limitless perfectibility of the nature of things, "of speaking of the process of ceaseless envisaging of ideal possibilities."

> The infinite God or the perfect God might with a minimum of speculation be taken simply as a symbol of the limitless wealth of possibilities inherent in existence.[57]

The similarity between the approach of Phenix and that presented in this study comes out clearly in his conception of God. God is not a determinate object. God is

> more like a disclosure of the underlying nature of everything experienced. . . . God is the name applied to a set of definite and intelligible *aspects* of the world made apparent in the experience of everything in it. God is a kind of *dimension* or complex of dimensions made manifest in all our experience.

Further, the approach taken by Phenix is similar to the minimal model in the attention given to the problem of unity and plurality of God. Sometimes Phenix uses language such as "God is the name applied to a set of definite and intelligible *aspects* of the world." Here, the concept of "set" seems to be a unity constituted out of a variety, the question remaining of the degree of underlying unity constituting the set. At other times Phenix will assert:

> that God is one and not many means that the various experiences by which the meaning of the word "God" is defined are not separable.[58]

It seems as if his meaning is that the five human experiences of change, dependence, order, value and imperfection always occur together. Thus, while there is a complexity to our experience of God (namely, the diversity of these experiences), there is also a unity to this experience (namely, the inseperability of these experiences). This is a greater degree of unity than that postulated in the minimal model elaborated here.

Another major difference between our two approaches is that for Phenix the aspects of the world which constitute God are present in every experience. In the vision articulated here, the experiences may be quite different and do not have each of these five aspects. These experiences do have a generic similarity, the character of transcendence.

The minimalist approach of Phenix also comes out in his rethinking of omnipotence. Here his minimalist approach yields what Phenix calls an "experiential definition."

> According to the experiential definition, the omnipotence of God simply means that the experience of change, dependence, order, value and imperfection reflect the nature of *all possible existence*.

His minimalism is also present in his reconception of the personality of God.

> To say that God is personal, therefore, means simply that the experiences by which God is defined are ones in which there is direct involvement and relevance to persons.

> Creativity, sociality, intelligence, freedom and transcendence—these major characteristics of personality—are exactly the five elements involved in the fundamental religious experiences by means of which God is defined. These experiences are ones in which personality is most fully realized. This means that the experience of God is the essence of experiencing what it means to be personal. . . . The world as it meets one in religious experience is a person-producing and person-enhancing world.

Note the parallel in the last sentence to the definition of God of Shailer Mathews:

> God is our personification of those cosmic forces which have produced us as persons and with which we can have personal relations.[59]

IV. Continental Thinkers

1. Kant

Important historical antecedents of the minimalist position are found in the work of Immanuel Kant. Clearly, the epistemological and ontological context of the present approach is vastly different from that of the Königsberg thinker. The philosophical orientation here does not concern itself with the possibility of synthetic *a priori* judgments or with the distinction between noumena and phenomena. Nor are our conclusions set forth as universal and necessary conditions of knowledge or morality. The concept of the divine in our minimal model is quite different from that which Kant criticizes and that which he finally outlines. Nevertheless, Kant is a great watershed in Western culture and his spirit blows through this book, even though his vocabulary and many of his conclusions are rejected.

With the clear understanding that the minimalist approach is profoundly indebted to Kant and yet that our intellectual great-grandfather would hardly recognize his descendent, let us look at four of Kant's themes which have borne fruit in this constructive statement.

1) Kant gave a prominence to the role of the knowing self. Our approach rejects the clear distinction between form (supplied by the knower) and matter in epistemology (as well as other dichotomies, such as between perception and understanding and between the theoretical and practical uses of reason) and also rejects the corresponding assertion of universal and necessary synthetic judgments. We live in a world as understood by post-Newtonian physics and non-Euclidean geometry.

The interrelationship of knower and known becomes, in our approach, the openness of the self to this worldly transcendence. Specifically, in our model of divinity this theme appears as reciprocity between the imagination which abstracts and unifies the minimally transcendent resources and ideals on the one hand and these resources and ideals on the other. Historically, in between Kant and the present philosophical construction is the transactionalism of John Dewey.

2) Kant rejected the great Western tradition of proofs for the existence of a supreme being of which we have knowledge by rational argument. This was elaborated clearly in the Dialectic of the *Critique of Pure Reason*.[60] Historically this gave a great boost to discussions of both a limited deity and minimalist thinking, in that traditional arguments for a Supreme Being are severely challenged. Kant, however, would probably reject the ideas of many of those who adopt a minimal divinity as still using the theoretical employment of reason improperly.

Hume also challenged both revelation and reason as avenues to a knowledge of God, but his work seems not to have been as much of a challenge which the American sources of our approach felt should be answered as Darwin or positivism were. Neo-orthodoxy generally can be seen as another attempt to avoid Kant's rejection of revelation and rational arguments for God. The neo-orthodox approach was not by a minimalist reduction as by a retreat ("return" they would say) past the tradition of natural theology and orthodoxy to Biblical (and Reformation) roots. The result is a conception of God's self-revelation and a non-theoretical, non-objective reception of this revelation through faith within the divine-human encounter or decision for the kerygma. This result is an attempt to avoid arguments for the existence of God and the theoretical use of reason which Kant had rejected.

My own rejection of the approach of Karl Barth and Emil Brunner, and even of the neo-orthodox aspects of Paul Tillich,

Rudolf Bultmann and the Niebuhr brothers is due to the fact that:
a) a maximally conceived God is assumed by this approach, exceeding the bounds of our alternative stance of reticence, and
b) there are different alleged loci of revelation, and thus no non-
question-begging answer to the questions. Why should Christ be
chosen over Torah or why not the Qu'rān over Christ? (Granted that
Christ, to Christians, appears with New Testament warrant as the
culmination of Jewish longings. But the Messiah crucified is hardly
the fulfillment of Jewish expectations when looked at from the
other end of the telescope. Furthermore the Qu'rān tells us that
Muhammed, not Christ, is the seal of the prophets.)

3) Although Kant rejected not only the traditional proofs for the
existence of God but all theoretical knowledge of God, he did recon-
ceive the approach to God and the blockage of the Dialectic of Pure
Reason was avoided by making God a postulate of practical reason.
By "postulate" Kant meant a necessary condition of our moral activity (which activity itself seems both inevitable and, from a Kantian perspective, rational). At the same time that our approach to
God was reconceived as a necessary presupposition of moral reasoning, Kant narrowed the focus of the concept of God to a guarantor of
happiness in the afterlife for the morally virtuous.[61]

In our idea of this-worldly transcendence the rejection of rational proofs for God and theoretical knowledge of a supreme being is
accepted. In this sense the general argument of Kant's rejection of
the transcendent use of reason (in the Kantian sense of transcendent, that is, God as an idea of pure reason) as well as the antinomy
of the idea of a First Cause is accepted by minimalism. Our ontological reticence is very similar to Kant here. However, not only
is our minimal model rather different from Kant's reconceived
God, but his third postulate of practical reason, God as a necessary
condition of morality, is also far from our viewpoint. Our notion of
the provisional and tentative nature of our model and of all proper
ideas of the divine is such that we seek hypothetical, not categorical, positing. This is far removed from Kant. James and Meland
have come between us and the late eighteenth century with the result that a hypothetical and tentative affirmation is now much
more acceptable.

4) As is well known, Kant's major thrust in religious inquiry
has been the moral approach to God. God is the guarantor of the
perfect connection between morality and happiness. Within the
bounds of ontological reticence, however, we disagree. (Here we join
a great chorus of dissent, but our minimalism is not simple positivism or classic empiricism.) A guarantor of such unity between

morality and happiness is beyond proper ontological modesty. The very language of "*summum bonum*" rings false. Furthermore, given both our sense of plurality and our restriction to this very ambiguous world, we have no knowledge or even hint of such a unity. Finally, immortality is neither a matter of knowledge nor of practical belief, given our ontological restraint.[62] Kant wanted to keep religion within the bounds of reason and morality. Bernard Meland, from whom I have learned much, thought that this was too restrictive. In part, my acknowledgement of the real aspect of the transcendent is an attempt to expand the bounds of reason.[63]

However, Kant's emphasis on the moral has been retained in our approach, although with a difference. Our notion of ideal transcendence is strongly moral in focus, but the following three qualifications are important. 1) Our notion of ideal transcendence is broad enough to include non-moral ideals, including the pursuit of truth and beauty, although there is probably a strong moral concern to these pursuits. 2) The pluralistic aspect of minimalism rejects the unity of the attainment of these ideals in a *summum bonum*. 3) Clearly this-worldly, minimalistic naturalism cannot accept the idea of an infinite time of striving which Kant postulates for a person to reach these ideals. 4) In addition, our notion of actual and finite transcendence has a sense of receptivity to real resources which is lacking in Kant, for whom "will" was a key word, not "grace."

Many of us are in debt to Kant for showing us a way around Hume's radical skepticism in religious inquiry. However, the approach outlined in this book keeps within the ontological restraint which Kant followed only in the theoretical use of reason. Therefore, my answer to Hume is radically different from that of Kant. Also the glimpses of this-worldly transcendence are not restricted to a moral use of reason. (Indeed, Kant's God is further restricted to being an auxiliary of an individualistic, quasi-eschatological schema.)

5) Kant's approach rests on an investigation of the necessary conditions of human activity: theoretical, moral and aesthetic. This investigation is a major source, ultimately, of our ideal transcendence, particularly when combined with Kant's own ontological reticence. However, when he distinguished between the transcendent object and the transcendental conditions of reason, his conclusion does not have the minimal rigor which is advocated in this study. The minimalist approach extends Kant's distinction between the regulative and constitutive use of ideas to the moral sphere and beyond to all ideals.[64] This extension is one of the chief differences

between Kant and the minimal model. We should not leave Kant without a brief reference to the fact that the notion of "situation" in the minimal model owes much to Dewey and Wieman. This notion, clearly in Dewey, is a revision of Hegel's organicism which, in turn, can be traced to a general concern with organismic thinking, one of whose sources is Kant's Third Critique.

2. Feuerbach

At first glance there appears to be a similarity between the minimalist approach and that of Feuerbach. The appearance is significant enough to warrant a brief discussion.

Feuerbach is helpful in suggesting that there may be significance to religious language and the doctrines of traditional theology, even though there is no God other than that projected by the human imagination. Feuerbach is also helpful in stressing the role of projection in shaping the notion of God and of the role of human ideals as the material for the process.

A clear difference between the minimal model and the position of Feuerbach is that the notion of actual transcendence developed here, although inner-worldly, refers to real resources of growth and restoration in the world. These resources, while working in interaction with an individual or even a group, have an objective existence, in the sense of coming from outside the person or group, indeed, from outside the perceived situation of the person or group. By "objective" here is not meant the agreement of competent observers. In the sense used here the body and the deeper recesses of the mind may on occasion be objective in relation to the self. Feuerbach, on the other hand, does not refer to any resources with a reality independent of the self or its group. The distinction between actual and ideal transcendence made in the minimal model is an attempt to avoid the major weakness of the stance of Feuerbach and the general position of the Humanist movement. That weakness is a closure, at least in the theoretical sphere, to resources beyond the human situation as perceived, as understood by currently available categories, and as managed by current means for present values.

In the second place, it would appear that Feuerbach's notion of God is very similar to that of ideal transcendence in the minimal model. With the understanding that this is only the ideal aspect of transcendence, not the real aspect, there is a similarity. There are some differences, however.

Feuerbach's God is a projection of *idealized* humanity. I conceive of ideal transcendence as a projection of unrealized goals.

Unless I am misreading the existential situation, there is a lure, a dynamic element which many people have found in religion which I find lacking in Feuerbach. Allied to this lure is a healthy sense of judgment, even of unworthiness, arising from a sense of unrealized possibilities, lost opportunities, and perverted choices.

Finally, Feuerbach overlooks the problem of the plurality of the imaginative projections. In each of these three areas John Dewey is a somewhat better guide than Feuerbach, although Dewey himself does not seem surefooted when exploring religion.

3. Ricoeur

Paul Ricoeur is a complex thinker with a wide range of interests, sources, and dialogue partners. Perhaps most widely known for his *Symbolism of Evil* and his study of Freud's interpretation theory, he has been intensively studied by a number of Biblical scholars for his hermeneutics of the parables. As a Husserl scholar, he has developed a new approach in phenomenology, formulated a complex philosophical anthropology, written a detailed history of metaphor theory, engaged in a running battle against structuralism, and devoted considerable attention to the tasks of hermeneutics.

For the purpose of placing of philosophy the inner-worldly transcendence in its context, concentration will be on two articles written by Ricoeur in the late 1960's: "Freedom in the Light of Hope" and "Religion, Atheism, and Faith."[65] These two articles touch clearly on the themes of our book. They are places where he treats religion, not hermeneutically (as in *The Symbolism of Evil,* the Parable studies, or *Essays on Biblical Interpretation*),[66] but reflectively, attempting to say how the results of the hermeneutical task can be appropriated today.

1. There is a strong echo between the note of tentativeness in the philosophy of inner-worldly transcendence set forth in this book and Ricoeur's concepts of a "post-religious faith" or of "thinking according to hope." Ricoeur does not fully explicate these concepts, but the general direction may be garnered from the two articles. Apparently they are akin to what Ricoeur in *The Symbolism of Evil* referred to as "post-critical naivete," or "second naivete."[67]

Postreligious faith or faith for a postreligious age is the type of faith which is possible when the false gods of accusation and consolation are overcome through the critique of atheism. What we have in "Religion, Atheism, and Faith" is a three-stage dialectic. First there is an explication of the God of religion and the functions of accusation and consolation which this God performs. Then there is the consideration of the critique by the atheists, particularly Freud and Nietzsche, opening the way for a faith apart from accusation and consolation.

It is not quite clear whether "thinking according to hope" in "Freedom in the Light of Hope" is the same as postreligious faith in "Religion, Atheism, and Faith."[68] They are parallel in that they both belong to the postcritical, postreligious stage, but differ in that the latter is faith, the former is philosophical reflection.[69]

There are two themes in Ricoeur's discussion of hope. First, the difficulty that hope presents to thinking is not a lack of meaning, but an excess of meaning. This ties in with Ricoeur's notion of the "economy of superabundance" (see below). Thinking according to hope will only be an "approximation" to what is hoped for. Postulated immortality, for example, is only an approximation to the hope for resurrection.[70]

Second, thinking according to hope parallels postreligious faith quite clearly in that the transcendental illusions which are an ever-present temptation to thinking must be purged. The critique here is not that of Freud and Nietzsche but that of the Dialectic of Kant's first *Critique*. Since "the domain of hope is quite precisely coextensive with the region of transcendental [*sic*, not transcendent] illusion," the Dialectic of pure reason is necessary because it introduces such a critique which is "indispensable to an *intellectus spei*."

> I hope, there where I necessarily deceive myself, by forming absolute objects: self, freedom, God . . . The Kantian concept of the transcendental illusion, applied to the religious object par excellence, is one of inexhaustible philosophical fecundity.

The difference between the Kantian critique and that of Feuerbach or Nietzsche is that "there is a legitimate thought of the unconditioned."

> The transcendental illusion . . . does not proceed from the projection of the human into the divine but, on the contrary, from the filling-in of the thought of the unconditioned according to the mode of the empirical object. That is why Kant can say: . . . reason limits the claim of sensibility to extend our empirical, phenomenal, spatio-temporal knowledge to the noumenal order.[71]

Clearly there is an echo here between my this-worldly transcendence and Ricoeur's postreligious faith. It is not merely the extension of "empirical, phenomenal, spatio-temporal knowledge" to the unconditioned which our minimalism rejects, it is the very legitimacy of thinking of the unconditioned at all. In the appropriation of Kant which underlies my minimalism, the Dialectic of the First Critique takes precedence over that of the Second in this sense: God as a postulate of practical reason is seen to be a variant of God as demonstrated by theoretical reason and, hence, falls under the strictures of the Dialectic of the Ideal of Pure Reason.

Ricoeur says little of God when he is reflecting in the postreligious mode. There is plenty of critique of the precritical conception of God as the source of accusation and consolation, and much of the hermeneutics of the Biblical symbols of fatherhood, hope, and the parables of the Kingdom, but little reflection on what all of this would mean for a philosophical reflection on the nature of God. Is this reticence to speak of God, except critically and hermeneutically, a general reluctance to speak ontologically about God? This reluctance seems to be an echo of minimalism's ontological reticence.

2. A second echo between Ricoeur and the philosophy of this-worldly transcendence is the rejection of the god of "corrupt" religion. The two poles of religious feelings are "the fear of punishment and the desire for protection." It is the god of "corrupt" religion who punishes and consoles. While the minimal model would go beyond rejecting the god of "corrupt" religion to reject almost all conceptions of god, there is an echo between these two concerns. Both Ricoeur and the minimal model seek to root out the conception of a supreme source of accusation and consolation.

When Nietzsche and Freud are brought together, Ricoeur sees them as developing a new type of hermeneutics, a critique of "cultural representations considered as disguised symptoms of desire and fear."[72] This critique will displace the god of "onto-theology,"

> the god of metaphysics and also the god of theology, insofar as theology rests on the metaphysics of the first cause, necessary being, and the prime mover, conceived as the source of values and as the absolute good.[73]

Likewise the analysis of consolation results in a displacement of the god who functions as "the ultimate source of protection." God, conceived as father, is "not only the figure who accuses; he is also the figure who protects. Now he responds . . . to our desire for protection and consolation, and the name for this desire is nostalgia for the father."[74]

3. Another echo between Ricoeur's thinking and the philosophy of openness is his concept of the "logic of super-abundance," the category of "how much more."[75] This is apparently one of the key themes which Ricoeur finds in his hermeneutics of the New Testament and which he utilizes as a key concept in his reflections on ethics and history. Here the echo in the philosophy of openness is the notion of transcendence.

Ricoeur focuses on Romans 5 with its repetition of "how much more" and the abounding of grace. The obverse of "how much more" is the category of "in spite of," in spite of actual reality, including death. This "logic of surplus and excess" is to be deciphered "in daily life, in work and in leisure, in politics and in universal history." It is an openness to new creation, a "passion for the possible."

At this point Ricoeur sees himself diverging from an existentialism which contracts freedom "within an experience of present, interior, and subjective decision."[76] Instead, it opens up freedom for social and political justice.

Ricoeur's theme of openness to new creation finds a strong echo in the notion of openness to resources of healing and renewal. There is a strong analogy between a recognition of superabundance, a passion for the possible, and the sense of transcendence, both actual and ideal. And Ricoeur's sense of freedom for justice finds its counterpart in transcendent resources opening up new concrete possibilities of pursuing the obligation of justice.

The divergence between Ricoeur and the philosophy of this-worldly transcendence comes out clearly, however, in the ease with which Ricoeur can speak of Resurrection and the denial of death.

While we cannot do full justice to the insights of Ricoeur in these articles, including his fascinating interplay between Kant and Hegel, his treatment of the relation between philosophy and hearing (or tradition), and his important discussion of the pathology of hope, we can see that the minimalist approach has analogies to Ricoeur's rejection of the god of onto-theology.[77]

4. Tillich

The notion of transcendent norms in the minimal model owes much to Paul Tillich's notion of the unconditional basis and goal of the human pursuit of meaning. However, this viewpoint is radically transformed within this minimal model, since the unconditioned element in culture is deprived of its status as an ontological ultimate and reconceived as a collection of regulative ideas whose pursuit is worthwhile.

According to Tillich, there is an unconditional element in human theoretical and practical acts of meaning. It is the power of being which is also:

> the basis of truth, because it is the transcendence of subject and object. It is the basis of the good, because it contains every being in its essential nature and . . . the norms of every ethical command.

But although it is the basis of the truth and the good, it is not itself the object of any act of truth or goodness.

> This 'being' transcends everything particular without becoming empty, for it embraces everything particular.[78]

It is to be noted that the unconditional element is not reached by thought or achieved by action. The unconditional is not the object of meaningful acts, whether of knowledge or of conduct. It is rather the basis of meaningful acts which, apart from the concrete contents of these acts (for it is the *un*conditioned), gives rise to these acts. It is the *veritas ipsa* and the *bonum ipsum* which is independent of any conditional judgment concerning the *veritates* or the *bona*. It is present as an unconditional certainty, whenever conscious attention is focused on it, although it is not the special content of any act of meaning.

> Every creative act of spirit is, in its intention, directed toward the *unconditioned form*. The unconditioned form does not exist, however; it is the expression for the fundamental relationship between thought and being. . . . Being is the import, the reality, the unconditioned meaning that gives reality and meaning to every particular form. Therefore, every spiritual act of meaning-fulfillment bears in itself the Eros for the unconditioned meaning.[79]

All of the functions of culture involve the interaction between subject and object and therefore rest on the *prius* of the separation between subject and object, which is the unconditional element toward which culture strives and which is yet present giving meaning to the actual products of cultural creation. Thus,

> the prius of any individual comprehension of meaning is the unconditioned meaning itself, . . . the prius of every form of meaning

is direction toward the unconditioned form, and . . . the prius of every import of meaning is the unconditioned import.[80]

Thus the unconditional is both the goal and the basis of every act of grasping or creating of meaning.[81]

Tillich classifies cultural activities into the four functions: the cognitive and aesthetic on the theoretical side and personal and communal creation on the practical.[82]

There is a gap between subject and object which it is the intention of the cognitive and the aesthetic to overcome. It is this intention where the unconditional element in *theoria* comes in. "Truth" is the name of the reunion of the subject and object in the cognitive realm. In the esthetic realm it is "beauty" or, better, "authentic expressiveness."

Praxis is the transforming or shaping function of culture, the opposite of *theoria* as the receiving or grasping function. *Praxis* likewise is divided into two parts, excluding the technical realm. These parts are the creation of persons and the creation of communities. Corresponding to truth and expressiveness as goals of *theoria* are "humanity" and "justice." Humanity is "the fulfillment of man's inner aims with respect to himself and his personal relations," in short, "the fulfillment of human potentialities" in individuals. Justice is "the fulfillment of the inner aim of social groups and their mutual relations . . . the aim of all cultural actions which are directed toward the transformation of society."[83]

In all of the functions of culture there is a gap between subject and object, a gap which it is the intention of *theoria* and *praxis* to overcome. This gap is never finally bridged under the conditions of existential estrangement, but the drive, the intention toward bridging it is the unconditional element which the receiving and transforming acts of culture attempt to realize. At the same time this intention to realize the unconditional is successful to the extent that the estrangement between subject and object is overcome, for that which is the goal of every cultural act also undergirds and is present within every such act as that which precedes the split between subject and object.

Within the different realms of man's encounter with reality—the cognitive, the ethical, and . . . the aesthetic and the social-political—he finds structural absolutes without which life in these realms would be impossible. . . . In each of these structural absolutes there is a point of self-transcendence toward the Absolute itself, the ground of being. . . . In the cognitive encounter this point of self-transcendence is being-itself; in the ethical encounter it is love in its character of *agape,* which contains justice and combines the absolute and the relative. In other words, we have shown by analytic description the presence of absolutes within the universe of relativities and have pointed to the ground of everything absolute—the Absolute itself.[84]

The notion of transcendent norms in this model represents a selective appropriation in a naturalistic framework of Tillich's concept of the unconditional element in human search for meaning. I do not claim that this translation is exhaustive and without remainder. I do claim, however, that it represents a way of deepening the naturalistic framework through a genuine learning from Tillich.

The first move is to note the structure of Tillich's concept of this unconditioned element. There is a duality to Tillich's concept: the unconditioned is both *"prius"* and "goal" of every act of meaning. I take *prius* or, as I prefer, "presupposition," to mean that there is validity in every particular act of meaning. In the theoretical sphere, for example, even skepticism presupposes the validity of the act of skepticism. I take "goal" to mean the ideal towards which all search for meaning strives.

The second move is to specify the meaning of "unconditionedness" in both the presupposition and the goal of every act of meaning. On the one hand, since the *prius* is the validity presupposed in *every* act of meaning, this validity has no conditions. In short, it is unconditioned. On the other hand, the goal is a standard towards which the act of meaning strives. It is a never-attainable ideal. Since it is never attained, it also has no conditions. It is unconditioned.

The practical consequence of all of this is that all of our endeavors after meaning are worthwhile, since there is validity in every act of meaning. At the same time we need to remain unsatisfied with every attainment, since no accomplishment is ideal. This blending of relative worth with continual striving is the answer to both despair over meaninglessness and the fanaticism of assuming ultimate attainment.

In different functions of meaning Tillich refers to the unconditional as "truth-itself," "beauty-itself," and "the good-itself." The third move is to note that Tillich sees an identity between "truth-itself," "beauty-itself," and "the good-itself" and between these and "being-itself."

Our selective appropriation of Tillich involves an exploration of some common experiences of the pursuit of value which have the dual structure of unconditioned *prius* and unconditioned goal. This search will be fruitful, thus confirming the significance of Tillich's approach. However, within our naturalistic framework we shall question the unity of "truth-itself," "beauty-itself," and "the good-itself." While there can be an imaginative identification of these goals, the value of doing so is limited. Furthermore, the unity of these axiological goals with "being-itself" is explicitly denied within the naturalistic framework.

The humane endeavours of reflective inquiry, art, the moral life and social responsibility sometimes involve the pursuit of meanings which transcend the situation. Reflective inquiry, for example, may search for a truth not yet attained and art attempt to create a beauty or form not yet made.

We can also affirm within our naturalistic framework that these humane endeavours often involve the presupposition that the pursuit is worthwhile, that significant attainment in its direction is possible no matter what failure or disappointment may meet the specific results of the pursuit of the goal. But within our framework we cannot speak of an objective correlate to this presupposition of significance. To do this would also be an illegitimate move beyond the evidence. We must be reticent to speak of the *prius* of meaning as an ontological ultimate. The *prius* of the pursuit of meaning is our sense of the worthwhileness of the pursuit of meaning.

Those who dismiss the ultimate as an illusion have missed an important point. There is at least something going on in the belief in the ontological or religious ultimate that is usually lost when it is dismissed as an illusion. This something is the function which the ultimate plays in our pursuit of value. Given our modest model, what we can legitimately affirm is not an ontological or religious ultimate but rather the continually transcendent presupposition and goal of the pursuit of value.

In concluding our sketch of the historical context of this religious naturalism, we note that our treatment of the ideal aspect of transcendence owes much to H. Richard Niebuhr's analysis of radical monotheism in science and democracy. The chief difference between our analysis and that of Niebuhr is that he identifies the unconditional with the God of radical monotheism, which is a full-fledged transcendent reality. Our ontological caution does not allow us to grant such an ontological status to the unconditional goal of the pursuit of values.

A number of other thinkers have explored the ideal aspect of transcendence but exceeded proper ontological reticence. Josiah Royce used a number of arguments for the unconditional presupposition of all rational inquiry, from his first argument from the possibility of error on to his last argument based on the need for a universal community of interpretation. Charles Hartshorne argued that all our pursuits of meaning presuppose the existence of God. Following Hartshorne, Schubert Ogden developed the idea that all moral affirmations, in fact any assertion of "the foundational value of freedom or anything else rests on the assurance that the world is finally meaningful and that our striving to realize values is not simply vain." Bernard Lonergan and Emerich Coreth argue for the unconditional basis of theoretical inquiry by using a transcendental method which focuses on the presuppositions of theoretical inquiry. Recently Charles Winquist has used this procedure as one aspect of his multi-faceted approach.

These thinkers all argue from the necessary presuppositions of rational or moral inquiry to affirm the ontological reality of the ground of such a presupposition. The ontological reticence of our minimal model, as argued in the third section of Chapter One, rejects the possibility and the necessity of this move.[85]

CHAPTER THREE

THE ETHICS OF OPENNESS

In one sense the moral imperative of a philosophy of openness to this-worldly transcendence is easy to state as an abstract principle. One should be open to situationally transcendent resources and be open and committed to challenging ideals. Since such openness and commitment involve a continual process of correction, even radical transformation, it is preferable to add the word "critical." Thus the basic moral principle of this philosophy is that we should be critically open to situationally transcendent resources and critically open and committed to challenging ideals. In short, *we should adopt and continually nurture a stance of critical openness and commitment.*

I. Discernment of Worth

The first half of this principle is openness to the real aspect of transcendence. This openness involves receptivity, involving among its modes an active and disciplined receptivity, to the creative qualities entering into a situation. This receptivity to creative qualities is a discernment of worth, a cherishing of value, a sensitive appreciation of caliber and need. The epistemological parallel to sensitive appreciation is discussed in the next chapter as sensitive discrimination.

Emphasizing the discernment of worth helps pull us out of the trap of subjectivism. A common approach in our time has been to create a dichotomy between judgments of fact and value judgments, relegating value judgments to the domain of the arbitrary and even meaningless. Value judgments are then *merely* opinions and, while you have a right to your opinion, in the end your opinion is no better than anybody else's opinion. As a result, value judgments, including moral judgments, are frequently regarded as arbitrary and subjective.

However, when discernment of worth is taken as a guiding concept, the approach is different. Events and objects do have various types of worth, including triviality or baseness. These are, to a considerable extent, objective characteristics of these events and objects. True, they are not as cleanly objective as some observation statements may be. However, when ordinary conversation refers to something as gross, trashy, or evil, this is usually not arbitrary or misleading. It does tell us something, often very important, about the way things are. There is room for error, individual preference, and cultural difference. Such room, however, does not make such judgments arbitrary or mere subjective opinion. When someone tells us, "the steak at Barney's is rather nice," we can act appropriately on the basis of the communication. This statement could be true and, of course, false. But the possibility of error does not make it subjective. It makes it corrigible.

The term "worth" is chosen for a variety of reasons. It places the emphasis on the objective quality, value, importance or significance of the object (event, process, person, thing). To be sure, "worth" involves a transaction. It will always be the worth of some object to some person, group or organism in some situation. Worth requires discernment or appreciation. On the other hand, the term "worth" focuses on the objective pole of the transaction.

Thus the term "worth" draws attention to the objective pole of the interaction, that is, to the contribution that the worth-ful object makes to a subject which deems it worth-ful in that context or, if not to the contribution of the object, the term draws attention to the worth which the object has to a wider community of appreciation. That is, the term "worth" is intended to focus attention on the merit of the object, even though the subject cannot be ignored.

Our term "worth" is intended to signify, to some extent, what John Dewey meant by valu*able,* as distinct from valu*ed.* As I understand it, for Dewey nothing can be valuable without some subject to appreciate its value. However, the valuable is distinguished from the valued by reference to an appreciation of its relations to its context, specifically the conditions and consequences of the object. I differ from Dewey at two points. First, I see the valuable as distinguished not only by the context of the object, but also by a larger community of appreciation. Thus, if I cannot appreciate something, but competent and reflective judges can, it may be that there is something valuable which I have not yet learned to appreciate. While Dewey does not speak here of a community of appreciation, he does refer to the possibility of growth in taste or appreciation. My second distinction from Dewey is that my notion of worth is intended to signal that the appreciation of value is not clearly empirical, in a scientific sense, but includes aesthetic sensitivity. In other words, I understand the appreciation of the worth of the valuable to go beyond the publicly observable and operationally definable canons of scientific procedures as normally understood. Dewey's language about value is not always as clear about this as he is in *Art as Experience*.

The term worth is thus used to indicate that judgments of value are often not arbitrary or mere opinion. It is further used to focus on the properties or qualities of the object itself, even though such a focus is a partial abstraction from the total context. Finally the term is used to point to, indeed encourage, an attitude of openness to the object, the opposite of an attitude of manipulation. This is akin to Buber's I-Thou attitude, although it does not accept his extreme and clear-cut distinction between an I-Thou and an I-It orientation.

Finally the term "worth" also suggests that a) the importance or significance of the valuable object may be more than presently expressed in gesture or language and b) this importance or significance may be more than can be presently discerned. The term has a heuristic thrust, calling for further openness to and exploration of the worth-ful object in its context.

Judgments about worth need not be subjective. They do have a personal component, as do all judgments. When a person seriously makes an appraisal of value, she is personally underwriting the judgment, backing it with her personal commitment. But such a commitment does not mean that it is subjective in the sense of being arbitrary or privatized. In addition to Bernard Meland's concept of appreciative or sensitive awareness, here used in a moral context, I have been stimulated by Daniel Maguire's "ethical realism," in which he speaks of the "experience of the value of persons and their environment," of the perception of their valuableness. Also Douglas Sturm has been engaged in some fruitful reflection on a "relational understanding" of experience with particular reference to the use of Meland's work in ethics.[1]

Discernment of worth also takes us beyond the no-harm principle. There is a tendency in discussions of moral philosophy to give preference to the no-harm principle, as opposed to the principles of beneficence or justice. For one thing it is much easier to decide on what doing harm is than what doing good is. Furthermore, there are always the problems of meddling, of making someone dependent, or of depleting one's own resources when attempting to be helpful. Doing no harm is easier to mesh with respect for autonomy and individual rights than is doing good. In fact, doing no harm often means doing nothing at all.[2]

However, when worth is discerned there often is more that is expected of us than doing no harm to the worthful thing or event. We may be called on to protect or defend it. Or we may be called to nurture, reinforce or enhance it.

This is both theoretically and practically more ambiguous than the application of the no-harm principle. Rather than having a fairly clear obligation not to harm, we have a more open-ended and indefinite responsibility to protect and enhance. Further, the problems of interference, dependency, and self-sacrifice enter the picture. Nevertheless, the addition of these problems only complicates the situation. It does not alter the fact that the discernment of worth challenges, at times even obligates us, to take an active role in the defense and furtherance of worth in the world.

This emphasis on the discernment of worth helps us see that moral rules need to be respected, not venerated. It helps us to treat moral rules as valuable tools, without falling into either moral dogmatism or relativism. The key point is that rules are abstract while worth is concrete. The abstract can never fully specify, descriptively or prescriptively, a concrete situation. Worth overflows rules. Even when we have rules, Dewey would remind us that the task of inquiring if and how they apply has just begun.[3] There are answers, but we won't find them in the back of the book.

To say that rules are abstract and therefore do not exhaustively specify concrete obligations or responsibilities, is not to say that they are to be treated lightly. Even though we may not know how to apply the rules, or even though they may not apply to a specific situation, does not mean that they are dispensable. It is not true that anything goes. Worth needs to be respected and nurtured. Most moral rules, whether naively held or reflectively thought through, involve respecting, protecting, and sometimes nurturing worth. Any moral rule with *prima facie* applicability should only be overridden carefully and regretfully, with a sense both of the danger in that situation and of the danger of weakening of general respect for morality. The web of moral practices is a delicate fabric.

Making discernment of worth a basic moral commitment will not solve all our theoretical or practical moral issues. We will still be faced with genuine moral dilemmas. We can make mistakes in our assessments of worth. However, it will help us from being dogmatically committed to rigidly held moral rules on the one hand or to a reckless moral relativism on the other.

II. Loyalty to the Universal Community

The second half of our basic moral principle is that we should adopt and nurture a stance of critical commitment. Such a stance implies continual corrigibility and growth and also universal loyalty. Corrigibility means an acknowledgment of failure and a willingness to forgive, since everyone falls short in these quests for value. Also, from the basic moral principle that we should adopt and nurture a stance of critical openness and commitment, it is a short step to the imperative that we should widen our loyalty to include the whole human community and beyond to include the universal community of all life and worthy inanimate things, in short, to the universal community. By "worthy" I intend to exclude dangerous organisms and objects, such as mosquitoes and broken glass. Such exclusion is both morally and ecologically fraught with danger, but it must be done. This will be a recovery, on a naturalistic basis, of the theocentric drive toward loyalty to the Lord of being.[4]

1. The Drive Towards Universal Intent

In the accountable life of humanity there is sometimes evident a movement of self-judgment and self-guidance which moves toward reference to the universal community. The societies which judge us are often self-transcending societies, and frequently the process of self-transcendence does not stop until the total community of being is involved. This process of transcendence is sometimes noticeable in our political life in a democracy, for the transcendent reference group in a democracy can be widened until it includes a community which refers beyond itself to humanity as a whole and beyond that to the total community of being.

Our imperative is to nurture and encourage this incipient movement toward universal intent, to critically commit ourselves to this process of self-correction and widening of intent.

Much of this notion is a naturalistic appropriation of Richard Niebuhr's conception of radical monotheism, although I draw also upon George Herbert Mead, Josiah Royce, and Jonathan Edwards.[5] The orientation of radical monotheism, as Niebuhr conceives it, derives the worth of the self from the same principle by which all things exist. It accepts the value of whatever exists. Its cause for the sake of which it lives is both the principle of being and the realm of being.

> Such universal loyalty . . . is loyalty to all existents as bound together by a loyalty that is not only resident in them but transcends them. . . . Hence universal loyalty expresses itself as loyalty to each particular existent in the community of being and to the universal community.[6]

There is here an Augustinian emphasis that whatever is, is good, since it derives its existence from that which is both the source of existence and of value.

> Monotheism is less than radical, if it makes a distinction between the principle of being and the principle of value; so that while all being is acknowledged as absolutely dependent for existence on the One, only some beings are valued as having worth for it.[7]

Richard Niebuhr is most insistent that the full force of the Christian's confession is that of a God who is transcendent in a radically different way than any other value-center. He states this as the difference between henotheism and radical monotheism. Niebuhr is quite correct that the family of Judeao-Christian (and, we add, Islamic) experiences of God can be explored most adequately by clearly delineating the radical nature of monotheism. Niebuhr is also correct that there are analogies to this in certain areas of our secular life. I shall appropriate this in my naturalistic outlook through the notion of critical commitment to ideal transcendence, a concept derived from Niebuhr's notion that our sense of responsibility widens continually until we feel under the judgment of a universal community.

There is also a pseudo-universal intent, what Niebuhr calls a non-radical monotheism often mixed with radical monotheism. Henotheism involves a closed society as a value-center. Now when this closed society fills the whole of existence, so that nothing is actually excluded, it will appear to be a radical monotheism, a universal faith with loyalty to the realm of being. But often there is an incipient henotheism present which becomes apparent as soon as

an out-group is distinguished. An example of this pseudomono-
theism is the glorification of a civilization.

> A civilization is . . . always one among many. Where it is the value-
> center . . . then science and religion, art and economics, political
> and economic institutions, ethos and ethics, are valued as mani-
> festations of the ongoing life of the civilized society.[8]

Another example of this cryptohenotheism is to be found in the
religions of humanity.

> The religion of humanism, starting as a protest against the doubt-
> ful assurance and the partial loyalties of closed societies, ends
> with an enlarged but yet dubious and partial closed-society faith.[9]

Niebuhr also finds that naturalism, while more inclusive than
humanism, is a closed-society faith.

> Being is greater in extent than nature as is indicated by the place
> naturalism must accord to ideals that attract and compel men,
> which, it believes, somehow emerge out of nature yet are not actual
> in it.

As examples of naturalistic henotheism Niebuhr cites John Dewey
and Spinoza. His view is that:

> naturalism remains henotheistic in its refusal even to entertain
> the possibility that there are provinces of being not accessible to its
> special methods of understanding, in its reduction of all value to
> value-in-relation-to-nature. Into its faith loyalty an element of
> polytheism also intrudes, expressed in the manifoldness of ideals
> to be served.[10]

While we cannot here enter into a detailed reply to Niebuhr's
criticism of naturalism, the enterprise of inner-worldly transcendence is, from one perspective, an attempt to overcome the henotheism of naturalism. Whether this is logically consistent is a matter
for others to judge. Clearly, however, our notions of appreciative
awareness and discernment of worth are attempts to move beyond
"special methods of understanding," by which Niebuhr apparently
means the scientific method.

Of each of these ways of faith Niebuhr claims that:

> each excludes some realm of being from the sphere of value; each is
> claimed by a cause less inclusive than the realm of being in its
> wholeness.[11]

2. Universal Loyalty in Democracy

We now focus our attention on Niebuhr's attempt to discover
universal intent and ideal transcendence in the struggles of universal and partial intent within democracy.

Niebuhr finds that the modern nation-state seeks to elicit loyalty from its subjects, not just fear as a state seeks, or even love as
a clan seeks. Further, the nation seeks not just fidelity to itself. The
patriot is related to his country, not merely as a community of persons, but as a community plus that to which the heroes, co-patriots,
and posterity of the nation refer. Niebuhr uses the notion of a triad
here. The cause is the third element to which the patriot and his
co-patriots, the other two elements, refer.[12] This cause is both a
community and that to which the community refers. At one point
Niebuhr uses the examples of democracy in America, true religion
in old Spain, and communism in Russia.[13]

> A democratic patriot in the United States, for instance, will carry
> on his dialogue with current companions, but as one who is also in
> relation to what his companions refer to—representatives of the
> community such as Washingtons, Jeffersons, Madisons, Lincolns,
> etc. Responsive to his companions he is also responsive to a tran-
> scendent reference group. . . . But now the transcendent reference
> group . . . represent(s) not the community only but what the com-
> munity stands for.
>
> In Spain . . . the national-state . . . was believed in as the servant
> of the true Catholic religion. The United States and France came
> into being in their modern form as devoted exponents of democracy
> and the rights of men. Germany sought its unity as well as its
> power as the exponent of culture. Under the Czars Russia drama-
> tized itself as Holy Russia . . . and its Messianic sense has . . . in-
> creased with the substitution of international communism for
> Orthodoxy. . . . The British Empire consciously carried the white
> man's burden while they enjoyed the perquisites of dominion. . . .
> In all these nations the loyalty of citizens has therefore had a dou-
> ble direction: on the one hand it has been claimed by the transcen-
> dent end, on the other, by the nation itself as representative of the

cause. . . . To affirm that the only real interest of nations is self-interest and that all references to great causes is hypocrisy, is to . . . discount many phenomena in our political existence. It is also to break apart . . . elements that in human life appear only in indissoluble union—such as self-interest and social interest or conscience and the will-to-power.[14]

In Niebuhr's analysis, loyalty in our political life seems to be largely the henotheistic variety, making the community the center of value. There has also been a monotheistic strain which, though seldom dominant, has often been in conflict with political henotheism.[15]

Niebuhr analyses this mingling of henotheistic and monotheistic strands by using the notion of a dual rootage of many of our democratic ideals in these two strands. One root of religious freedom, for example, was the desirability of compromise among conflicting religious groups. This was a henotheistic relegation of religion to a secondary place behind political loyalty. The radically monotheistic root of religious freedom is the recognition that religious faith takes precedence over all other loyalties,

> the acknowledgment that loyalty to God is prior to every civic loyalty; that before man is a member of any political society he is a member of the universal commonwealth in which he is under obligations that take precedence over all duties to the state.

These two roots are illustrated nicely in the Macintosh case. Macintosh was born a Canadian, had served as a chaplain in World War I and spoken on behalf of the Allied war effort. Teaching at the Yale Divinity School, at the age of forty-eight he filed for his United States naturalization papers. In response to the question to be answered by each applicant, Macintosh said that he would be willing to take up arms in the defense of this country, but that "I should want to be free to judge of the necessity." Later, expanding on this, he wrote:

> I do not undertake to support "my country, right or wrong" in any dispute which may arise, and I am not willing to promise beforehand, and without knowing the cause for which my country may go to war, either that I will or that I will not "take up arms in defense of this country." . . . He was ready to give to the United States all the allegiance he ever had given or ever could give to any country, but he could not put allegiance to the government of any country

before allegiance to the will of God. . . . He recognized the principle of the submission of the individual citizen to the opinion of the majority in a democratic country; but he did not believe in having his own moral problems solved by the majority. . . . He was willing to support his country, even to the extent of bearing arms, if asked to do so by the government, in any war which he could regard as morally justified.[16]

Chief Justice Hughes' dissenting opinion included the following statement illustrative of radical monotheism:

> In the forum of conscience, duty to a moral power higher than the state has always been maintained. . . . The essence of religion is belief in a relation to God involving duties superior to those arising from any human relation.

Justice Sutherland, in the majority opinion, illustrates the principle of henotheism:

> government must go forward upon the assumption . . . that unqualified allegiance to the nation and submission and obedience to the laws of the land, as well those made for war as those made for peace, are not inconsistent with the will of God.[17]

Another example of the monotheistic strain in our political life is the concept of the limiting and balancing of power. Again Niebuhr finds a dual rootage. One root is the need to find a compromise among rival claimants to power in order to ensure national welfare, making national loyalty supreme. The monotheistic root is:

> the conviction that ultimate power belongs to God and that . . . finite power . . . works destructively if it is not guarded against the constant temptation to make itself infinite, totalitarian, and god-like.[18]

This dual rootage is also illustrated by questions about law and contracts. Is the source of law the social will or the will of God, a structure of right pervading the entire realm of being? Are contracts to be enforced because they are needed for the regulation of economic practices or are they sacred because God is faithful and thus requires and makes possible promise-keeping among people in all their relations? Other examples of conflict between henotheism and radical monotheism are found in such principles as the sacredness of treaties, government by law rather than by men, the acceptance of majority rule, and respect for the rights of minorities.

A final and important example of the struggle between henotheism and radical monotheism in political life is found in the belief in the equality of all persons. As a faith statement, in Niebuhr's analysis, it expresses confidence that all people have worth because of their relation to a common center and it expresses a pledge that people will respect each other's rights. This confidence and pledge seems genuinely monotheistic because of its universality and its reference to a common source of value. However, it is sometimes accepted on the basis of a nationalistic social faith which does not accord equality of rights to those who are not citizens.

In summary, our democratic policies are carried on under the influence of rival forms of faith.

> In henotheism the voice of the people is the voice of god. . . . Loyalty to nation is the supreme loyalty of citizens and governors. On the other hand the democratic process may be carried on within the context of monotheistic faith. Then no relative power, be it that of the nation or its people as well as that of tyrants, can claim . . . total loyalty. The power that has brought a nation into being has also elected into existence its companion nations; and the rights of such nations . . . are equal. . . . Men will accept the relativity of all their judgments and continue in their striving to make political decisions that express their universal faith.[19]

The major contribution which Niebuhr makes to our effort is his analysis of an obligation to universalize loyalty within our common political life, an obligation which, if followed to the end, would result in a loyalty to the universal community. This incipient universal intent seems visible when political life is looked at from the standpoint of radical monotheism. Within our philosophy of this-worldly transcendence we find this universal intent to be a naturalistic analogue of radical monotheism.

> A democratic patriot . . . will carry on his dialogue with current companions, but as one who is also in relation to what his companions refer to—representatives of this community such as Washingtons, Jeffersons, Madisons, Lincolns, etc. Responsive to his companions he is also responsive to a transcendent reference group and thereby achieves a relative independence from his immediate associates. . . . But now the transcendent reference group . . . represent(s) not the community only but what the

community stands for. Ultimately we arrive in the case of democracy at a community which refers beyond itself to humanity.... When we educate children to become responsible citizens in Western societies we seek to relate them to such founding fathers ... who make their statement out of a 'decent respect for the opinions of mankind.'[20]

Niebuhr speaks of a movement of self-transcendence which cannot stop until the universal community is reached.

> To the monotheist believer ... there seem to be indications in the whole of the responsive, accountable life of men of a movement of self-judgment and self-guidance which cannot come to rest until it makes its reference to a universal other and a universal community, which that other both represents and makes his cause.... The societies that judge or in which we judge ourselves are self-transcending societies. And the process of self-transcendence does not come to rest until the total community of being has been involved.[21]

This incipient tendency toward universal loyalty involves self-criticism, a kind of perpetual dissatisfaction. In moments of universally responsible action we try to evaluate our actions as they would be judged by

> representatives of universal community, or by the generalized other who is universal, or by an impartial spectator who regards our actions from a universal point of view, whose impartiality is that of loyalty to the universal cause.[22]

We do not always act from this point of view, of course, but in critical moments a radical monotheist does ask about ultimate causes and ultimate judges.

The claim made here from the perspective of religious naturalism is that the ideal aspect of transcendence also involves this notion of a universal intent and an ultimate cause, that is, that we should widen our loyalty to include the universal community. The ethical implication of this is that we should nurture this universal intent, that we should judge ourselves and our projects from such a universal viewpoint. This is involved in commitment to ideal transcendence.

3. Mead's Generalized Other

Niebuhr draws upon previous analyses of the social nature of conscience and selfhood, particularly that of George Herbert Mead and Josiah Royce. Mead's concept of the generalized other involves the notion that there are two crucial stages in the development of a self, that of play and that of participating in a game. The difference is that in a game the child must be aware of the attitudes of all the other players.

> The attitudes of the other players which the participant assumes organize into a sort of unit, and it is that organization which controls the response of the individual. . . . The organized community or social group which gives to the individual his unity of self may be called "the generalized other."[23]

Niebuhr has some significant criticism of Mead. The first is that Mead does not adequately underscore the reality of conflict between various generalized others. If, as Mead admits, we are members of many communities, the points of view of the generalized others of these communities often conflict. Hence the need for a transcendent reference group, particularly a universal community, from the perspective of which these conflicts can be adjudicated. Second, the generalized other is not always disinterested, but may be committed to a cause and thus seems disinterested or impartial in relation to the self.[24]

Mead did sketch the notion of a higher reference group which could transcend the generalized other. We find this idea attractive because it shows that the idea of universal intent is natural to a naturalistic outlook.

> The only way in which we can react against the disapproval of the entire community is by setting up a higher sort of community which in a certain sense out-votes the one we find. A person may reach a point of going against the whole world with the voice of reason. . . . But to do that he has to speak with the voice of reason to himself. He has to comprehend the voices of the past and of the future.[25]

4. Royce and Loyalty

Josiah Royce developed a method of transcending partial loyalties through his maxim of loyalty to loyalty: be so loyal to your own cause as thereby to serve the advancement of the cause of universal loyalty.[26] Niebuhr criticized this notion in that it is not loyalty to which we should be loyal, but rather the universal community. Anticipating this criticism, Royce moved from loyalty to loyalty, the loyalty which loves the loyalty of the stranger and the enemy, to a conception of the brotherhood of all the loyal. To this community in ideal all men belong. It is not realized empirically, although there is an historical tendency toward it. Christianity knows this universal community as "the Beloved Community." Through this concept of loyalty to the universal community Royce sought a reinterpretation of central Christian ideas, using *Romans* as a particular source of motifs. In particular no one can be loyal to the Beloved Community except as a gift of grace. This grace comes when One who initiates or inspires loyalty arrives. The ideality of this universal community in one sense gives it an abstractness. In another sense, the fact that it is not empirically realized means that it transcends any specific community. This is a part of the note of transcendence in Royce. The fact that we can be devoted to lost causes shows that we seek a unity too good to be visibly realized at any one moment in the world. From within our naturalistic orientation we use the concept of intention toward an ideal and transcendence and loyalty to the universal community as our analogue to Royce's concept of a universal community.[27]

5. Edwards and Benevolence to Being

Jonathan Edwards is a good example of a monotheistic thinker with a theocentric orientation who developed a notion of a universal community.

> True Virtue most essentially consists in *benevolence to Being in general* . . . that consent, propensity and union of heart to Being in general which is immediately exercised in a general good will.[28]

For Edwards this benevolence to Being in general is primarily love to God who is the greatest and best of beings. But it is also a love for all beings (or at least intelligent beings), except for those cases where the love of a being is not consistent with the highest good of Being in general, when that being is an enemy to Being in general, for example. Niebuhr draws upon Edwards as one of his theological sources for using the idea of the universal community of being as a way of contrasting radical monotheism with henotheism. Edwards expresses this by saying that benevolence to a person or private system rather than to the whole society of beings is a private affection and not benevolence to being in general, unless subordinate to a love of God and benevolence to being. Such a private affection will dispose a person to enmity against being in general. It will set up

the private system against being in general, just as the setting up of
one prince disposes the followers of that prince to enmity against
the true sovereign. Indeed, it not merely disposes to enmity against
being in general, it is itself an attitude of enmity.[29]

Where Edwards speaks of private affection Niebuhr speaks of
henotheism, and where Edwards speaks of a private system Niebuhr speaks of a closed society. Royce would agree with this distinction, but does not take such great pains to insist upon it, perhaps
because he has his roots in idealism while Edwards and Niebuhr
stem from a tradition of exclusive monotheism.

My discussion of the imperative to widen our commitment and
concern to the total universal community of all life and worthy inanimate things has been an attempt at a retrieval within a naturalistic framework of Richard Niebuhr's theocentric drive toward
loyalty to the universal community of being based on loyalty to the
Lord of all beings. With my ontological reticence I do not speak of
the Lord of all beings, however. I am aided in this naturalistic appropriation of Niebuhr by Mead's concept of the generalized other,
by Royce's maxim of loyalty to the universal community, and by Edwards' notion of the universal community of being. To be sure, our
minimalist ontological modesty requires that this notion be treated
as a regulative idea, imaginatively entertained, bereft of reference
to the Lord of being of Edwards and Niebuhr and of the universal
community of interpretation of Royce.

There are further problems which we cannot solve here. One of
these is the relationship between particular obligations and responsibilities and the general responsibility to the universal community
and its members. We shall discuss this briefly below when we consider the tension between universal and particular love in various
cultures. A second problem concerns the "strange work of love"
which may have to withhold support, threaten, punish, and even
use violence or capital punishment (although I question this latter).

III. Care for Sisters and Brothers

Another set of implications which follows from our philosophy
of openness to this-worldly transcendence concerns care for others.
Action in accordance with a discernment of worth and openness to
ideal transcendence implies not only a willingness to refrain from
harming others because of their intrinsic worth as persons, but also
a positive degree of respect, defense, care and nurture. This is an

orientation ready to listen, to respect, to accept the other's intrinsic worth as a person and to appraise the other's merit impartially. No specific directives follow from the principle of discernment of worth, but some directions do. Besides maintaining openness to the divine, we are also to care for others in the universal community. This will be a prudent care, since we are not to waste ourselves foolishly. It will be a self-regarding care, since we ourselves are a part of the universal community and since our respect for our own worth protects our weaker brothers and sisters who may be more ready to drop the burden of responsible selfhood. It will be a critical care, since it is all too easy to find a false fulfillment in life by abnegating ourselves for another, by following any messiah who calls. Nevertheless, it will be a care which is ready, at the appropriate time, to sacrifice ourselves.

1. A Life-Style of Service

This means a life-style of *agape,* of service, an appropriate willingness to concede in a conflict, to be a servant. It means a sense of humor towards ourselves, a willingness to compromise, to adopt a giving attitude. It does not seek martyrdom, but is ready for self-sacrifice if need be.

How far is it possible to travel down this road? Can we bear the cost of discipleship in this secular and naturalistic *imitatio Christi* (for we must acknowledge the Christian roots of this viewpoint)? The impossibility of this task is no excuse for refusing to attempt it and to pursue it as far as we can. In addition, it is imperative to maintain an openness to situationally transcendent resources of strength and healing, lest we end up with a martyr complex and resentment.

What does this mean for us as we enter the twenty-first century? Again, there are no directives, but there are directions. It means that we are called on to adopt a servant role, a style of *agape* and giving love. We are called upon to heal and serve the world. This means to be concerned in a sophisticated and active way about the world's hunger, for example. This means to be willing to restrict our production and consumption for the future. This means to be willing, persuasively or militantly, to challenge corporations and political and academic institutions which are careless with the well-being of persons. This means to love persons in a society dominated by technique. This means a life-style which challenges the leading of public opinion. This means a life-style fostering creative interchange.

To adopt such a stance means to have a sense of lightness about one's own program and one's own importance. As we enter into the period of increasing conflicts between rights and claims for rights, it means being willing to concede, negotiate, and compromise as much as to persuade, challenge, or champion. Yet this also means that we cannot do this to the point of loss of self-respect, lest it become masochism and self-deprecation. Paradoxically, one's own rights cannot be waived where that will cause a further deterioration in human rights in general. And of course, the work of sacrificial love may cause us to come to the defense of another's rights.

Finally, this stance leads one to a willingness to sacrifice one's life for discerned worth where and when necessary, although it does not lead to a martyr or suicide complex. Those who actively resist evil, as Bonhoeffer or Martin Luther King, Jr. witnessed, know that the final liberation is liberation from the fear of death. Those who are ready to go the whole way receive all of life authentically. But who can claim to be capable of this?

2. Jesus as Paradigm

It is clear that the life of Jesus, at least as understood from within our perspective, operates in a paradigmatic fashion here. I am reluctant to make this explicit, for two reasons. However, honesty and the transparency of the fact lead me to this acknowledgment. The first reason for hesitation is that it increases the probability that I will be seen to argue for a stance of caring because of a prior commitment to the Christian paradigm, that I'm a Christian at heart with a nostalgia for the old Christian story. However, as I hope to make clear in the sequel, the model of Jesus serves not as a warrant for the stance, but as an example. The model is chosen, I claim, autonomously, because of its intrinsic worth, not out of a prior commitment to it. The second reason for hesitation is that the selection of any paradigm is likely to be divisive, separating oneself from those who follow different models. For this reason I wish to redouble my tone of tentativeness. The mention of this paradigm should not be divisive. It is rather an exercise in honesty, in the self-understanding that comes from acknowledging one's own historical roots. We all speak with an historical accent, including the children of the Enlightenment who claim to speak with none. As I argue in Chapter Four, there is an historical rootedness to all inquiry. I believe that the imperative of prudent care follows from the openness to discerned worth and the challenge of the ideal aspect of inner-worldly transcendence. In principle, anyone of whatever persuasion should recognize and accept this. However, to assume that this will indeed happen would be the most foolish sort of naivete. It is better to recognize the Christian roots of this imperative, with a touch of irony, rather than mistakenly claim the universal validity of this imperative and the hard-headedness and hard-heartedness of anyone who refuses to accept it. This principle of prudent care has Christian roots. However, it is offered with great tentativeness for thoughtful consideration by anyone of whatever persuasion who thinks in a language with whatever historical accent.

It must be acknowledged also that this paradigm is a late twentieth-century Christ, or at least a Christ as appropriated by a late twentieth-century naturalist. The old quip that the researchers for the historical Jesus looked down a deep well and saw their own reflections is not so far off the mark here. Actually, I wish to make a clear distinction between meaning and significance. As far as we can ascertain, Jesus clearly did not talk about prudent love. This is not what he meant at all. Much of his ethical viewpoint is rejected or ignored in this naturalistic interpretation. And he clearly did not have a minimal model of deity. However, what Jesus meant and what his significance is for our purposes are two different things. It is not that we see our own reflection at the bottom of the well. It is rather that his significance comes through a dialogue between the historical figure (as faithfully reconstructed as possible, but nonetheless reconstructed from our perspective) and our own viewpoint. This will be our own appropriation of the (reconstructed) original meaning. This dialogue allows, indeed requires, both our own autonomy and the integrity of our inner-worldly naturalism and also the challenge of the figure who comes to us from the past.[30]

3. Other Traditions

The principle of prudent care for others in a universal community of moral responsibility should be capable of appropriation by those guided by other paradigms, although the emphases, accents, and symbolic forms will vary. For someone rooted in the Torah the accents will be different. Justice will probably be a more dominant tone than love. But the concern for the weak and oppressed, for the widow, the orphan, and the stranger at the gates will produce a stance that will be very similar to the servanthood and *agape* in our paradigm. Above all, our paradigm cannot be set up as superior to that of Israel in either an orthodox Christian typological fashion or a liberal view of evolutionary development from Old Testament to

New. Our paradigm is offered for serious consideration, but only in a dialogue where the other partner is treated, not tolerantly, but as one whose view might be right and whose view will definitely have much to teach.

The secular humanist will claim to speak without an accent, to have no "positive" elements in her outlook, as the argument used to go. She will claim to have stripped the kernel of universal morality free of all husks. There is some truth to that. However, the humanist speaks from a particular historical situation and intends, but does not achieve, universal validity. She is rooted in twentieth-century Western culture, with roots in the Enlightenment and perhaps earlier. Her values at their best should be close to ours, although perhaps not with the possibility of sacrificial care. The guarded admiration accorded Kant's *Religion Within the Bounds of Reason Alone* by the writer indicates the historical affinity of religious naturalism in a minimalist mode with the Enlightenment roots of some secular humanists. It also indicates our departure from Christian orthodoxy.

Again, there will be affinities with the Hindu view of *ahimsa* and with care for all levels of existence. The Hindu accent, as well as the Buddhist, speaks much more clearly of a responsibility to all levels of existence, of a broadening of the circle of concern well past a henotheistic concern with the human community. Nevertheless, as Śri Aurobindo emphasized, there is a danger of self-absorption and neglect of the material basis (or "life") of existence in this Hindu paradigm.[31]

In Buddhism our principle of prudent care comes closest to the Mahāyāna notion of the compassionate Buddha and the vow of the Bodhisattva to save all sentient beings. Whether the non-attached love of the Buddhist is preferable to the love implied in our notion of care and concern is a matter of debate. It is not clear that the traditional Christian notion of love is superior. Love can be a misleading or suffocating item. This is one reason why I have used the term "care" rather than love as my dominant category.

Our principle of prudent care is very close to the traditional West African notion of responsibility to significant others. The West African image of the self is that it is much like a web. The self is not enclosed within the body, but a part of it which we could call the "life-force" resides in the persons with whom you have to deal. Thus each of us is responsible to enhance the life-force of the other which resides within us. The life-force in another person, of course, is very vulnerable, and much of the underlying principle of traditional

African healing involves discovering who is tearing down your life-force and in working through a ceremony of reconciliation to restore inter-personal relations.[32] The concept has its merits. Our view would have a greater emphasis on the universal community. The traditional African view emphasizes the concreteness of real inter-personal relationships. This is a needed emphasis to restore the balance of those who destroy their loved ones in their love for mankind.

Also our principle of prudent care has close affinities to the Moslem notion that Allah is the All-merciful, the All-compassionate. In practice this is focussed in the command to practice alms, one of the Five Pillars of the Faith. This notion of alms has often been institutionalized in Moslem history, with all the accompanying virtues and dangers of institutionalization. Also alms-giving can lead to a perpetuation of a system which creates paupers in the first place. But who are Westerners to talk? Again, our ethics of prudent service will be similar to the Islamic ethics of compassion, with our notion of readiness to lay down one's life being more radical, yet tempered by our notion of prudence.

In the cultures stemming from K'ung tzu (Confucius), our principle of prudent responsibility will be quite at home. There is a graded scale of degree of obligation in the Confucian ethic worked out along the Five Great Relationships. This makes it similar to the traditional West African ethics, except more formalized. Like the African model it has the advantages and disadvantages of acknowledging positions of superiority and inferiority. Like the African it also has the strength and weakness of stressing the priority of proximate relationships. Here the ethics of Mo Tzu form a valuable point of debate with the traditional Confucian ethic.[33]

In sum, when our stance of prudent care is placed beside other major stances with their historical-cultural traditions, points of contact and divergence appear. Many of these traditions agree in going beyond the minimalist no-harm principle which some ethicists make central today. Many speak of a type of compassion, of care for the oppressed, of a vow to save all creatures. And the differences are also important. There is a difference in the native soil: Torah, Qu'rān, Jesus, Upanishads and Gita, etc. These historical roots are important and are not mere husks. They penetrate the kernel. There are also clear differences in the degree of universality of concern and whether there is a priority of concern for those close at hand. There are differences as to whether a formal or informal, emotional or dispassionate concern is called for, whether justice, love or whatever is the key category. The point I wish to make here is that our principle of prudent care for others is a part of the current global dialogue (or shouting match) among varying ethical viewpoints, that most go beyond the no-harm principle, and that all, including the secularists who deny it, have historical roots, the examination of which is important, if for no other reason than to achieve a responsible autonomy by a creative fidelity in relation to these historical models.

4. Autonomous Appropriation of Traditions

We have been using the Christian moral approach as a stimulus in our philosophical work. Indeed, the roots of this total philosophy in the monotheistic traditions should be obvious. It is also clear that these historical roots are utilized in such a loose way that they are hardly recognizable. This is not the first attempt to use autonomous reflection to appropriate a religious tradition. However, it is important to remind ourselves of this since some philosophers, whose view of their historical roots hardly stretches past the seventeenth and eighteenth centuries, forget how important this autonomous appropriation of a religious tradition is in the philosophical task.

Apart from Plato and Aristotle, Kant, Hegel and Schelling were early pioneers in developing a hermeneutics of autonomous appropriation.[34] Particular stimulus to our hermeneutical approach has come from Josiah Royce and Henry Nelson Wieman.[35] Whitehead's notion that the occasion creates itself out of a chosen appropriation of its past is very much in the background here.[36] Ricoeur's very sophisticated approach to philosophical reflection on symbol and text has provided much grist for my mill.[37] Similarities to Gabriel Marcel's notion of creative fidelity and Martin Heidegger's concept of the appropriation of a tradition seem important.[38] Polanyi's notion of each generation in science, and in culture generally, renewing and transcending its tradition forms an interesting parallel with Heidegger and Marcel.[39] Increasingly I am coming to form a dialogue in my mind between the modernist Biblical scholar, Shirley Jackson Case, and the hermeneutical philosopher Hans-Georg Gadamer. At first glance, these two historians seem to take different approaches to the dominance that the tradition or the present age should have in determining the appropriation of the significance of our traditions. I think, however, that a genuine fusion of horizons will result in a chastened and deepened modernism.[40]

What I do believe I have indicated is that there is ample precedence in philosophy for the creative and autonomous use of a religious tradition.

5. *The Persuasiveness of a Life of Service*

I have been trying to elaborate a moral orientation of a life ordered by a vocation of service and self-giving dedication. Whether this type of life-orientation has value or is imperative cannot be demonstrated. It perhaps can be apprehended. Some comments are in order about the persuasiveness of this stance.

There is an attractive power to the extraordinary and ordinary exemplars of this life-style. Also it is probably true that there is a hierarchy of needs, perhaps not rigid, but very real. This moral approach of service and dedication may be more persuasive to those whose basic needs are largely met. It is easier to love when you are loved. The claim that all persons deserve respect will be much more persuasive to a person who respects herself. Finally there is a real sense in which life becomes meaningful through service. This may not be the only way of organizing meaning to life, but it is definitely one way. Royce knew this through his reflections in the unification of the self through loyalty.[41] There is, of course, a real problem of being dedicated to a cause that collapses. Royce did not face the problem of divided loyalties, just as Mead did not face the problem of conflict between the generalized others of different communities to which a single self may belong. This raises the question of whether there needs to be any ultimate cause at all to which we are devoted. We shall answer this question negatively when we treat Langdon Gilkey in our last section.

IV. *A Plurality of Values*

An important aspect of the metaphysical reticence of our naturalism is the recognition that there is a plurality of ends, a multiplicity of values. Simply put, you can't have your cake and eat it, too (unless, of course, you bake two cakes, but then you've used time, energy and money to bake two cakes rather than do something else). There is no all-inclusive unity or harmony of ends. There is, however, a degree of compatibility between many ends. It is often possible to bake a cake and read several pages, to eat a small piece and diet sensibly. But there is no ontological or eschatological realm where all goods can be achieved in totality and unity or all values made compossible. There is no Big Rock Candy Mountain. The imagined unity of values in the ideal aspect of Transcendence is a regulative idea. It has the pragmatic function of inspiration and lure. However, when specific choices are made in particular situations, the plurality of ideals becomes apparent, sometimes painfully. Then choices and trade-offs must be made.[42]

For example, liberty and security are different ends. It is possible to have a political system providing for a degree of both. They are compatible to a degree. But they are not maximally compatible. You can't have maximum liberty and maximum security. You can give precedence to one value over another, of course, but that is precisely to indicate that you are willing to have less of one because you value the other more. The trouble with many political world-views is the simplistic way in which they assume that by following their program all good things will come. Part of the realism of John Rawls and the Great Dissenter, Oliver Wendell Holmes, Jr., lies in their sense of the necessity of choice and in the choices for liberty and freedom which they did make.

Choices have to be made. In economics, apparently, you can't have maximal employment and control inflation. In medical care, you can't have maximal technology and adequate care for everyone.[43] Or, if you do, you won't have sound bridges, day care, and the necessary (or imagined) defense spending. Or, if you do, you won't be able to keep down taxes and reduce the deficit. In the real world, to maximize A you frequently have to cut back on B.

The plurality of ends and the incompatibility of maximal realization of many of them has been stressed for two reasons. First of all, our reference to the ideal aspect of transcendence in the sketch of a minimal model of transcendence refers to the imagined unity of ideals. This will be a false abstraction, dangerous in practice, unless the plurality of values is recognized in concrete situations of choice. The imagined unity of ideals in the ideal aspect of transcendence has a regulative, emotional and devotional function. It is not meant to preempt the use of intelligence and careful decision making in concrete situations. In the second place the recognition of a plurality of values is one way of achieving a critical stance towards any ideal. To know, for instance, that a strong program of law and order may erode civil liberties and vice versa, is to provide a sense of critical detachment and a willingness to be corrected which is crucial in social policy. Otherwise you have all the dangers of touters of a panacea.

V. Beyond Fanaticism and Despair

As we face the twenty-first century, one of our chief problems is our oscillation between a sense of futility in view of the enormity of our problems and a fanatical sense that we have the answers. The stance of critical openness and commitment is an attempt to speak to this issue.

The answer to despair is courage. Such a courage must not come from the selective perception of optimistic culture-Christianity (whether liberal or fundamentalist).[44] Instead it must come from a struggle in the midst of despair and discouragement.[45]

The notion of courage which seems most appropriate comes into focus through a comparison with Tillich's analysis of courage. Tillich is correct that courage involves a facing of despair, a struggle with the reality of discouragement. In addition, while it is important to make a decision to be courageous, to "screw one's courage to the sticking place," both Tillich and our analysis agree that courage can be assisted, can have roots. However, Tillich sees courage as being ultimately rooted in the infinite ground of being. In our analysis courage is rooted in whatever finite resources are available. A word of reassurance from a fellow companion can sometimes have tremendous power. There are a variety of possible sources for courage, including diet and ritual. These can be studied from various psychological and sociological perspectives. Any coach, parent or teacher needs experience in the art of encouragement. And, of course, there are dangers in utilizing the resources for courage, ranging from chemical dependency to propagandistic manipulation.

Courage, in our analysis and that of Tillich, functions as an alternative to defeatism, much like hope in future-oriented theologies, except that neither Tillich nor our analysis make Christian symbols of Resurrection or *eschaton* central in the personal struggle with despair. In the moment of discouragement, there is often doubt about the meaning and validity of symbols, including symbols of hope.

Courage by itself easily becomes fanatic. As we move into the twenty-first century we need a sense of judgment as well as of courage. We need a critical No as well as a creative Yes. Not only the destructive and evil aspects of our life, but also the solutions we use to resist these evils and solve our problems need critical judgment. We need an Archimedean point from which to criticize our culture. The interlocking surface of our one-dimensional society needs to be broken by a transcendent depth. We need the power of negative thinking, of the Great Refusal.[46] In a technological society, where the answer to the problems created by technique is more technique, this judgment upon our remedies is important. We cannot suspend technique, for that itself is a technique. But we do need to "lighten up," and to question our answers. A critical commitment to the challenge of transcendent goals and ideals can provide such a stance of questioning. It will not give us specific answers, but all specification needs to be challenged anyway.

The transcendent No needs to be spoken not only to obvious evil, but even to our efforts to ameliorate our condition. People of integrity and good will can have uncritical attachment to a cause. This is dangerous and potentially destructive. The danger lies not only with a lack of courage, but also with an uncritical acceptance with which the True Believers follow the New Messiahs that claim to solve or at least cope with our problems.[47] There are Ayatollahs of the mind in every country. The Archimedean point of transcendent challenge is a judgment on all human attempts at creation and preservation of meaning, a vantage point enabling us to see the ambiguity of all of our good efforts.

There is a theocentric tradition stretching back at least to the eighth-century Hebrew prophets. This tradition includes the great prophets, Jesus and Paul, Augustine, the Islamic tradition, Luther and Calvin. In our century this tradition was revitalized by Paul Tillich and Reinhold and Richard Niebuhr. These three, as well as my teacher and friend, Langdon Gilkey, have been particularly influential in shaping this approach.[48] Ronald H. Stone's insightful studies of Tillich and Reinhold Niebuhr have been especially helpful in this regard.[49]

Part of the purpose of this book is to develop within the framework of naturalism this sense of transcendent judgment and support. My claim is that the transcendence contained in the ideal and real aspects of the divine can provide such an Archimedean point. These representatives of the theocentric tradition would reject the possibility of significant transcendence within naturalism, but this is partly because they have only studied the earlier naturalists, such as Santayana and Randall, for whom transcendence only applies to ideals, and Dewey, whose steps towards an adequate conception of naturalistic transcendence are barely articulated.

As we approach the twenty-first century our twin dangers are apathy and fanaticism. The transition in the United States from the '60's to the '70's to the '80's was partly a veering from the Scylla of uncritical attachment to rebellion and counter-rebellion to the

Charybdis of indifference and protective apathy. The need is to move beyond this oscillation into a critical courage, a courage which faces the pathos of despair and moves beyond it, and yet which is self-critical, avoiding fanaticism without falling into paralysis. Courage beyond apathy and despair, and self-criticism beyond fanaticism and blind loyalty are needed as we move in these perilous times. We need the courage to be, to create, and to take judgment upon ourselves.

Who is sufficient for these things? No one, of course. Yet we can seek strength in the dark night of the soul, not by evading it, but by wrestling with the nameless fears. Courage will not come automatically, certainly not by deciding to have it. But a nurtured stance of openness to resources of renewal can put us in touch with unexpected and unmanageable, situationally transcendent or superior processes which can support, encourage, and strengthen. This, combined with a nurtured stance of openness to correction, is the answer of a naturalism of openness to despair and fanaticism.

VI. Beyond Egocentricity

Critical openness to situationally superior resources and critical commitment to continually challenging values lead the self beyond a preoccupation with itself. A stance of critical openness and commitment will help in overcoming the tendency toward egocentricity. This tendency is ever present.

> The problem of subjective existence . . . preconditions every sensory life for a sinful existence: i.e. a life absorbed in the demands of the ego, compelling the orientation of energies around the self.[50]

Commitment is a reaching beyond egocentricity. However, by itself it can intensify self-preoccupation, as the object of commitment becomes part of the propriate structure of the self. As the dialectic of law and grace in the theocentric tradition clearly shows, obligation to reach beyond the self can result in deeper attention to the self-effort. An openness to the other aspect of transcendence, the real resources available for healing and renewal, can provide a release from self-preoccupation. In traditional language, grace can heal where law cannot.

> The assurance of grace—this abundance of concrete goodness in existence which awaits our capacity to receive it—is the objective

datum that can release the ego from its preoccupation with protective procedures. This is always relative, to be sure. Subjectivity is never completely overcome; but the intensity of the focus may be tempered.[51]

VII. Liberation and Transcendence

A philosophy of inner-worldly transcendence is a this-worldly orientation. It is clearly not escapist. On the other hand, the point made by Herbert Marcuse that many empirical studies of social conditions lack the power of negative thinking, the power of a critique of those conditions, is well taken.[52] This-worldly orientations often lack a prophetic or critical rejection of present conditions. They can also discourage a reaching out for resources and power.

There are two key elements in any theory or praxis of liberation which openness toward inner-worldly transcendence can bring into play. One is a challenge to the status quo and its ideological rationalization. The other is an openness to resources of renewal.

On the one hand openness to continually transcendent values is a challenge to the acceptance of present conditions. The never-fulfilled imperatives of care for others and of loyalty to the universal community provide cutting edges to the attitude of openness to transcendent challenge. The stance of openness to challenge represents an attitude always ready to question the self-deceptions of any theory or worldview, including especially any view satisfied with the progress being made. It is an equal opportunity critic, challenging without discrimination. This means that the dogmatisms of liberation movements are themselves subject to criticism. For example, Cornel West's critique of Leninism and Stalinism apply broadly, as he clearly intends them to.[53]

On the other hand every serious concern for social and personal freedom requires courage. Apathy often stems from despair. The stance of openness to situationally transcendent resources is an attempt to speak to this. Often resources are available, but outside of the situation as perceived. An attitude of despair or rigid self-discipline can effectively close off the appropriation of these resources of renewal. A prophecy of doom can be self-fulfilling, while expectancy can be a catalytic factor in the generation of resources. Besides this, a stance of openness can loosen up the rigid seriousness and lack of humor that too often infects movements toward betterment.

The philosophy of openness to the immanent divine is only a vision of transcendence. It does not provide a detailed picture or program of what needs to be done. It is not intended to do so. It calls for an attitude, not a substitute for hard investigation and painful effort. Apart from a more concrete picture of present conditions in the life of an individual or group it cannot even supply a direction in which to move. It is on the side of neither the liberal, the conservative or the radical. Just as the idea of justice of John Rawls is compatible with a free enterprise or a socialist economy, depending on a more concrete economic theory to specify its directives, so the philosophy of this-worldly transcendence is compatible with a variety of political and economic theories.[54] What it does do is to encourage a willingness to ask questions, to dream, to imagine alternatives. What it does do is to encourage attitudes of intelligent receptivity to challenge and a readiness to respond to unexpected resources.[55]

I have not drawn out all of the implications of an ethics of sensitive discernment for ecological stewardship. A moral viewpoint resting on an appreciation of value suggests that our moral responsibility extends further than humanity. This is one of the limitations of basing the moral community on moral agency (Gewirth, Kant, Nozick, Rawls). While enlightened self-interest would be a better foundation for ecological trusteeship than short-sighted pursuit of profit, our responsibility for this planet with its fragile web of life needs to include an openness to transhuman value. Such an appreciative openness will not solve our ecological dilemmas, but it can provide a challenge to narrow specie-ism. Here too, we need to be open to continual challenge so as to overcome apathy and to be open to resources of transformation to ground our courage.

CHAPTER FOUR

A GENEROUS EMPIRICISM

There has been a recent revival of interest in American radical empiricism, partly as a way to escape the horns of a dilemma. One position seems to be that we need a secure starting point and the correct method in order to achieve true and certain, or at least reliable, knowledge. For some people the only other position seems to be that since we cannot achieve this foundation and method, we cannot know anything with any degree of certainty. The first position can, with some degree of justice, be said to be motivated by the anxiety to achieve certainty, the so-called Cartesian anxiety. The second position often generates either a feeling of despair or of celebration. The dilemma is that both positions face difficulties, the first because it appears impossible to achieve, the second because it leads to theoretical and moral skepticism.

Radical empiricism is seen by some writers like William Dean and Nancy Frankenberry to be a way to break through this dichotomy.[1] Granted that there is no secure method or starting point. On the other hand, we are not left wandering in the dark or the irrational or foundering in a morass of subjectivity. Note the title of Richard Bernstein's book, *Beyond Objectivism and Relativism*.[2] Rather we are able to grope and explore our way into the complexities of life. The mood here seems to be neither an oscillation between anxiety and certitude, or between celebration and despair. The mood seems to be rather that of courage and caution.

In this chapter I wish to share some methodological musings as my contribution to radical empiricism, that is to say, to empiricism generously conceived. I offer four main points and two brief historical sketches. My main points concern: (1) the importance of sensitive discernment, (2) the transactional nature of experience, (3) the historical rootedness of empirical inquiry, and (4) the relationship between the language of inquiry and the language of devotion. The historical sketches are of the radical empiricism of Henri Bergson, Gerald Birney Smith, and Bernard Meland.

I. Sensitive Discernment

William Dean urges that we develop an affectional sensibility as a way into the full dimensions of a valueful history.[3] My elaboration of the concept of sensitive discernment is intended as a step in this direction.

Openness to situationally transcendent resources and continually challenging ideals calls for openness in perception. I call this sensitive discernment or, following Bernard Meland, appreciative awareness. This discernment is a type of perception which is receptive to the full range, complexity, and uniqueness of data. As such it is sensitive to situationally transcendent renewal or criticism. It is the reaching out of awareness to the transcendent elements in the immanent.

In our day observation is often shaped by the requirements of the scientific outlook. Sensitive discernment does not require the rejection of the scientific approach and its type of perception. But appreciative awareness does involve a broader and more sensitive type of perception. My concern here is to sketch a broader empiricism that includes scientific observation but also recognizes the validity of other types of perception. William Dean's suggestion that we need to supplement the scientific with an historical model of knowing is a helpful starting point.

Scientific observation is narrowly focussed. Science is interested in particular types of data and looks for the kinds of data which meet these interests. There are at least five needs of science which influence the types of fact we look for. These include: (1) the testing of particular hypotheses, resulting in directed observation, searching for data to confirm or disconfirm a particular hypothesis; (2) isolated systems with soluble problems, leading to a fairly restricted range of observations; (3) quantified or at least precise language, leading to a search for quantifiable data or facts capable of being stated with precision; (4) correlation among variables, leading to the search for manipulable or at least isolable variables; and, (5) operational definitions leading to the search for publicly repeatable data observable by any competent, unbiased observers. Each of these needs of science leads to the search for a particular kind of data, whereas sensitive discernment encourages a broader type of observation.

These needs of science make awareness of transcendence difficult when they are dominant. They narrow down concern to manageable problems, tending to reduce meanings and data to the quantifiable, the repeatable, and the statistical. Likewise when the goals of prediction and control become dominant, an attitude opposite that of sensitive openness can very well be fostered.

The attitude of openness to transcendence encourages sensitive discernment. It is not limited by the needs of science, although it does not oppose the use of scientific procedures as a complementary attitude with different ends.

For example, appreciative discernment is not directed observation seeking to test a particular hypothesis nor does it seek for an isolated system. Rather, it is a broad awareness, scanning whatever is present, sensitive to processes of renewal from whatever quarter, open to fresh signs of worth. Of course hypotheses concerning renewal and worth can be tested, but the scientific attitude, while legitimate, is not the only valid approach to pursue and may not be most conducive to appreciation and healing.

Sensitive discernment does not restrict itself to quantifiable data or data capable of being recorded with precision. It is sensitive to all occurrences. It does not glorify the vague and indistinct. Nor does it deny the value of scientific method. But it refuses to restrict observation by the canons of precision and measurement.

Appreciative awareness is not primarily concerned to sort out and manipulate the variables in a situation. It is appreciative of resources of healing and gifts of kindness. The transcendent is not manipulable, hence it can be lost in an emphasis on analysis and manipulation. Nor does transcendence halt receptivity until the variables can be sorted out and properly isolated. It does not prevent the study of variables, but its primary thrust is receptive, not analytic.

Science requires publicly repeatable observations by unbiased observers. Appreciative awareness is receptive to transforming resources and challenging worth regardless of whether they are repeatable. Again, sensitive discernment and the scientific attitude are complementary and need not be mutually restrictive.

Science often seeks to understand in terms of past conditions or overarching theory. Sensitive discernment seeks to appreciate and receive help and criticism. This divergence in aim leads to a difference in type of fact apprehended. The data of appreciative awareness are more inclusive. The needs of science are legitimate but are not the only demands which can legitimately shape our perception.

It should be clear from this discussion that when I identify the philosophy outlined here as a type of religious naturalism, I am not counting as one of its essential characteristics the affirmation that scientific methods are the only legitimate approach to exploring our world. This is an empiricism generously conceived. My conception of naturalism, while it does affirm that there is only one world and that values and explanations must be found therein, does differ from the more restrictive methodological monism of some of its expositors.[4] Recently Larry Churchill has insisted on the importance of moral sensibility in medical ethics. This parallels our concept of sensitive discernment.[5]

Any assertion of the value of appreciative perception must take pains to avoid irrationalism and obscurantism. Sensitive discernment and directed, focussed observation are complementary. Thus the attitude of openness encourages scientific inquiry. Science, at its growing edge, can help nurture an attitude of continuing openness. It embodies a principle of self-criticism and can be an aid in understanding and using resources of renewal, provided that the attitudes of certainty and manipulation do not become dominant. To encourage appreciation is not to glorify the irrational. The mystical, the occult, the intuitive are not to be pursued as higher types of knowledge.

Sensitive discernment is a normal human ability which can be nurtured or impoverished. How this encouraging or deadening occurs would be an important study, an inquiry which itself would call for sensitive discernment as well as scientific rigor. Education, occupation, and recreation all must play a part in the process of enhancing or weakening sensitive awareness. One factor in the nurturing of appreciative discernment is surely the development of an adequate theory of inquiry, a generous empiricism.

II. Three Proponents of Sensitive Discernment

One of the claims made in this chapter is that all thinking is historically rooted and that it is well to explore one's own tradition carefully to assess its resources and problems. In line with this claim, it needs to be explicitly recognized that the generous empiricism developed in this chapter is situated firmly within the tradition of radical empiricism, including William James and Whitehead. This tradition need not be explored in detail here. Frankenberry and Dean have recently done this in expert fashion.[6] However, I do wish to spend time exploring the thought of Bergson, who is not explicitly treated by Dean or Frankenberry, as well as the thought of G. B. Smith, and of Bernard Meland, partly because they need to be better known and partly because Meland especially has exercised a profound influence on my own thinking.

1. Henri Bergson

Dare Bergson's name be mentioned today? This once-popular salon lecturer's name has become associated with fuzzy thinking, even with a fascist glorification of power. (He did, however, refuse special treatment from the French government, renounced his honors and privileges, and registered with his fellow Jews to wear the yellow armband under the Nazi occupation.)[7] He definitely deserves our attention. In the first place, whatever his shortcomings, he was a key figure, through James, Whitehead, Wieman and Meland, in the development of radical empiricism and process thought generally. When I encountered Bergson's *Introduction to Metaphysics* it was the first major challenge for me to classical British empiricism. In the second place, some of his critics are one-sided and shrill. Scholars like Pete Gunter and Milič Čapek have recently been attempting to present a more balanced view of Bergson. Nonetheless, there is in Bergson either the potential or the appearance of a potential to move in the direction of obscurantism and the occult, a tendency which British and American romantics share with Bergson, possibly through a common rootage in Schellings's *Naturphilosophie*. This potential, or even the appearance of such, needs to be resisted.

To begin our exploration of Bergson, we need to examine his fundamental bifurcation of reality into matter and life, the former characterized by the absence of organization and growth, the latter by their presence. For him time is efficacious and real, producing novelty in life. Organized living bodies, as distinct from aggregates of simples, grow in a true sense. (This parallels Meland's view that complex relationships or Gestalts produce novelty.) Matter, however, is not organized and is decomposable into parts over which time slips without penetrating. The future states of closed systems of matter are calculable, but only because such systems are abstracted from larger systems which include organized matter. Thus an omnipotent mind could not predict the future, only the future of certain closed systems.[8]

Novelty and life require recognition by a special cognitive approach, namely, intuition. For intuition the new is unforeseen growth. For intellect, on the other hand, the new is merely a rearrangement of parts. This concept of a special cognitive approach adequate to novelty, along with support from other sources, encouraged Meland to develop his concept of appreciative awareness, although without sharp bifurcation between the static and the dynamic and definitely without the sharp dichotomy between intelligence and intuition or appreciative awareness.

Bergson's concept of intuition is not obscurantist. It is that of a mode of awareness which is "disinterested, self-conscious, capable of reflecting."[9] Rather than being opposed to science, Bergson was trying to develop "a philosophy which would submit to the control of science and which in turn would enable science to progress."[10]

Pete Gunter has effectively challenged the conventional interpretation of Bergson as an irrationalist who attacks intelligence.

> Bergson's practice, however, refutes this interpretation. . . . Evolutionary theory and aphasiology provide only two of many instances in which Bergson departs from his presumed ideal of intuition as the perfect negation of human intelligence. Throughout his writings one finds the persistent bringing together of scientific knowledge so as to form the most coherent possible scientific world-view.
>
> The intuition at which we have arrived can be tested. . . . (Not that it is) a question of immediately verifying or falsifying Bergson's putative insights. The scientific uses of intuition require time for their maturation . . . and they involve not so much the details of verification as the broad conceptual framework with which science approaches, and makes sense of, these details.[11]

A key passage from Bergson which supports this view is from *Creative Mind.*

> Philosophy then must be able to model itself upon science, and an idea of so-called intuitive origin which could not manage . . . to cover the facts observed outwardly and the laws by which science joins them to each other, which would not be capable of correcting certain generalizations and of rectifying certain observations, would be pure fantasy.

Gunter sees Bergson's intuition as an active and controlled attitude.

Bergson's intuition is a form of reflection. . . . This form of reflection is carefully controlled and involves an intense effort of concentration. . . . If we are to have an intuition, therefore, we must be fully active and highly conscious.[12]

An important aspect of Bergson's concept of intuition is the questioning of established habits of thought. As construed by Milič Čapek,

the Bergsonian intuition . . . begins with the attitude of distrust for the accepted modes of thought. . . . This attitude of distrust originates in a vague awareness of certain experiences incompatible with the accepted modes of thought; the essence of intuition is precisely to bring these vague and rather implicitly felt data into a clear focus and to show that the new forms of understanding thus created are superior to the old ones.[13]

As Mary Christine Morkovsky phrases it when discussing how this idea is reflected in Bergson's later treatment of an open society:

Men who are intelligent and free and unwilling to repeat mechanically are a threat to closed societies. But they are the only ones who can bring about an open society. They do not overthrow obligation but rather respond to another type of obligation which is not slavish custom but an appeal to self-surpassing.

This self-surpassing is the same as, or at least akin to, the lure of continually challenging ideals in the minimalist model of transcendence.

The conventional interpretation of Bergson's concept of intuition as irrational and anti-intellectual is incorrect. When Bergson challenges the concept of "intelligence" he has in mind a very specific method of a mechanistic type based on the outlook of Euclid and Newton. In the words of Gunter, for Bergson intelligence is

not reason in its traditional definition but a partial and limited function of the human mind: a set of habitual responses to a world presumably well known. The disinterestedness, openness, flexibility and profundity customarily associated with reason are for Bergson attributes not of intelligence but of intuition.[14]

Bergson's concept of intuition needs to be appreciated as a key source for the attitude of sensitive discernment. Correlated with this is his recognition of the dynamic and interrelated nature of life. At the same time as these two appreciative notes are made, his dichotomies between intelligence and intuition and between matter and life are too simple. This issue is addressed in part in the discussion below concerning the continuum between the language of inquiry and the language of devotion.

Finally, Bergson was not careful in the way he expressed himself. You can always expect superficial readers and you need to take what steps you can to guard against them. While Gunter and Čapek seem correct to me in their more balanced view of Bergson, radical empiricism should not be allowed to become an excuse for obscurantism and irrationalism through the careless expression of its proponents.

2. G. B. Smith

An important root of our notion of sensitive discernment is to be found in the later writing of Gerald Birney Smith, teacher of theology at the University of Chicago in the first three decades of the twentieth century. A brief statement of his mature view can be found in his article, "Is Theism Essential to Religion?" referred to in Chapter Two.[15] In particular both the tentativeness of all propositional expressions of sensitive discernment and what I shall call below the transactional character of experience are affirmed by Smith.

He urges a

> frank recognition of the fact that our religious relationship to what we worship in our cosmic environment must be empirically stated, and our conception of God must be formulated in tentative terms which grow out of that experience, rather than in terms of a prior philosophy assumed to be final. Men may believe in God without being able to define God.

The exact meaning of "empirical" is not clear here, but from the context it seems to indicate a concern for experiential concreteness and for a rejection of a definitive, apodictic and *a priori* method. Smith buttresses this stress on the tentative character of our conceptions of God by a reference to what Ian Barbour would call "critical realism" in our understanding of scientific language.

> The testimony of religious souls points to a real reciprocity. It is, of course, true that epistemological analysis will destroy a naively

realistic conception of the other side of this reciprocal experience. But epistemology has done this for the physical world so often that we are ceasing to be disturbed by the inevitable "egocentric" factor in any interpretation. We are quite willing to recognize that our conceptions of physical reality are symbolic rather than descriptive. Nevertheless, so long as we can continue to use them in our actual dealings with the world, we have no practical doubt as to the objective existence of that world. Is not the case somewhat similar in the realm of religion?

This emphasis on the reciprocal or transactional character of experience is strongly affirmed by Smith.

This definitely involves a concern with concrete data of experience.

> Theologians in the near future will adopt a more inductive approach to the problem of defining the nature of the cosmic aspect of religious worship. . . . The character of God will be found in the experienced reciprocity between man and his environment rather than in the realm of metaphysical causation. The modern trend in theology is decidedly in the direction of exploring mysticism rather than in a dependence on philosophy.

Here there is general agreement between Smith and our approach. The best way to approach a conception of the divine is through an exploration of experiences of transcendence, rather than through rational argumentation to a metaphysical principle of sufficient reason. To be sure, I am not opposed to the philosophical task of attempting to clarify our notions, although they must remain tentative. Hence this entire enterprise might be thought of as a philosophy, although a philosophy of openness rather than of closure. Also, the the term "mysticism" seems a little out of place, but this may be a linguistic fashion. If anyone wants to refer to openness to transcendent realities as "mystical," I hesitate because of the baggage connected with that word, but suggest that perhaps the dispute may be purely verbal.

Smith hints at a conception of religious language appropriate to this sense of mystery.

> A theistic theology seems to many a person to belittle the religious relationship by fitting it too neatly into the categories of human logic. Poetry, symbolism, wordless adoration, seem more truly to interpret our relationship to the cosmic order than does a system

depicting precise theological control. Do we really want to believe
in a God who is too completely rationalized?

One can't help but believe that Smith would be interested in and
profit from the current discussions of metaphor, myth, and model.
Also, his thrusts at theism would need to be tempered in today's climate of discussion where many revisionist theologians are quite
concerned with a proper placing of mystery. One further point needs
to be made. The minimal model of divinity sketched in this book is
an attempt to be faithful to the spirit of tentativeness affirmed by
Smith and by his student, Bernard Meland. However, it is set forth
in technical language with attention to precision of language.
Hence, if the provisional character of this model is forgotten it will
be completely misunderstood. It is intended as fully hypothetical in
character and its intent is misunderstood if its provisional character as a model is overlooked.

In an address on "The Nature of Science and of Religion and
their Interrelation" Smith suggests that the basic task in the education of religious leaders today

> calls for the literary and poetic and philosophical (in the large
> sense) temper rather than the technique of the scientist. Science
> must perforce be precise and analytic. It is compelled to invent
> technical terms in order to get away from the vagueness of popular
> language . . . . We desperately need religious utterances which re-
> flect what we believe to be true concerning man and his world, and
> at the same time suggest the emotional and ennobling significance
> of those truths.
>
> In our modern schools of religion . . . as yet there is little appreci-
> ation of the fact that religion at its best furnishes a noble aesthetic
> interpretation of the meaning of life.

Clearly here "aesthetic" does not have the connotation of fictive as
it does for Santayana or those with an emotive theory of language.
In surveying the field of religious training, Smith feels that

> what is supremely needed is a group of scholars who know the
> field and the meaning of the personal emotions and loyalties in-
> volved in modern religion . . . and who will help to bring to self-
> consciousness the socially shared aspirations of those who have
> burned the bridges of pre-scientific theology behind them, and who
> want the meaning of religious living in the modern world to receive .

> its due literary and esthetic expression. . . . Religious leaders can-
> not look to the scientists to help formulate the meaning of reli-
> gion. . . . In the last analysis, religion is an art rather than a
> science.

It is interesting that while science has aided in the dissolution of
old beliefs and opened up vast reaches of the unknown universe, religion must seek artistic expression, because science attempts a
precision which cannot convey the richness of religious meaning.

3. Bernard Meland

The concept of sensitive discernment as developed above owes
much to Bernard Meland's notion of appreciative awareness. By
this concept Meland is trying to denote a way of apprehending reality that will be open to a fuller dimension of the world than is usually available to most of our thinking.

> This act is . . . holistic and appreciative, aiming at opening one's
> conscious awareness to the full impact of the concrete occurrence.
> It is very much like allowing one's visual powers to accommodate
> themselves to the enveloping darkness until, in their more recep-
> tive response . . . one begins to see into the darkness and to detect
> in it the subtleties of relationships and tendencies which had
> eluded one.[16]

The ideal of thinking is generally held to be rational thought with
its criteria of clarity and precision. However, claims Meland, much
of the world is too complex to fit into our clear and distinct ideas. He
does not deny their importance, but he does wish to assert that
there is more to the world than can be grasped clearly and precisely.
True and radical empiricism will grant these complexities instead
of reducing its view of reality to a truncated version of the world,
manageable but lacking in full concreteness.
    This awareness of the penumbra of complexity and concrete-
ness which surrounds the luminous area that we clearly know is
what Meland calls appreciative awareness. It is not a special fac-
ulty. It is an attempt to be more fully aware. It utilizes emotion, not
to lose objectivity, but to perceive more fully, as in the empathetic
understanding of a person or culture. It may be that the insights so
gained must be communicated in poetry, images, even myth rather
than analytic language.

In his effort to avoid obscurantism Meland insists that appreciative awareness can be trained and disciplined. It can be criticized.

Appreciative awareness itself is not an experience of transcendence. However, appreciative awareness is the way to the recognition of the concrete appearances of the transcendent.

Intellectual effort has an egoistic tendency to "enclose the mind within the bounds of the limited data available to the human situation at any given time or place."[17] Appreciative awareness is "an orientation of the mind which makes for a maximum degree of receptivity to the datum." It attempts to counter the illusion of intellectual egoism "that the categories are at hand with which to exhaust the meaning of this object."[18] To pursue inquiry with this presupposition is to simplify the data until they fit our clear and distinct ideas. Perceptiveness is sacrificed to precision.

Speaking of dealing with persons in legal matters or with countries in a diplomatic or military situation, Meland asserts:

> Thinking definitively is always motivated by some functional purpose. The object in such instances is not to understand the person or object, but to deal with it. . . . The penumbra of mystery and meaning . . . is ignored.[19]

In Meland's oft-repeated phrase, "We live more profoundly than we can think."

> Living or dying, and the human responses to these occurrences, are more complex than reflections about them or than any intellectual query involved by them.[20]

Appreciative awareness goes beyond a dichotomy between the rational consciousness and the moral consciousness, both of which suffer, in Meland's view, from the attempt to reduce reality to manageable proportions. Here Meland follows Schleiermacher's concern to locate religion beyond the restrictive measures of a rational or moral basis for religion. Meland traces the emphasis on rational consciousness back to Aristotle, while the emphasis on moral consciousness received chief expression in Calvinism, pietism, Kant, and the Ritschlian tradition.[21]

Religion itself can be narrow and confining. On the other hand, appreciative awareness can deepen religious sensitivity.

The difference between a religious mind cribbed and cabined within its own unclarified and undisciplined emotions, and a spirit that is free and forgiving is often a matter of sensitivity, proportion, and vision . . . . It is difficult to see how it could be attained except through the exercise of the appreciative consciousness.[22]

There is something subjective about our categories of rationality. The way beyond this egoism is through a perception that is broader than rationality. Such perception involves feelings, not understood as subjective moods, but as a total awareness, as the broadest possible involvement in the concrete datum. Consciousness is essentially a selective and focussing process, while feeling is able to grasp the rich texture of relations as well as any feelings in the datum, if it is a sentient being.[23]

The body is "less individuated than the conscious mind," and even apart from the sense organs, is

a threshold to the deeper stratum of organic being. . . . It literally relates the individuated life with the fuller context of living, both in the realm of nature, including the deeper creative passage, and in the social matrix. . . . The human self, when it becomes totally atuned to the fullness of being which reaches it . . . thinks and feels with its body.

Sensitive awareness "is the intellect widening and extending its depth and range to the level of feeling without losing its conscious focus." This is "more profound than thought, and more disciplined and directed than sheer sensation."[24]

Appreciative awareness includes a sensitivity to past evaluations in one's culture, valuations which tend to persist and to merge with the individual's mind and total organism.

Experience . . . is never simply a subjective event, but a happening within relationships that takes on public character with social consequences. . . . It is necessary, therefore, to speak of experience as the individual response to events, together with an accumulation of effects in duration within a structure of experience . . . . Although this larger structure is continuous with the individual structures of personality, it gathers into itself the persisting, protoplasmic character of institutional and other corporate processes. . . . All that has entered into the public and private decisions of a people . . . resides as a persistent datum in what I would call the structure of experience.

This structure of experience is far too complex to come into human consciousness, for it relates to us to the totality of events, including God.

> The full . . . content of the structure of experience . . . no human consciousness can know. It is a depth in our nature that connects all that we are with all that has been within . . . our culture. It is a depth in our nature that relates us as events to all existing events.[25]

By emphasizing feeling as a corrective to rationality, Meland is attempting to be more, not less, objective. What is felt are not subjective states, but the complex texture of the datum unavailable to the narrow focus of reason. Appreciative awareness has "an explicit cognitive concern," and implies an awareness "toward the end of *knowing* the reality *out there* in its own right."[26]

Appreciative awareness is an act of acquiring the meaning of a person or event through empathy and identification. Empathy is a "transcendence of egoistic barriers . . . the capacity of an individual to feel into a situation."[27]

> Identification . . . implies more than a cognitive appropriation of the meaning of the object within a given frame of symbolization. . . . It may extend beyond the subjective act of feeling into the event and assume the nature of real discernment into the solidarity of events.[28]

The use of feeling in appreciative awareness is not to be dissociated from the cognitive use of reason. Sometimes Meland makes this point by saying that appreciative awareness and critical inquiry must alternate.[29] At other times he speaks of appreciative awareness as itself involving analytical concern. There are three dimensions of this awareness. The first is "the reach toward the object . . . unaffected by the intrusion of the conscious ego." The second is:

> the appropriation of the object, relating it to the conscious ego, implying both its fragmented form through symbolization and its undifferentiated form.

The third is discrimination.

> This act is analytical; though it does not involve extricating the datum from its context . . . (for) an event is never properly known apart from its context.[30]

Another passage introduces aesthetic appreciation, a type of aesthetic awareness, treating both the object or referent of appreciative awareness and the intermingling of analysis and empathy. The art critic

> may have to study the work painstakingly to grasp all the subtle meanings that are being communicated to him, but his judgment of the balance of good and bad is as instantaneous as vision. . . . It is . . . the exercising of an ego whose vision has undergone the discipline of discriminating and enjoying certain values. Appreciative awareness is thus both objective and subjective.

In illustrating his assertion that "discernment of quality . . . is an act of appreciative awareness," Meland refers to reading, music, selecting a teacher, voting, ethical choice, and deciding a religious issue.[31] He uses a similar melding of empathetic understanding with rational inquiry to refer to understanding an alien culture.[32]

Rooted in process thought, Meland sees reality as characterized by interrelatedness, the persistence of the past, and the possibility of novelty. This makes each occasion inexhaustible by rational categories. Our concepts are to be held tentatively. Hence the appropriateness of appreciative awareness as perception open to complexities and anticipation of novelty.

Reality is characterized by novelty.

> Reality is unfinished . . . time makes a difference . . . mobility is the basic category . . . creativity is occurring . . . time is real. . . .
> The Appreciative Consciousness begins in a recognition of the metaphysical fallacy which inheres in the concern for fixity, and issues in an art of life which sees beyond the appeal to one's own securities.

However the past persists in interrelationship with the present, so that there is "both constant change and the persistence of past attainment."[33]

Reality is also characterized by the interrelatedness of events, the social or organic nature of reality. "Relations extend every event indefinitely." Reality is both transitive and relational, "a dynamic context of interpenetrating orders of meaning."[34] The interrelatedness of the datum makes it conceptually inexhaustible. Our concepts are to be held tentatively, subject to revision.

There are different levels of emergence in the world which yield to different kinds of inquiry. A different method is applicable where physical behavior is dominant from where personal life appears.

This does not involve the refusal to use descriptive analysis, but it does insist that it become allied with a more sensitive inquiry using appreciative awareness at the higher levels. In this approach

> perceptiveness assumes the kind of primacy which precise calculation acquired under Newtonian physics . . . (where) structure meant mechanism or an ordering of meaning which was permanently given, so completely, in fact, that mathematical science could describe, measure, or predict its character.[35]

Meland feels appreciative awareness is particularly apt for the study of persons, institutions, and God. In sociology statistics help, but do not illumine the subtle resources of insight or of pathological resistance to understanding. The novelist and the humorist are often the shrewdest analysts, because of their perceptive curiosity and sympathetic understanding of motives and hopes.[36]

The kind of inquiry which uses appreciative awareness "can be awakened and nurtured just as surely as discipline in logical analysis or precision in scientific thought." Appreciative awareness is not to be separated from concern with fact and structure, for this would make it "a special form of intuition or act of faith that sets aside empirical and rational inquiry as being irrelevant to its deeper knowledge."[37] Just as exact thought can breed deception, inexact thought can breed error and indulgent sentiment, much as love without the restraint of law can be sordid or sentimental.[38] Appreciative awareness, like art appreciation which is a particular mode of it, requires discipline and discrimination.

> One brings to bear upon the object or the event the full play of one's critical powers, being receptive at the same time to what is given in this object such that one's critical powers may also stand under judgment. . . . How else does the critic grow in sensitivity and discrimination except as he profits by his continual association with competent, creative effort, exercising his judgment in relation to it? . . . (Art criticism) remains a valid blending of the subjective powers and psychic distance.[39]

When Meland wrote about appreciative awareness in the early 1950's he could indicate that the affective processes, which form the basis of this wider awareness, are neglected in our culture, except for exploitation by commercial interests. He noted that churches appeal to these processes, but do not nurture them in significant ways.

He saw these processes as stimulated constantly, but as neglected by education. Since the late 1960's there has been more of a concern in American culture for feelings, but his point that they need discipline remains valid.[40]

> Attaining this kind of discernment would require, ideally, a slow process of nurture in which feeling (empathy), imagination, and critical reflection would be simultaneously quickened and related.

Without discipline

> the appeal to the appreciative consciousness will result in nothing more than a relaxing of intellectual effort. . . . Appreciative awareness . . . is the intellect fully informed by feeling and by awareness of the context of relations in which meaning has formed.

Meland continues in asserting that criticism

> has the effect both of restraining irresponsible expression and of eliciting from creative imagination . . . disciplined effort. . . . Understanding does not necessarily involve complete and continuous detachment. It may require a degree of distance in alternation with a measure of involvement.[41]

Recourse to sensitive awareness is a sound realism. The person in whom appreciative awareness is feeble will "impress the limited and circumscribed meanings of his own valuations upon whatever he encounters."

> The Appreciative Consciousness is the indispensable guide to understanding any problem, situation, crisis. . . . The unexpected happens, often not because the facts give no hint of the outcome, but because there were no eyes to see or to attend to these relational and transitive factors.[42]

III. The Transactions Between Experience and Language

Nancy Frankenberry points out that we need a theory of experience.

> Empiricism has always stood for the justificatory need to ground all knowledge in experience. But as such it is a thesis in search of

an adequate *theory* of experience. "Experience" is not an easy word
to introduce into today's intellectual climate, however. It is so slip-
pery and overworked, at the same time. It is one of those words
that, as Humpty Dumpty noted, ought to be paid overtime because
it does so much work.[43]

1. Experience as Transactional

My proposal is that we think of experience as a transaction. A
transaction between what? We must be careful how we state this,
lest we reify the end points of the relationship, lest we falsely abstract from the activity of experience to substantive agents and
things. There are a variety of terms we could use, all of them dangerous if taken with misplaced concreteness, each of them helpful in
pointing to aspects of experience that we wish to highlight.

Experience can be thought of as a transaction between self (itself a product of choices made in the context of social and genetic
legacies) and world (itself both construct and material constructed).
Experience can also be thought of as a transaction between organism and environment (both of which are themselves social processes). Experience can also be thought of as a transaction between
language (an inherited yet flexible medium) and lived feelings intermingling with relatively clear perceptions.

However we speak (in language which is inherited yet flexible,
a language which we modify even as we speak), experience is best
spoken of, I think, as a complex interaction. Most likely, experience
is not a passive affair. Whatever it is, the self is not a *tabula rasa*.

On the one hand, probably there is little or no pure experience
unclarified or untainted by tradition, language or theory. There
may be occasional points of brute pain or immediate feeling or sensation unmediated by language, concept or tradition, but if there be
such points they are of passing moment and little meaning until
they are interpreted. Most of our experience is not of such points but
of various transactions between ourselves and our world in which
we recognize "the dentist's drill coming," "an infected needle over
there," "I'm sick to my stomach," "my alarm clock buzzing," or "the
morning sun coming out."

Any points of pure experience, if there be such, cannot be used
as epistemological anchors, sure foundations to solve our practical
(or our philosophical) problems.

On the other hand, we are not out of touch with our world. It is
not language all the way down. Or rather, it is language in transaction with our world (and ourselves). The litany of terms invoked

above, from "dentist's drill" to "morning sun" are clearly linguistic, inherited social constructs, but they can be used appropriately (or inappropriately) in relation to dull ache-whine-dentist's face-light above-chair around, etc. or in relation to coffee smell-warm feeling-bright light-remembered dream-thoughts of projects, etc. (or the absence of these).

We are not wholly adrift in a linguistic sea. We may have no anchors or sure foundations, but we do have fallible, yet often rather helpful, feelers, clues and hints which may be sharpened or which may become misleading. As the chair rocks it may be helpful to note that other clues point to an earthquake. "Earthquake" is a socially inherited linguistic construct, but sometimes it is appropriate not to fall on one's knees to placate God but instead to run out of the building in case it collapses. There are no guarantees. It may not be an earthquake, but shelling, and the street may be filled with combat troops.

Experience is a transaction. Language is part of the transaction. The linguistic structures may help or may hinder. Sensations and feelings are also part of the transaction. They may be helpfully understood or not. There are no sure foundations which are guaranteed to get us out of trouble, practically or philosophically. But while there are no guarantees, it still pays to pay attention.

In another contribution to the discussion, Nancy Frankenberry has detected a problem in radical empiricism which she calls "the linguistic gap," the problem of whether lived experience as the pre-reflective experiential basis of knowledge is expressible in language. To the degree that lived experience has a non-discursive character, it lacks the determinateness to function epistemically. But to the degree that it is determinate enough to function epistemically, it seems to be conceptual and no longer simply felt.[44] She has put her finger on a crucial problem. She is also correct in her proposal that:

> radical empiricism should recognize a reciprocal and even codeterminate relation between experience and language.[45]

There is no basic priority to either which can settle the problems of faith or inquiry. There is the on-going process of self-critical faithfulness. I suggest that an acknowledgement of the transactional character of living in relation to both immediate experience and inherited language is a way of recognizing this codeterminate relation and avoiding the linguistic gap.[46]

2. Transactional Realism

Further, I suggest that an historical empiricism can enter the present debate about realism and define itself as a transactional or anticipatory realism. By transactional realism I mean that we are often in touch with the world (indeed, the world is in touch with us), although we may misunderstand or misinterpret the clues in the touchings. The moral of the story of the blind men and the elephant is not just that they were blind and thus mistaken, compared to an accurate and total vision. The moral is that they were in touch with the elephant and, if as smart as many seeing-impaired people whom I know, they would be able to improve their understanding of the elephant through a variety of means. (I leave it to my readers' imaginations as to how they did that. Remember, they were blind, not dumb.) Deliberately, I use the word "improve", not "correct." The word "improve" has less of a connotation of the possession of a clear standard in terms of which to correct. (In that sense, I do not correct my students' essays. I suggest ways to improve them.) To be sure, we could ask whether "improvement" does not imply a standard in terms of which we can judge the improvement. I think that we do not *have* a clear sense of a standard. What we have is a courageous hope that the standards that we dimly grasp are not too misleading. Transactional realism is an anticipatory realism, a realism of hope.

I distinguish anticipatory realism from most contemporary statements of realism.[47] As a tentative statement of anticipatory realism I mean the following: the attempt to revise or correct theories, visions, or images by further exploration of experience is worth pursuing, while the present results of such attempts are worth relying on when necessary, although we do not have the hope of a definitive answer (which would be the end of the process). In short, the process of revision is worth the effort, even though we do not hope to reach the answer, and acting on the results so far attained is worth the risk. The claim is not that our theories and models, when true, map the world as it really is, but that the process of revision toward what the world really can be is worth the struggle, even though we will never know how adequate the mapping is. The claim is, further, that when our theories, models and visions have been subject to appropriate scrutiny, despite our propensity to error, they are worth the risk of relying on, acting on, living by.

Such anticipatory realism would see correspondence between idea and object as a regulative, not a constitutive principle. Regulative here means that anticipatory realism provides encouragement, not a strategy or a criterion for inquiry. We can approximate truth, or, better, we can become more adequate in our surmising. There is no way of showing this; that is, there is no superior view or impartial spectator above the history of the subject-object transactions to decide between competing theories and visions. Our guide is pragmatic adequacy which is itself subject to revision and hence is not a definitive test.

As a side comment, may I say that the instrumentalism derided by contemporary realists does not seem to be the position of Dewey. John Dewey's theory of knowledge has been referred to as a transactional view.[48] That is, he sees a continuing interaction between knower and known. On this processive view, knowing does not constitute the reality of what is given to the knower (in this many statements of realism are correct), but knowing is involved in constituting the object of knowledge. "Objects of knowledge *in their capacity of distinctive objects of knowledge* are determined by intelligence."[49] In order to grasp Dewey here, it is important to note that the term he uses is "object *of* knowledge" (emphasis added). When Dewey speaks of an "object," he refers not to what is given, something there, but to the result of inquiry. Dewey's example is that of a doctor examining a patient.

> Now, in the degree to which the physician comes to the examination of what is there with a large and comprehensive stock of such possibilities or meanings in mind, he will be intellectually resourceful in dealing with a particular case. They ... are ... the means of knowing the case in hand; they are the agencies of transforming it, through the actions which they call for, into an object— an object of knowledge.[50]

The process of inquiry will give us a ruptured appendix or a kidney stone as the object of inquiry. They are objects or "objectives" of inquiry.[51] "For the working scientist, 'objects of knowledge' mean precisely the objects which have been obtained by approved processes of inquiry."[52]

To add to the possibility of misunderstanding Dewey, he attacked the realism of his day in *Essays in Experimental Logic*. The thrust of his attack was first that the realism of his day assumed an epistemological bifurcation into *res cogitans* and *res extensa*, rather than continuing interaction between knower and known. The second point of his attack was that the then current realism also tended to assume that every presentation of anything to a person was a type of knowledge. Thus immediate presentation would be called knowledge by these realists.

Dewey's favorite term for his approach to a theory of inquiry, "instrumentalism," is misleading, for it has taken on the connotation that ideas are *merely* instruments. However, the term originally conveyed the notion of an interaction or, better, a transaction between knower and known. An instrument involves activity. This might be called a "transactional realism," or even a "processive" or "anticipatory realism." Given both the historic ambiguities of the term "realism" and the current debate over realism in the philosophy of science, perhaps the term should not be used. However, one value that the term does have is that it indicates that for Dewey the knower is reciprocally related to more than her own ideas or language. The processive or anticipatory note points out that for Dewey the knower is not so much starting from the real as moving towards the real. At any rate, Dewey in his later writings found the term "transaction" to be helpful. As an insightful current interpreter of Dewey has written:

> One must not think of 'organism' and 'environment' or 'self' and 'world' as separate and separable entities which come together and then 'interact' (it was over such confusions that Dewey adopted the term 'transaction' for his more customary 'interaction').[53]

Given the tentativeness, even minimalism, of at least some radical empiricists in religion, why do I affirm the thesis of anticipatory realism, minimalist as it is? Why speak of revising or correcting theories if we are not making any assertions about the world anyway?[54] The answer is that we are making assertions about realities, assertions which we affirm are (probably) more adequate to these realities than other assertions. Dewey makes assertions about the religious quality of experience, Meland about realities dimly apprehended in sensitive awareness, and I speak of the appreciation of situationally transcendent worth and the acknowledgement of situationally transcendent challenge. For all my minimalism and tentativeness I wish to affirm that the appreciation of this worth and the acceptance of these challenges are not stupid or mere gambles. The realities which we dimly perceive and the theories which we develop concerning them, when subject to appropriate scrutiny, are worth the risk of living by, despite our propensity to error and fantasy.

Whether this anticipatory realism qualifies as a variety of realism, it is clear that a self-critical empiricism will be an historically critical, culturally aware empiricism. Gadamer is correct that recognizing the historical rootedness of inquiry is both real and even helpful. Distortions by this historical rootedness can be lessened, even if not denied, and we are responsible for that. On the other hand the cultural and historical roots need be accepted neither with resignation nor with chauvinism. They do need to be examined.

An historically critical, anticipatory realism adds the note of responsibility to critical tentativeness. It is a self-critical stance which is willing to assume responsibility for choice without foundations. Perhaps my own situational rootedness as a parent and teacher with administrative duties helps me to see the importance of this stance. It is a stance which accepts Nietzsche's challenge to reevaluate all values but which in turn challenges his flirting with arbitrariness and nihilism. This stance is designed to remedy the lack of nerve which can come from relativism. For example, Richard Rorty's view of philosophy as kibitzing in the conversation of mankind shows a reluctance to shoulder responsibility for the task of philosophy as a search (a constantly revisionary process without incorrigible foundations) for wisdom or at least insight. His comments on the dispute between Galileo and Cardinal Belarmine and on why fascism is wrong display an implicit lack of nerve. His point in the Galileo-Belarmine dispute is that after Galileo the standards of rationality have changed so that we can now agree with Galileo, but that at that time no neutral rational observer would be able to decide between the two sides, since the adoption of standards of rationality is not a matter of neutrality. This over-simplifies the problem. Granted that standards of rationality change, Rorty is operating with a false dichotomy. He assumes that either a neutral observer could get the one correct answer (which is a foundationalist position) or that it is merely a matter of the upholders of the older standards dying off and a new generation taking over. But this dichotomy between foundationalism and a temporal relativism overlooks the possibility that there can be strong but not conclusive arguments. Indeed, at the time of the dispute people were persuaded by strong arguments to change their views. Without a recognition of the partial strength of rational arguments Rorty has nothing to say to the worst excesses of the New Age people who wish to bring in yet new standards. Are we merely to accept any new standard because it is new? Are we to say that the choice between human rights and fascism is merely a matter of fashion?[55]

We are faced with a variety of situations in which our choices must supervene on the choices of others in, for example, parental or administrative situations, or else we must refrain from intervening. Granted that a Taoist policy of doing nothing is often appropriate, there are times in the transactions of life where not to intervene is likely to be more destructive than if we do. There are a multitude of situations where substituted judgments or transnational or transcultural judgments are called for. We need courage to act, because arrogance and guilt are both terribly real. Openness to self-criticism and self-review is a rare quality, nationally or individually. Readiness for a self-critical responsible engagement is also rare, since self-criticism can lead to abdication of responsibility. An historically critical empiricism, an empiricism flavored with an anticipatory realism, can help us to shoulder the responsibilities with appropriate gentleness and self-critical caution.[56]

3. The Objectivity/Subjectivity Dichotomy

Much of the debate in both philosophy and wider circles today concerns the relationship between objectivity and subjectivity. This debate is often raised in terms of an either-or dilemma: we either have starting points and methods for solving questions of fact and value or else, where we do not, we are left floundering in a morass of unjustified opinions and arbitrary preferences.

The dynamic, transactional nature of experience which has been elaborated here, the view that we are in touch with the world and that our exploration of this world is an on-going, revisionary process, shows that the choice between epistemological security and despair is a false dichotomy. For there is a third option which reveals both horns of the dilemma to be extreme positions.

The modern viewpoint was that if we cannot in principle achieve objective certainty, then we are left with arbitrary subjectivity. Modernism affirmed the autonomy of inquiry in relation to state, church, and tradition. However, modernism failed because it did not realize that its empirical (Locke) or rational (Descartes) starting points were not innocent, pure, and free from doubt or question.[57] In contrast, the traditions of pragmatism and radical empiricism in American philosophy and theology emphasize the continuous reconstruction of experience. This reconstruction is not an arbitrary construction (as many of the postmodernists, especially the deconstructionists, would hold), because the world restricts the range of possible constructions, the past constrains the domain of allowable interpretations. The blind men did not think that they felt a blossom, a bird, a dustball or a swamp.

There is a third option between certainty and despair, between objectivity in the sense of methodological security and subjectivity in the sense of arbitrariness, between a value-free world and the values projected onto the world by speculation, emotion, and wish-fulfillment. Between certainty and despair there is a reasonable hope. Between security and arbitrariness there is choice working with partial reasons, with a preponderance of evidence, with partly warranted premises yielding probable conclusions, in short, with weighted wagers. Between a value-free world of fact and mere opinions, feelings, and biases, there is an affective openness to, a sensitive discernment of, the significance of the world. The world is full of meaning and worth, beauty and terror, and an affectively responsive openness to this world, a feeling-into, a genuine sympathy can discern, with error and distortion, the values and significance that are in the world.

An example of the difficulty which occurs when this third option is neglected or undeveloped is the difficulty which faces Richard Rorty in arguing for his social preferences. For Rorty, since there is no foundation on which to stand in order to fight against such pathologies as fascism, we are left with a mere matter of preference.[58] As Dean suggests in a different context, we are left with no rational way to choose between the third world and the Third Reich. But surely a sensitive discrimination of the actual differences of worth between the third world and the Third Reich will not leave a serious moral doubt for most persons of normal moral maturity, even though their discernment may be ambiguous and clouded. To say this is to invite neither foundationalism nor cultural provincialism.

4. Proudfoot's Challenge to Empiricism

A recent significant study by Wayne Proudfoot criticizes the definition of religion in terms of any common core experience. This might seem to challenge both the centrality of experience in the methodology of generous empiricism and also the triadic description of religion which I offered in Chapter One as a delineation of the common core of religion. I believe that it does not.

Proudfoot claims that defining religion in terms of a common religious experience is an invalid procedure. According to him, an experience cannot be specified without reference to words or concepts. Further, it is not true that experience is more primitive than words or concepts. Proudfoot takes ordinary perception as an instance.

> Ordinary perceptual experiences also assume beliefs. They presuppose beliefs about the causes of experience. One would not identify an experience as a perception in the face of evidence that the appropriate causal relation between the object perceived and the experience itself was lacking.[59]

If it is true of ordinary perception that an experience cannot be identified without reference to words or concepts, it is certainly true, Proudfoot continues, of that mystical experience which many empirical theories of religion claim to be at the core of the varieties of religion.

> Ineffability and noetic quality, the two marks that James regards as jointly sufficient for the specification of a mystical experience, function to insure that any experience identified as mystical will be anomalous with respect to any determinate description. . . . Far from being more primitive than words, concepts, and beliefs . . . the experience cannot be specified without explicit reference to these criteria.[60]

I believe that Proudfoot's challenge to the uncovering of a common core of religious experience does not affect my description of the triadic experience common to the religions. This traidic experience I described in Chapter One as a polarity of blessing and judgment or gift and challenge plus the dimension of transcendence. The sketch of the triadic experience of transcendence is not an attempt to sketch a pure, unmediated experience prior to words, but to offer a hypothetical sketch, at a fairly abstract and general level, of common elements of experiences which are intertwined with, not separate from, words, symbols, rituals, institutions and all the observable phenomena of religion in culture and personal life. I do not speak of a common experience prior to or underlying its manifestations, but of a generic similarity among a variety of cultural-personal phenomena. This generic similarity seems to indicate an intentional reference to a transcendent dimension with a polarity of blessing and curse, of support and challenge, of creation and judgment. The minimal model is offered as a theoretical description of these phenomena, a model with existential implications.

Proudfoot suggests that concepts not only are needed to identify an experience but may even be considered to be constitutive of them.

> The assessments and interpretations are formative rather than consequent. The suggestion that fear and anger are simple impressions has seemed plausible to many. If they are not simple but

assume rather sophisticated conceptual distinctions and judgments, then a similar analysis is surely required for the complex
affections with which phenomenologists of religions have chiefly
been concerned.

As Proudfoot concludes,

> an experience that has been evoked by carefully chosen rhetoric
> and by assuming a cultural tradition informed by theism cannot be
> taken as evidence for a unity that is independent of our concepts
> and beliefs.[61]

What Proudfoot is attacking here is an empiricism of pure experience. However, a transactional understanding of experience
never denies the formative power of language and traditions. The
appeal to experience that I am making is not an appeal to an untainted experience that shall establish a sure foundation for religious inquiry. Rather I am seeking to explore, to uncover, to enrich
experience with my minimal model, my ideas, my philosophy and in
turn seek to show that experience as thus actively explored will in
turn throw light on and give further support to the model, the ideas,
the philosophy.

A generous and radical empiricism, as I seek to employ it, does
not focus on feeling alone, but on overcoming these false separa-
tions. Some feelings are feelings into a situation and merge into intellect and moral insight. The appeal is not to pure experience to
provide the answers. The appeal is to a growing experience to become more supportive in our search for deeper answers as this experience itself is nurtured and educated.

Proudfoot argues further that causal claims are imported by
the theoreticians of religious experience into their description of the
experience. Thus Proudfoot claims that three illegitimate steps are
taken by Otto, a key representative of this approach. In the first
place the very description of religious experience which is offered by
Otto rules out naturalistic explanation prior to inquiry. In the second place the language of Otto's theory, instead of describing the experience, actually creates it. Finally Otto invokes a non-natural
explanation (the *numinous*) to explain the experience which was
not only identified, but actually caused by, the non-natural description. Is this a serious challenge to the approach I take here? No, for
my approach differs significantly from that of Otto. In the first
place, the minimalistic approach does not preclude empirical investigation and naturalistic explanation. It welcomes it. However, it is

open to the possibility that there will still be inexplicable creation and re-creation, to be identified as situationally transcendent resources. It is Proudfoot who has shortcircuited inquiry by deciding that non-naturalistic explanation is illegitimate. If I am not mistaken, that is an implicit assumption underlying his analysis. Should it occur that such unpredicted and unmanageable (and at least temporarily unexplained) healing and renewal never occurs we will revise our theories. But we find no reason *a priori* to preclude such situationally transcendent resources. Nor do we find reason to abandon the stance of openness and expectant waiting for such resources to occur, even though they may not come.

In the second place our intention is not to evoke or create the sense of situational transcendence with this theory, although it is possible that theories can evoke or create experiences. We must be careful and cautious with our theories, just because they can create erroneous or misleading experiences. But to be cautious is not to throw in the towel and admit that theory causes all experience. If theory is experience-laden, it need not be theory-caused. Even if an experience is "created" by a theory, the experience need not be a distortion or a misrepresentation. It may be that the theory removed prejudice or helped open us to novel experience.

Indeed, our minimalist approach, far from evoking an experience of situational transcendence, may possibly have closed off experience of the numinous, the holy, or God's grace and glory. This would not be the first time that a theory has radically altered the likelihood of an experience. We see fewer ghosts and visions of Christ and Mary today. And none of my Western acquaintances have seen Krishna. Such a narrowing of experience may be fortunate or unfortunate, depending on whether it is seen as a cleansing or an impoverishment. But it is an inevitable result of changes in theory and our overall world view. You cannot get rid of theory in favor of pure, unadulterated experience. What you can do is to attempt to deepen and enrich theory with experience and to clarify and criticize experience through theory. In part, this book is an elaboration of a theory which seeks to clarify and criticize religious experience, not to evoke it.

As for Proudfoot's third criticism of the approach taken by Otto, the minimalist model defended here does not offer a non-natural explanation of the sort Proudfoot presumes. What I offer in my minimalist conception is a description together with a suspension of an explanation or, better, a description which allows openness within a naturalistic outlook which eschews theistic explanations for religious experience. In other words, it is an attempt to develop a theory which will not short-circuit or preclude experiences of the transcendent.

Finally, Proudfoot maintains that there is a far greater variety of religious experience than the claims to elaborating a common core of such experience can encompass. However, our triadic description of the experience of transcendence is at a level of generality which should, in principle, encompass the significant varieties, apart from some borderline cases. My triadic description seeks to discern a generic similarity, not a monolithic common core or essence.

5. Lindbeck's Challenge to Empiricism

George Lindbeck's *The Nature of Doctrine* might be construed as another serious contemporary challenge to the radical empiricist understanding of the role of experience in inquiry being developed here. Lindbeck is trying to develop and defend a cultural-linguistic theory of religion and doctrine in which doctrines are to be seen as primarily second-order statements, as regulations or rules governing (but not specifying) religious affirmations. He wishes to set forth this theory as an alternative to the traditional cognitive theory in which religious language is basically propositional and to the liberal's experiential-expressive theory in which doctrines are expressive symbols of an inner religious experience.

According to Lindbeck's cultural-linguistic theory, religions are "comprehensive interpretive schemes, usually embodied in myths or narratives and heavily ritualized, which structure human experience and understanding of self and world" and which are used for the intention of "identifying and describing what is taken to be 'more important than anything else in the universe' and to organize all of life, including both behavior and beliefs, in relation to this."[62] To become religious, on this view, is to interiorize a set of skills by training and practice. To put it slightly differently, a religion is "a communal phenomenon shaping the subjectivities of the individual, not a manifestation of them."[63]

A key issue for Lindbeck is whether religion should be seen as the product of the experience of the divine (the experiential-expressive theory) or whether, as he claims, religion produces the experience.[64] Lindbeck briefly grants that there is a reciprocity between "inner" experience and "external" religious and cultural factors and claims merely to stress the latter as the primary factors.[65]

However, in his working out of the thesis he drops the recognition that there is an interplay between the "inner" experience and the communal-linguistic network of symbols and instead lays exclusive emphasis on the social network when he works out his analysis. Indeed, Lindbeck is quite explicit about the exclusiveness of his emphasis on the symbolic network, despite his brief disclaimer about the interplay of the "inner" and the "outer." Since symbol systems are primary, there are no uninterpreted or unthematized experiences. For Lindbeck an experience, by definition, is something of which one is conscious, a key difference from radical empiricism which is willing to speak of emergent meanings, vague feelings, and a penumbra surrounding conscious clarity. An experience, further, depends on its being symbolized, and all symbol systems have their origin in interpersonal relations and social interactions. Lindbeck suggests that there are no purely private symbolizations and therefore no private experiences, or, as a less strong and perhaps more defensible claim, that it is not necessary to utilize the hypothesis of private experience in order to understand religion.[66]

Lindbeck's insights are valuable, but he overplays them. Seeing doctrine as a second-order activity which indicates rules for religious affirmations is a helpful approach, although I think that the distinction between first- and second-order language may be hard to sustain consistently, especially in analyzing the history of doctrine. Also the recognition of the role of social symbols in the formation of experience is an important insight and a helpful corrective to the isolated individualism of much liberal and existentialist thought.

A more adequate approach would maintain, using Lindbeck's terms, that there is an interplay between "inner" experience and "outer" religious and cultural factors. To use terms which I prefer, there is an interplay between the social network of symbolized experience and the individual creative use of it in explaining one's own experience. Further, by not recognizing the transactions between symbols and the world, Lindbeck has no room for the exploration of the world through a disciplined and open sensitive discernment. It would be difficult to say which has primacy, the personal or the social, nor is it important to do this. However, Lindbeck has not made a strong case for his denial of the significance of the personal.

In Lindbeck's theory, religious language is intratextual or intrasemiotic, that is, it is a second-order language. It says nothing either true or false about the object of religious language, about God, for example.[67] Lindbeck says that this cultural-linguistic theory does not imply a rejection of epistemological realism, since theology and doctrine are second-order language. But this intrasemiotic approach in effect means that the extrasemiotic relationship can be ignored.

Lindbeck wishes to avoid the alternative of relativism and foundationalism. However, intratextuality seems relativistic, turning religion into incommensurable intellectual ghettoes and leaving the choice between religions arbitrary, since there is no foundation from which to evaluate competing claims. But Lindbeck wishes to assert that the antifoundationalism which is a corollary of his approach is not identical with irrationalism.

Lindbeck suggests that we have learned from Kuhn and Wittgenstein that the norms of reasonableness are too rich and subtle to be specified in a general theory. Rather reasonableness is analogous to the unformalizable skill of the artist or the linguistically competent. Intelligibility and credibility come from competence in a skill, not from a theory. Coming to believe is parallel to learning a language. One does not use argumentation in learning a language, but once one has learned to speak the language, argument becomes possible. Thus while religious language is invulnerable to definitive confirmation and refutation, it can be argued for.[68]

Such arguments will not involve which theory of the Trinity, for example, best corresponds to the real nature of God. No one can answer that question. Rather the best theory of the Trinity will be the one that best organizes the data of Scripture and tradition with a view to its use in worship and life. In other words for Lindbeck confirmation and disconfirmation of religious assertions occurs through the accumulation of successes or failures in making coherent sense of relevant data.[69]

We need not take the time here to assess the general validity of Lindbeck's theory when applied to religious language and doctrine. I do wish to suggest a difference between his approach and the minimal option set forth in this book.

I agree that religious language is not subject to "no doubt about it" confirmation and "knock down" refutation, but I maintain that it can be argued for. Further, I agree that much of what counts as reasonableness is too rich and subtle to be specified, that it has aspects of an unanalyzable skill.[70] However, when Lindbeck talks about success in the organization of data, his data are texts, not realities to which the text refers. The problem is his intrasemiotic stance. I wish to affirm that there is something outside the text; there are extrasemiotic realities to which language, including religious language, often refers. However, I do wish to qualify this assertion in two significant respects.

In the first place the realities to which religious language refers, in my understanding of language, are not "things" or "entities," spiritual or otherwise. Rather these are realities with certain qualities. These realities are either forces with the quality of being creative or healing and also of being unexpected and unmanageable, that is, situationally transcendent, or else they are ideals of truth, beauty, humanity and community with the quality of being continually beckoning.

In the second place I am not affirming that we have an unthematized experience, a prelinguistic or prereflective experience which is the *fons et origo,* foundation or Archimedean point from which to test assertions, a superior perspective from which to look down and compare language and reality. There may be prelinguistic experience, but it would represent a limiting case and can function in no wise as a foundation or test. Yet I do wish to affirm the reality, often vaguely discerned and subject to error, of such transactions with experience as often reconstruct it towards a more adequate knowledge, understanding, or insight. Just because we do not have a definitive vision of the world whereby to test our language does not mean that we are isolated in our language, out of touch with an experienced world.

IV. The Historical Rootedness of Empirical Inquiry

All inquiry is historically rooted. A theory of experience needs to affirm this both in theory and in practice. A truly generous empiricism, a radical empiricism, will distinguish itself from earlier British empiricism by moving beyond the centrality of the five senses and by widening the sensationalistic paradigm of knowing to include an historical model of knowing. A generous empiricism will recognize that present experience is, to a large degree, a reconstruction of past experience. This reconstruction is not arbitrary because the past informs it and restricts its range. Not only has William Dean helped me to understand this, but his work is part of the contemporary context of this book, particularly this section.

Thus experience is a chain or series of interpretations. The study of both individual growth and human culture is the study of such chains. Indeed, I would say that our experiences of the divine, of the situationally transcendent and continually challenging, are always rooted in past interpretations. The root shapes and limits the growth of the plant. It does not determine it. Although I hesitate to say that God is a chain of interpretations, as Dean suggests, I will agree with his language that God (or the divine) is known as one knows the evolving character of a friend (or, given my uneasiness about personal religious language, as we learn the evolving character of friendship), through a series of successive steps. Thus I feel the need for a serious and self-conscious study of the history of these interpretations. This is the importance of the historical study of religion and culture. This is also the reason for the importance of the retrieval of the socio-historical study of religion of the "early Chicago school," not only because Ames and Mathews are influential in the formation of the religious naturalism in this book but also because of the intrinsic value of this approach in studying the chains of religious interpretations.[71]

Does historicism undercut empiricism? Does an acknowledgement of the historical rootedness of empirical inquiry invalidate the claims of empiricism as a mode of religious inquiry? As a way of focussing these questions, the "historical consciousness" of Hans Georg Gadamer is taken as a viewpoint from which to examine two exponents of empiricism in religious inquiry.[72]

Let us start with an exposition of Gadamer's thoughts on the role of "pre-judgments" and "productive-history" in understanding and his judgement on the "naivete" of modern scientific consciousness. Next, let us examine Henry Nelson Wieman and Bernard Meland, two thinkers in the tradition of radical empiricism, to see whether they can escape Gadamer's charge of naivete. Then Gadamer's thesis of the universality of language will be, in turn, challenged by Meland's concepts of "bodily acquaintance" and "sensibilities."

A fundamental thesis of Gadamer is the all-pervasiveness of language. "Language is the fundamental mode of operation of our being-in-the-world." We never escape language. Language is the matrix of all our interaction with the world. "In all knowledge of the world, we are always already encompassed by the language that is our own." Indeed, Gadamer speaks of language as "the medium in and through which we . . . perceive our world."[73]

As an aspect of this fundamental thesis, Gadamer asserts that in all understanding the power of "productive history" (Linge's translation) is at work. To explicate this notion, let us examine

Gadamer's interesting and controversial concept of the role of prejudice (or "pre-judgment" as my translation of *Vorurteil*) in understanding.[74]

According to Gadamer, all understanding involves prejudgment. Here he is deliberately challenging the position of the Enlightenment. Indeed, we might say that this challenge marks Gadamer's differentiation of his postmodern stance from that of the modern or Enlightenment stance.

> This is the point at which the attempt to arrive at an historical hermeneutics has to start its critique. The overcoming of all prejudices, this global demand of the enlightenment, will prove to be itself a prejudice, the removal of which opens the way to an appropriate understanding of our finitude.

> It can be shown that the concept of prejudice did not originally have the meaning we have attached to it. Prejudices are not necessarily unjustified and erroneous, so that they inevitably distort the truth. In fact, the historicity of our existence entails that prejudices, in the literal sense of the word, constitute the initial directedness of our whole ability to experience. Prejudices are biases of our openness to the world. They are simply conditions whereby we experience something—whereby what we encounter says something to us. This formulation certainly does not mean that we are enclosed within a wall of prejudices and only let through the narrow portals those things that can produce a pass saying, "Nothing new will be said here." Instead we welcome just that guest who promises something new to our curiosity. But how do we know the guest whom we admit is one who has something *new* to say to us? Is not our expectation and our readiness to hear the new also necessarily determined by the old that has already taken possession of us?[75]

It is important for Gadamer that pre-judgments often have the positive function of opening our understanding. Further, it is important for our understanding of Gadamer himself not to forget this positive function of pre-judgment or expectation. (It is precisely because I have chosen to challenge at the level of translation the negative connotations which the term "prejudice" acquired during the Enlightenment that I prefer the term "pre-judgment." Also the relationship between "pre-judgment" and "expectation" is brought out by this translation.)

> What is necessary is a fundamental rehabilitation of the concept of prejudice and a recognition of the fact that there are legitimate

prejudices, if we want to do justice to man's finite, historical mode of being. Thus we are able to formulate the central question of a truly historical hermeneutics, . . . where is the ground of the legitimacy of prejudices? What distinguishes legitimate prejudices from all the countless ones which it is the undeniable task of the critical reason to overcome?[76]

However, this is not a simple task. We cannot simply remove from ourselves the four idols of Francis Bacon. There is no simple method, Cartesian or otherwise, by which prejudice can be removed.

The prejudices and fore-meanings in the mind of the interpreter are not at his free disposal. He is not able to separate in advance the productive prejudices that make understanding possible from the prejudices that hinder understanding and lead to misunderstandings.[77]

Furthermore, distance in time between the interpreter and the object of investigation is not necessarily a gap which separates. It is also the medium of legitimate, helpful or productive pre-judgments which aid the process of understanding. Distance in time, in short, is the space for tradition.

Time is no longer primarily a gulf to be bridged, . . . but it is actually the supportive ground of process in which the present is rooted. . . . In fact the important thing is to recognize the distance in time as a positive and productive possibility of understanding. It is not a yawning abyss, but is filled with the continuity of custom and tradition, in the light of which all that is handed down presents itself to us.[78]

Here Gadamer uses as an example, to clarify and support his view, maturation of judgment about art which comes from temporal distance.

Everyone knows that curious impotence of our judgment where the distance in time has not given us sure criteria. Thus the judgment of contemporary works of art is desperately uncertain for the scientific consciousness. Obviously we approach such creations with the prejudices we are not in control of, presuppositions that have too great an influence over us for us to know about them; these can give to contemporary creations an extra resonance that does not correspond to their true content and their true significance. Only when all their relations to the present time have faded away can their real nature appear, so that the understanding of what is said in them can claim to be authoritative and universal.[79]

What we seem to have is a positive and a negative function of history. Negatively history gives us the distance to remove us from the pre-judgments of our own period. Positively tradition in history supplies us with productive expectations, with legitimate pre-judgments.

In addition to these two functions of history there is a third factor which can help overcome false pre-judgments. This is making these pre-judgments explicit. This is done, claims Gadamer, not in order to get rid of them, but rather to question and challenge them. And it is done, not by pretending to be free of them, but by opening oneself to the challenge of the text, by letting one's own pre-judgments be questioned by the text as a dialogue partner. The pre-judgments are made explicit, not by pretending they have been removed, but by bringing them into dialogue with the object of understanding, so that one's own pre-judgments can be made more explicit, examined, and perhaps challenged.

> It is only this temporal distance that can solve the really critical question of hermeneutics, namely of distinguishing the true prejudices, by which we understand, from the false ones by which we misunderstand. Hence, the hermeneutically trained mind . . . will make conscious the prejudices governing our own understanding, so that the text, as another's meaning, can be isolated and valued on its own. The isolation of a prejudice clearly requires the suspension of its validity for us. For so long as our mind is influenced by a prejudice, we do not know and consider it as a judgment. How then are we able to isolate it? It is impossible to make ourselves aware of it while it is constantly operating unnoticed, but only when it is, so to speak, stimulated. The encounter with a text from the past can provide this stimulus. . . . Understanding begins . . . when something addresses us. . . . We know what this requires, namely the fundamental suspension of our own prejudices. But all suspension of judgments and hence, a fortiori, of prejudices, has logically the structure of a question.

> The essence of a question is the opening up . . . of possibilities. If a prejudice becomes questionable, in view of what another or a text says to us, this does not mean that it is simply set aside and the other writing or the other person accepted as valid in its place. It shows, rather, the naiveté of historical objectivism to accept this

disregarding of ourselves as what actually happens. In fact our own prejudice is properly brought into play through its being at risk. Only through its being given full play is it able to experience the other's claim to truth and make it possible for he himself to have full play.[80]

Gadamer speaks of the challenge to a pre-judgment or preconception as a disruption. One of the ways such a disruption can come about is through a challenge in which the pre-judgment is rendered untenable or at least questionable.

> We are guided by preconceptions and anticipations in our talking in such a way that these continually remain hidden and . . . it takes a disruption in oneself of the intended meaning of what one is saying to become conscious of these prejudices as such. In general the disruption comes about through some new experience, in which a previous opinion reveals itself to be untenable. But the basic prejudices are not easily dislodged and protect themselves by claiming self-evident certainty for themselves, or even by posing as supposed freedom from all prejudice and thereby securing their acceptance. We are familiar with the form of language that such self-securing of prejudices takes: namely the unyielding repetitiousness characteristic of all dogmatism.[81]

This discovery of the true meaning of a text is an infinite, a never-finished process.

> If anything does characterize human thought, it is this infinite dialogue with ourselves which never leads anywhere definitively and which differentiates us from that ideal of an infinite spirit to which all that exists and all truth is present in a single vision.

> I want to argue for the pretention to universality of the act of understanding and of speaking. We can express everything in words and can try to come to an agreement about everything. That we are limited by our finitude and that only a truly infinite conversation could entirely actualize this pretention, is, of course, true.[82]

Gadamer often draws his examples of understanding from the interpretation of a written text. However, the object of understanding is ultimately the tradition in which we live. "We always stand within tradition."[83] Gadamer does not draw the deterministic implications which would seem to follow from this thesis of the situatedness of all understanding within tradition. Rather, we modify tradition by participating in its evolution.

> The fact is that tradition is constantly an element of freedom and of history itself. Even the most genuine and solid tradition does not persist by nature because of the inertia of what once existed. It needs to be affirmed, embraced, cultivated. . . . At any rate, preservation is as much a freely-chosen action as revolution and renewal.
>
> Tradition is not simply a precondition into which we come, but we produce it ourselves, inasmuch as we understand, participate in the evolution of tradition and hence further determine it ourselves.[84]

Tradition, however modified, is the source of the prejudgments which open up our understanding. The historical rootedness of inquiry is not just a limitation, but a positive source of understanding, a window which discloses as it frames a point of view.

> Just as the recipient of a letter understands the news that it contains and first sees things with the eyes of the person who wrote the letter . . . so we understand texts that have been handed down to us on the basis of expectations of meaning which are drawn from our own anterior relation to the subject. . . . Hence the first of all hermeneutic requirements remains one's own foreunderstanding, which proceeds from being concerned with the same subject. . . . We share fundamental prejudices with tradition. Hermeneutics must start from the position that a person seeking to understand something has a relation to the object that comes into language in the transmitted text and has, or acquires, a connection with the tradition out of which the text speaks.[85]

This leads to Gadamer's notion of "effective-history" or "productive-history."

> We are always subject to the effects of effective-history. It determines in advance both what seems to us worth inquiring about and what will appear as an object of investigation.
>
> In all understanding, whether we are expressly aware of it or not, the power of this effective-history is at work. When a naive faith in scientific method ignores its existence, there can be an actual deformation of knowledge. . . . This, precisely, is the power of history over finite human consciousness, namely that it prevails even where faith in method leads one to deny one's own historicality.[86]

Gadamer's notions of pre-judgment and of the productive-history of tradition correlate with his idea of understanding as a fusion of horizons. Pre-judgments constitute the horizon of the particular present, the limit of perception. This is not a fixed set of opinions. The horizon is continually being formed, in that we have to test our pre-judgments continually. A key part of this testing is understanding the tradition in which we stand. Understanding is the fusion of the horizons of the present and the past. In a tradition this process of fusion is going on continually, the old and the new constantly growing together to make something living. Therefore, the problem is not one of understanding the past in itself, but of expanding our horizons (horizon-fusion).[87]

Gadamer contrasts his outlook which affirms this viewpoint with that of the contemporary scientific outlook. As he sees it, modern science "stands or falls with the principle of being unbiased and prejudiceless." Gadamer feels that this principle of being without bias is naive. "The claim to be completely free of prejudice is naïve, whether that naïvete be the delusion of an absolute enlightenment or the delusion of an empiricism free of all previous opinions."[88]

Let us now examine two thinkers who employed the approach of radical empiricism in religion to see if they satisfy Gadamer's demands about the recognition of the historical rootedness of inquiry. For the moment let us assume the validity of Gadamer's approach. We begin with Henry Nelson Wieman.

Wieman takes standard scientific and common sense empirical inquiry as his key and models religious inquiry after it. Thus, there is but one method of separating truth from fantasy, and religious inquiry is a species of this method, differentiated from other inquiry by its object, not its methods or principles.

Wieman delineates four phases of empirical inquiry: 1) the emergence of an hypothesis, 2) the specification of this insight in precise and unambiguous language, 3) the elaboration of observable consequences through tracing the logical implications of the hypothesis, and 4) testing these consequences through the observation of (or failure to observe) these predicted consequences. In short, we have insight, specification, prediction, and testing. Note the importance of specification for prediction and testing.

> Seeking to specify as accurately as possible is what we understand science to be. . . . It is also the endeavor to discover under what conditions predictable events will occur.[89]

The distinction between religious inquiry and other empirical inquiry is based on the nature of the religious object. When the object of religious inquiry is specified, religious knowledge will be found to be a species of knowledge in general. The field of empirical inquiry is essentially homogeneous, in Wieman's view, and once the object is specified, there need be no further differentiation of method, other than added diligence in preventing error.[90]

The question of how to differentiate religious knowledge from other types of knowledge concerns the type of observable consequence we are looking for; that is, it is a matter of definition. We are looking for:

> What transforms man as he cannot transform himself to save him from evil and lead him to the best that human life can ever attain, provided that he give himself over to it in religious faith and meet other required conditions.[91]

Wieman speaks of two kinds of religious language: the language of religious inquiry, an intellectual language which seeks "precision by way of abstractions" and the language of worship or ruling commitment which expresses the "concrete fullness of being where alone can be found the values for which we live."[92] (The term "creativity," for example, is a term invented for intellectual inquiry.) Today especially, because of magnified power, we need correct descriptive statements in the language of inquiry giving us knowledge of the reality which can save. But these statements cannot comprehend the totality of life, love, persons, or creativity. In committing ourselves to the "creativity which transforms" we need both languages. Just as we need symbols to represent the mystery of the person we love, we need symbols to represent the mystery of the saving creativity because we are committing ourselves to the wholeness of that reality, not just to abstractions conveyed by correct descriptions. Thus, we can speak of God as a "person" in the language of love and commitment. Personal language is a falsification only when we insist that the full reality of the creativity is a person in the sense in which human beings are persons. Thus, correct descriptive statements about creativity and persons are true only as far as they go.[93]

Wieman cites as a crucial instance of the lack of agreement among observers the Biblical hermeneutics of Carnell, Tillich, Barth and Bultmann. One would expect, given Wieman's devotion to creative interchange, that he would welcome this disagreement. But he does not. The disagreement among these four does not result in creative interchange, according to Wieman, because "there is no agreement on the principles of inquiry nor on what to seek when they seek Christ."[94]

It is clear that Wieman demands two types of agreement: definitional agreement on the specifics of what is to be observed and observational agreement on what is observed. Now agreement on both definition and observations is possible in many types of argument. But it seems to me naive, in Gadamer's sense, to expect this agreement in many areas of human concern, including religious inquiry. Indeed, Wieman's exasperation at the four theologians is due to his unrealistic attitude in expecting agreement.

If Wieman were correct in his demand for definitional and observational agreement, why was it not forthcoming? Why didn't most enlightened observers come to agree with him? Was it because they hadn't been listening? Were they too committed to their supernaturalistic legacies? Was it because various psychological and sociological motives for remaining uncritical in religion remained dominant? Or was it because Wieman was unrealistic in his expectations? I am inclined to think that one aspect of Wieman's program was doomed, because of his unrealistic expectations as well as the tenacity of both supernaturalists and anti-supernaturalists, but that in a far deeper sense he was successful because of his contribution to the on-going process of religious inquiry, not least because he forced the issues of a naturalistic conception of God and of the empirical referent of God-language. He remains a key voice in the creative interchange of this century.

Wieman himself operated out of a specific religious tradition which affected his theoretical definitions. Could you expect a Mahāyāna Buddhist or a classical Vedāntist to agree with Wieman's definition of God as reality transformative of this world? Or a polytheist? Or many naturalists? There is a traditional Christian emphasis on transcendence, on the unity of the divine, and an anthropocentrism about Wieman's source of human good that indicates that he is operating out of a tradition which affects him the more because he seems, enlightenment fashion, to think that he has escaped from it. What a thinker operating in Wieman's orbit of meaning needs to do is to go back to the definitions of God that Wieman so fruitfully explored, to confront these with both the tradition from whence they came and with other traditions, in an ever-renewed attempt to refine these definitions, not pretending that we will at last get the one best definition, but that we shall together fruitfully engage in the on-going, never-ceasing process, with or without paradigmatic shifts, of clarifying new meanings of the divine and what we should look at to sense its working in our history and lives. In short, what is needed in the tradition of empirical religious inquiry is an abandonment of Wieman's foundationalism and a reconception of Wieman's definitions of God as tentative explorations, "working hypotheses" in an on-going process of inquiry. We need to shift Wieman's explicit methodology from a foundational empiricism to a self-conscious, on-going inquiry alive to both its empirical and its cultural dimensions.

I question the observational specificity of the empirical consequences of Weiman's hypothesis. For example, he suggests that creative interchange is distinct from defensive interchange.[95] But is the creative/defensive distinction specific and unambiguous enough that observers will agree which is which? Wieman would hold that the consequences of the creative event are specific enough, once they have been set forth in precise unambiguous language. I doubt it. The very data which should test it are axiological data, requiring agreement on values, agreement which is not forthcoming. Is creative interchange better than isolation in a hermitage (granted that there is a form of interchange there also)? How do we know, clearly and unambiguously, which type of several creative outcomes is better or best? Granted, there are some which are pretty bad. But I don't see an *experimentum crucis* enabling us to test the hypothesis that the creative event is the source of human good.

Another aspect of this critique of Wieman concerns his dichotomy between the language of intellectual inquiry and the language of devotion. This dichotomy represents a valid distinction of functions. However, this dichotomy oversimplifies a complex issue. On the one hand, the language of inquiry is not completely isolated from the language of devotion. "Creativity," for example, is not a value-neutral term and hence has elements of devotion. Wieman's language of intellectual inquiry is the language of a foundationalism which is certain that it can be error-free. It is probably more adequate to speak of a continuum between two types of language. This would probably be more honest, since it doesn't pretend that the language of inquiry is free of commitment and thus devotion to values. It is also more arduous, since it introduces intellectual work into devotion. To use Wieman's own analogy of language between spouses, granted that there are times for the language of love and times for the language of the intellect, do we really want love without thought and the best empirical guidance? Even at times of deepest devotion, empirical inquiry should seldom be set aside. That way lies the way of irresponsible sex, for instance. On the other hand, do we really want empirical inquiry without concern for the total human person? Surely you don't want a doctor or scientist making decisions about therapy or experiment to be solely concerned for empirical inquiry.

Wieman is right. There is a fullness of being beyond our language of inquiry. What he fails to see is that the language of inquiry never escapes completely the ambiguity, value-commitment, and contingency of the language of commitment and that the language of commitment should seldom, if ever, lose its intellectual discipline. We should replace the dichotomy with a continuum.

There are value-choices which must be made concerning health for which the term "health" is not absolutely clear and precise. At precisely what point does a "best interest" decision imply that it is time to shut off a respirator? At precisely what point can the parent of a child dying of leukemia say, "I will not allow my child to be used for a phase one drug test"? At precisely what point do we acknowledge that a controlled test of a cure for AIDS is over and we can give the people in the control group the new treatment? There is no precise point or choice-free procedure always available. I suggest that this is true in matters of health and in the transformation of the human condition, for which health is Wieman's metaphor.

Granted that some choices are clear-cut. Nevertheless, it is illusory to pretend that empirical inquiry and the language of intellectual inquiry will solve all issues. Can the choice between a Theravāda disgust of the sensual, a life of chastity in a vocation of service, a life of monogamous marriage or a lifestyle of polymorphous libidinal satisfaction be resolved by empirical inquiry? To say that all that we need to do is to find which of these four approaches will lead to the most creative interchange seems naive in Gadamer's sense.

Wieman studied history, of course. But his theory of religious inquiry, as I have tried to show, does not account for the role of a particular tradition in shaping inquiry. Nor in his practice does he spend time sorting through the effect that his own historical roots have on his thinking.

On the other hand, Bernard Meland can be taken as a case of a radical empiricist in religion whose theory and practice are clearly informed by a consciousness of the historical rootedness of inquiry. He was trained in the Chicago School of historiography, his dissertations involved careful sorting through of theological varieties, and he early read thoughtfully in cultural anthropology. Take almost any ten pages of Meland, contrast them with ten pages of Wieman, and note the richness of Meland's historical awareness, including attention to the variety of Christian types, the complex relations of religion and secularity on a global scale, and even the changes in the consciousness of poets.

Meland's conception of the structure of experience is an acknowledgement of the historical rootedness of inquiry very much akin to Gadamer's principle of productive history. The structure of experience refers to the persisting character of communal processes and valuations.

> What is at work in individual experiences has its counterpart in the culture at large, embracing the individual events of joy and tragedy and fashioning a communal structure of experience. Although this larger structure is continuous with the individual structures of personality, it gathers into itself the persisting, protoplasmic character of institutional and other corporate processes.... All that has entered into the public and private decisions of a people through the accumulative effect of valuations resides as a persistent datum in what I would call the structure of experience.[96]

Clearly, experience is social, not subjective as in classical British empiricism.

> Experience ... is always a structured occurrence. It is never simply a subjective event, but a happening within relationships that takes on public character with social consequences. It is at once something internalized as individual meaning and a social nexus of accumulative communities.[97]

Just as Gadamer thinks of tradition not as a strangle-hold on the present, but as a legacy with which the present must come to terms, so Meland thinks of the structure of experience as a sequence of valuations that must be appropriated or transmuted in the present life of the individual and community.

The rootedness of inquiry in tradition comes out strongly in Meland's concern for the place of myth in religious inquiry. For Meland, myth is "the human response to actuality in its ultimate dimension." Without sorting out Meland's distinction between the analytical and the relational uses of theological language, we may say that for Meland myth is

> a constructive tool by which the depth of the cultural experience can be theologically envisaged and organically related to worship and to religious inquiry.... Myth, therefore, is indispensable to a profound orientation of the human psyche ... and the source of our most discerning theological insight.[98]

Myth, like the structure of experience of which it is a vital ingredient, is differentiated according to its cultural matrix and thus provides varying soil for the roots of inquiry.

> The cultural conditioning of the mythical response, however, is inescapable. . . . All cultures have historically manifested some capacity to be expressive in sensitive and creative ways; but there are marked variations among them. . . . It follows that no culture deserves to be neglected in the search for a full grasp of the psychical depth and outreach of the human spirit; for each culture exemplifies the concrete nature of God's working within the range of its available structures.[99]

Meland's concern for the historical rootedness of inquiry comes out also in his emphasis on the tentativeness of all human efforts to grasp the truth.

> The structures of reason which we are able to formulate and employ are but tentative ventures in apprehending the meaning of those realities.[100]

This is a contrast with Wieman, who agreed that reality transcends language, but who hoped that what our thoughts could grasp would result in precise and unambiguous language.

I have tried to show that Meland, in both theory and practice, avoids Gadamer's censure of the naivete of a presumed innocence of empirical inquiry of its rootedness in a tradition, while Wieman does not so escape. I turn now to suggest that Gadamer's view needs modification on at least one point by Meland's approach. Gadamer's thesis of the universality of language is challenged by Meland's concept of the structure of experience or persistent feeling context. The universality of language needs to be modified by a recognition of bodily acquaintance and of sensibilities as unconscious appreciations and restraints.

Sensibilities, in Meland's view, are mostly not conscious and do not reflect the inheritance of language.

> Consciousness, to be sure, is a dominant element in human personality; but it is in association with visceral, sensory, affective processes. . . . Sensibilities . . . may rarely enter the conscious level. . . . They simply form the deeply laid restraints and appreciations in a person or culture which give rise to a certain character or quality of action. . . . They are like spirit—qualities of

response that arise slowly in human personality or in culture as a result of persistent affections or appreciations.[101]

Perhaps the non-linguistic dimension of inherited experience is set forth most clearly in Meland's discussion of the bodily character of our thought.

> Experience . . . is not so much an interplay of explicit sensory responses as a bodily event which conveys to the living organism, in a holistic way, its rapport and participation in the nexus of relationships which constitute its existence. Experience in this holistic sense is not immediately conscious, and much if it never becomes so; for it remains . . . a substratum of intimate organic acquaintance from which moments of conscious experience intermittently arise. . . . In attentive moments, bodily acquaintance acts both as a resource of accumulative experience contributing form and character to the immediate event, and as a barrier to meaning.[102]

Meland tries hard to prevent his acknowledgement of the penumbra of meaning surrounding what can be clearly envisaged from becoming a dichotomy between the clear and distinct on the other hand, and the vague and dimly apprehended on the other.

> We know by acquaintance through bodily feeling, or through the sheer act of existing, much that we shall never know in any explicit, cognitive way. The ultimate range of meaning is not a penumbra of mystery that simply supervenes experience; it is a mystery and depth of the immediacies themselves.
>
> The vision of attention shades off into obscuring horizons. . . . Depths and discontinuities harass the inquiring mind. . . . (Given) the complexity of existence . . . the bafflement of man's intellect is a fact of our existence.[103]

Finally I would like to raise the question as to what thinkers who find historical roots in radical empiricism can learn from this interplay with Gadamer. Empiricism has always been critical, but a genuinely self-critical empiricism would be, I suggest, an historical empiricism. At the level of theory it would explicitly affirm the productive as well as distorting power of the influence of the social structure of experience. At the level of practice it would explore in some detail the influence of these historical roots on present inquiry. It would also seek to challenge these pre-judgments with the understandings arising from within other cultural horizons.

V. The Language of Inquiry and the Language of Devotion

Two of the main issues concerning language are the relationship between language and experience and the relationship between the functions of language, for example, the referential or cognitive and the devotional functions. This second issue is sometimes put as the relationship between different languages, for example, the language of inquiry and the language of devotion. In a previous section of this chapter the former topic has been addressed. Here we turn to the relationship between the investigative and the devotional functions of language. By the language of devotion I include a type of language which has a social and historical dimension and yet has place for personal innovation. It is a language which could have expressive and evocative functions, including the avowal of commitment. In the term "language of devotion," I include a referential function. This referential function, even though minimalistically understood, is a key point in religious naturalism as I conceive it.

In many ways the modern context for this issue starts in the seventeenth century. The primacy which Descartes placed on clear and distinct ideas left a powerful legacy of concern for precision and clarity of a language.[104]

Schleiermacher sharply distinguished dialectical language (the language to be used in dogmatics) from poetic and rhetorical language, the sharpness of the distinction reflecting the sharp distinction he made between feeling (the true home of piety), knowing and doing.[105] Thus, although Schleiermacher secured a place for religion outside of Kantian practical reason and Hegelian speculative reason, in Schleiermacher's thought the proper language for the theoretical understanding of religion partook of the legacy of Descartes (with the systematic interconnectedness of propositions being a prime goal). Schleiermacher represented a classic and influential statement of the sharp separation of the languages of theory and of devotion and also of the importance of a theoretical language for reflecting on the object (or subjective feelings) of devotion.

A survey of the background of how the languages of inquiry and devotion are related would have to include Hegel's subordination of religious *Vorstellungen* to philosophy, Russell's seminal concern with the philosophical significance of symbolic logic followed by Wittgenstein's *Tractatus,* logical positivism's verifiability criterion of meaningful language (other than mathematics and formal logic), and the widespread refusal to grant cognitive significance to emotive language so well established in twentieth century Anglo-American academic discourse from sociology to literary criticism. There were, of course, contrary voices like the later Schelling's hermeneutical explorations of myth and Scripture and the briefly popular approach of Bergson. In theological circles we should have to discuss Bultmann's program of demythologizing, the impact of the *New Essays in Philosophical Theology*, and the absorption of the significance of the later Wittgenstein. Finally we would have to consider the concern by some theologians, at first almost voices in the wilderness but now well-established, to analyze the referential import of the translucent penumbra of religious language, including the older discussions by Reinhold Niebuhr, Paul Tillich, Bernard Meland and the more recent treatments so well done by many including Langdon Gilkey, Paul Ricoeur, Janet Martin Soskice, Sally McFague, Wentzel van Huyssteen, and narrative theologians.[106]

There is a domain of language beyond the clear and distinct or empirically verifiable. This usage I call translucent language in distinction from the area of clear or verifiable language, which I call the language of transparency. This translucent usage of language includes the mythic, the symbolic, the parabolic, the metaphorical, and, undoubtedly, more besides.

I offer here no theory of metaphor, model, myth, or symbol. What I do offer is a theory of how translucent language functions in relation to the transparent domain of language. While much of the current discussion of the relationships between the languages of transparency and translucency shares in the aftermath of the Cartesian emphasis on clarity and distinctness, there is a long history of theological discussion of the referential significance of translucent religious language. Mention might be made, among others, of Origen, medieval exegesis and theories of analogy, and Calvin.[107]

For the purpose of this chapter I shall focus on one particular area of the domain of translucent language, the area that I call, with Wieman, the language of devotion. The translucent domain is relevant to many areas of our experience, including those overlapping areas which we call affective, valuational, matters of insight, and the discovery of the meaning of life. I shall focus primarily on the language of devotion, although, with appropriate modifications, what I say could be applied to many of these other areas of the domain of translucent language. In similar fashion I shall concentrate on one area of the language of transparency which, also following Wieman, I call the language of inquiry.

1. My first claim is that the domain of translucent language, including particularly the language of devotion, not only can serve expressive and evocative functions, but it can also have referential import. The translucent is not opaque. It is obscure. This is a controversial claim, although not so controversial in American religious studies in the present decade. It underlies not only the possible use of exploring the translucent domain in the social sciences. It also raises the question of the referential import of all of the humanities and religious studies. Much of the value of recent work by McFague, van Huyssteen, Barbour and Ricoeur lies in their exploration of this area of translucent language.

This claim regarding the referential import of transulcent religious language has to be tempered by the minimalist restriction inherent in the ontological restraint of our naturalism. This means that the referential import is not to an ontological ultimate, but to the divine aspects of our experienced world, the situationally transcendent, unmanipulable and unforeseen resources of healing and transformation and the continually luring call of worth, values, and ideals.

2. My second main claim is that it is best to think of most or all of the domains and areas of language as continua. There is probably no sharp line between the language of transparency and the language of translucency. Nor, more particularly, is there a sharp demarcation between the language of inquiry and the language of devotion. To be sure, there is a recognizable distinction between a hard-core example of the language of inquiry (Schleiermacher's *Glaubenslehre,* Wieman's discussions of creativity, or the minimal model of transcendence, for example,) and a paradigm case of the language of devotion (the hymns of piety or the phrases of meditative self-dedication to the creative event). To use a metaphor of color, there is no sharp demarcation between yellow and orange, although we can find paint patches and color samples which are clearly orange or yellow (the kind often used to teach children their colors). There are borderline cases where one type of language shades over into another, much as there are shades of yellow-orange (for example, Schleiermacher refers to didactic language which could include poetic and rhetorical language).

It is often helpful to consider a type of language in theoretical isolation from other types. We often focus on the poles of continua for our ideal types. Thus we can distinguish the language of theoretical inquiry from the language of devotion and communal affirmation. However, this focuses on language activities which are not isolable in practice. To use an old phrase, they are distinguishable, even though not separable (shades of Chalcedon!). When we speak of the languages of inquiry or of devotion, what we are doing is focussing on an area where one particular function (or group of functions) is dominant. In so doing the language type is selected or defined by its function. In so doing we are also ignoring those parts of the picture which are not in the area of our focus at that moment.

3. The next major claim to be made here is that there is a complex and on-going interplay between language and experience and also between different types of language.

As background for this claim let us look briefly at the discussions concerning religious language by two major thinkers, Henry Nelson Wieman and Langdon Gilkey. Each found that religious language was involved in a two-way street, both receiving from and contributing to its polar opposite. Wieman and Gilkey differed, however, in how they tended to conceive of the polar opposite of religious language when they reflected on this topic.

Thus Gilkey focuses on the interplay between the language of myth or God-language and the experience of ultimacy. The relationship between the two is that the experience of ultimacy provides an empirical referent or anchor for the language of ultimacy. This is a polyvalent language, one referent of which is to ultimacy and the other referent to an aspect of the finite world which points to the ultimate. In a secular age, for which the traditional religious language has become questionable or meaningless, this empirical referent is the key to the meaningfulness of language about ultimacy. On the other hand the language of ultimacy illuminates and thematizes and thus nurtures the experience of ultimacy. In short, for Gilkey the polar interplay is that the experiences of ultimacy, when uncovered, provide empirical referent and thus meaningfulness, while the language of ultimacy illuminates and thematizes and nurtures the experiences. It should be noted in passing that there is a role for what I am calling the language of inquiry in Gilkey's thinking. Theology can use the language of inquiry to "uncover" the experiences of ultimacy which have been forgotten in a secular age.

There are a number of types of experience in which Gilkey finds an awareness of ultimacy. These include the awareness of contingency, of relativity of meaning, of temporality, of the ambiguity of freedom, and also certain elements in cognitive inquiry. He suggests that we first become aware of ultimacy when we experience our contingency, when we cannot find an ultimate source of our life. Then an infinite Void at the depths threatens all we are and do. We feel emptiness and anxiety, perhaps despair. A rival, the boss, the stock market, the latest news can become symbols of Fate, of an ultimate insecurity. The ultimacy of this threat gives the quest for survival and power its panicky and endless character with demonic possibilities. The search for job and financial security, status, office politics, career maneuverings, and professional jealousy all partake of this infinite dynamic.

There are also signs of a positive creative power. There is a joy in life, a sense of vitality, of fulfillment at the use of our powers, a joy in community and personal intercourse. These common experiences buoy us up, make us glad to be alive and refuel our existence. There is ultimacy in these experiences since: a) being is not one of our values but is the basis of them all, b) this sense of reality is given to us, not created or controlled by us, and c) it appears within us as the ground of what we are, unlike finite things which appear over against us.[108] These experiences of contingency and of vitality are common types of experiences of ultimacy. The language of myth speaks of the experiences of contingency in terms of Fate, while God-language can also speak of God as the Power which buoys us up in the midst of contingency.

For Wieman the interplay is between two languages, the language of inquiry and the language of devotion. The symbols of faith in the language of devotion provide concreteness to the language of inquiry, but must be translated into descriptive statements scientifically demonstrable. On the other hand, the descriptive language of inquiry provides a specification of the symbols of the language of devotion by specifying the constant structure (that which saves us as we cannot when we create the required conditions). Once this specification is made, the language of inquiry clarifies and criticizes the language of devotion. It provides clarity about the object of our supreme commitment, fashions a critical tool against the idolatry of created goods, and specifies the conditions we must meet if we are to be transformed. In short, for Wieman the polar interplay is that the language of devotion provides concreteness; the language of inquiry specifies, clarifies, and criticizes. For example, to speak of God as a "person" is to use devotional language, while to refer to "creativity" or "creative good" is to use the language of intellectual inquiry.[109]

What we may learn from this brief excursus into Wieman and Gilkey concerns first, what the polar opposite of religious language is and second, what are the contributions to be made by each pole to the other.

It is best, I think, not to speak of one polar opposite of religious language. There is a complex and on-going functional interplay between both language and experience and also between the parts of the language continua. Specifically, religious language is in constant dialogue with *both* language and experience, in particular the language of inquiry and the multifarious experiences of transcendence. Thus one could speak of a triangle, with experience at one corner, the language of inquiry at another, and the language of devotion at the third. There would be a reciprocal back and forth interplay, sometimes enhancing, sometimes deadening or distorting, between one corner and each of the other two. However, such a triangle is only a cross section of an on-going process, a snapshot as opposed to a movie film or video.

4. The next point to be made, tentatively yet with conviction, is that each apex of the triangle (language of devotion, language of inquiry and experience of transcendence) can enhance the other. There is a genuine functional interplay between the three. By speaking of an interplay, we explicitly claim that there is no foundational starting point, no first step in the processes of inquiry, of experience, of commitment. To explain this point, let us note first that language, both the language of inquiry and the language of devotion, can nurture and transmit experience. We all agree that language can transmit experience, or at least the reports of experience. But I wish to say that it can also nurture experience. I recall twice in my own experience my perception improved when I learned an appropriate vocabulary. Once was when I worked in a gas station and needed to learn to recognize the major models of cars. The other was when I started to learn the history of art. Language can also criticize experience. The language of inquiry is designed for this and often does a better job at criticism than the language of devotion. However, it is often a blunt instrument or badly used, so that ironically it is often the language of devotion that is most effective critically.

To repeat, language can enhance experience by nurturing, transmitting, and criticizing it. Besides John Dewey, Langdon Gilkey is very helpful here.[110] Gilkey maintains that it is myth, his rough parallel to our language of devotion, which thematizes and so nurtures and transmits the experience of ultimacy. However, I propose that the language of inquiry can also nurture and transmit the experience of transcendence. This is partly because the language of inquiry can help clear away unnecessary intellectual difficulties. It is also because the language of inquiry is seldom without an undertone of the language of devotion, as I claim below. Perhaps also there is a genuine theoretical entrance into the experience of transcendence, at least for some people.

On the other hand it is experience, in this context the experience of transcendence, which anchors and gives meaning to language. The tradition of radical empiricism has been intent on showing that this anchoring process must be more generously conceived than is done by a narrow empiricism. Gilkey is also helpful here and shows how ordinary experience often points to the dimension of ultimacy or, as I prefer, minimal transcendence (see Chapter Five).

The mention of Langdon Gilkey and radical empiricism indicates further that there is a back and forth interplay between language and experience. For the theoretical work of James, Dewey, and Gilkey was based on experience and in turn has helped their students and readers to further exploration of experience. Once more, to ask which comes first, experience or language, is like asking for the priority of the chicken or the egg.

Finally, the other two corners of the triangle, the language of inquiry and the language of devotion, can enhance each other. The language of inquiry can enhance the language of devotion by clarifying and criticizing it. In turn the language of devotion gives power and depth (we have to use translucent language here!) to the language of inquiry.

Let us make two shifts in focus away from Wieman's way of putting this. For Wieman the language of devotion is to be "translated" into the language of inquiry.[111] However, I suggest that a better description of the shift between the two languages is that the language of inquiry "construes" or "interprets" the language of devotion. For there is no translation between these languages without some loss and in English the connotations of these two words makes this clear. Also, there is a tentativeness to this process of moving between languages, a real possibility of error and approximation and an arduous process of reworking, all of which is brought out by the words "construal" and "interpretation."

Furthermore, Wieman stresses the function of specification. For Wieman the language of inquiry delineates a specific structure in terms of which the language of devotion receives clarity. I shrink from this term "specification." There is a sense of finality and definiteness to the term which I reject. I suggest instead using the term "exploration." The function of the language of inquiry is to explore the language of devotion. Further, Wieman wishes to specify in order to anchor language in an empirically observable structure on the perception of which observers will agree. This, as I have said above, is modernist naivete.

Rather than translating the language of devotion into the language of inquiry in order to specify its empirical meaning, I suggest that we are construing one language by another in order to explore its meanings.

5. A further claim is that experience and the two languages of inquiry and devotion can also distort or deaden, as well as enhance, each other. The interplay can be dysfunctional as well as functional. We are dealing with genuine ambiguity here. This makes our move beyond foundationalism even more clear.

Language can misrepresent experience. That we are all agreed upon. Also, language can deaden experience. This is not so often seen. We can concentrate on what we have been taught to experience and overlook what is there for us to experience. How often our interpersonal lives are experienced in terms of what we have been taught to expect rather than with the freshness of open eyes and hearts.

Further, language can stifle our openness to the experiences of transcendence. How often our religious lives are experienced in terms of what we have been taught by the teachings of the church rather than with the freshness of open hearts and souls. Even a philosophy, such as the one here explicated, can blind the eyes of faith.

On the other hand, experience can hinder language. It can be so confused, so chaotic and surprising that our language becomes stammering and obscure.

It is also clear that the languages of inquiry and devotion can hinder each other. The language of inquiry can weaken and impoverish the language of devotion. There is just enough truth in the charge that too much philosophy can find the weaknesses in the language of devotion and weaken faith. Indeed, it can be dysfunctional. How can you pray to "the ground of being," we used to ask with serious humor. For that matter, how can you call out in despair to "the collection of minimally transcendent factors in the universe"? (Actually, you don't pray to the set of minimally transcendent forces. But I do remind the reader that this minimal naturalism has been wrestled with by the writer in his own periods of anguish. There is blood surging through the veins of these apparent abstractions.)

Finally the language of devotion can clearly obscure and confuse the language of devotion.

The fact that experience and both languages can be dysfunctional does not mean that we should avoid any one of the three. Nor does it mean that we should ensconce ourselves in one of these three. Abuses should not keep us from the constructive uses. The interplay between experience, the language of inquiry, and the language of devotion is risky and requires courage, not a dogmatic glorification of one at the expense of the others.

6. We have maintained above that there is a continuum between the languages of inquiry and devotion. That means that there will be borderline cases. That should not be surprising. There is often a platypus, virus, or liquid crystal creating problems for the taxonomist. More seriously, we almost never get a pure type of language in isolation. To continue the chromatic metaphor, what we usually have is a dominant color mixed up with highlights and undertones. We have a functional mix. This situation is not deplorable. Rather, and this is the sixth point, it is both honest and helpful to recognize that the languages of devotion and inquiry are often mixed.

It is more honest. Honesty requires recognition that the polar extremes are seldom, if ever, pure. In part this represents the historical rootedness of all language. There is no neutral standpoint from which we may judge morally or theoretically. The notion of an impartial spectator is as fictitious in theoretical inquiry as in moral or social debate. Just as England cannot claim to be neutral in northern Ireland or the United States in the Middle East, so likewise there is no neutral area from which we make our judgments. Politically and morally we may strive to be impartial, but cannot claim to be. Just so, the language of inquiry may strive to be neutral. It may not claim to be neutral. This does not mean that we should glory in our biases. We should seek to minimize them. What we should never do is to claim that we have eliminated them. The value of the American jury system, when functioning at its best, is not that the people in the jury box are wise or without prejudice. It is that the procedure, if done well, minimizes the relevant biases of the officers of the court and the jurors off the street.

It is not only more honest to recognize that we seldom, if ever, achieve a separation of the standpoints and languages of inquiry and devotion. It is also more helpful to recognize this. It is also harder. It is both helpful and arduous to bring intellectual work into devotion, whether personal, social, or religious. It is also helpful and hard to bring devotion into intellectual work. There are times for love to be dominant and times for inquiry to be dominant.

However, do we really want love with no thought and the best empirical guidance? Even at times of deepest devotion, empirical inquiry is usually relevant. Without it lurks irresponsible sex or fanaticism. On the other hand, we do not want empirical inquiry without concern for the total human person. We do not want a doctor or scientist solely concerned for empirical inquiry making decisions about therapy or medical experimentation.

The languages of inquiry and devotion can be thought of as a continuum in which the polar opposite may be muted, but is seldom silent. Honesty requires the recognition that each pole is never pure and separate from the other. Adequacy requires attention to the importance of the language of the opposite pole when we are concentrating on one function. In short, we can concentrate on one of the poles of language, we cannot isolate it.

This discussion of the relationship between the language of theoretical inquiry and the language of devotion can be summarized by recapitulating the five claims.

1. Translucent language can have referential import, even though our minimalist naturalism restricts the reference of religious language to situationally transcendent resources and the continual challenge of community, beauty, and their sister values.

2. Functional uses of language, in particular the languages of inquiry and the languages of devotion, form a continuum.

3. There is an on-going interplay between the experiences of the transcendent and the language of inquiry and the language of devotion.

4. Language and experience both can enhance or hinder the other.

5. The two languages of inquiry and of devotion can also hinder or impoverish each other.

6. It is more honest and helpful to recognize that the language of inquiry and the language of devotion are seldom pure. There is no neutral standpoint, morally or theoretically, from which the language of inquiry can operate and the language of interpersonal or religious devotion should not be left unclarified and uncriticized by the language of inquiry for long.

As a final point I wish to say that we need both languages. While we seldom, if ever, can have a pure language of inquiry or a pure language of devotion, there is room for both. This reflects the alternation in our life between critical distance and passionate involvement.[112] William Dean is half right. Openness to the complexity of experience is more important than clarity, finding truth more than avoiding error. This is correct for the exploratory phase of inquiry. But there is also a critical phase of inquiry in which we need to be concerned with clarity and avoiding error.

What I wish to reiterate is that even in moments of critical inquiry and in moments of devotion and commitment, the other moment is usually present as a penumbra or undertone, and it is both honest and helpful to recognize this.

Therefore a generous or radical empiricism has room for working models or hypotheses. We need to recognize that definitions of God are provisional and experimental approximations, "working hypotheses" in the on-going search for understanding and insight. Such a working hypothesis is offered in the first chapter of this book as a minimal model of transcendence. This and other working hypotheses bring tentative clarity and temporary specification to our thinking about the object(s) of our devotion.

The problem with the conceptual theism of Shailer Mathews is that he tended to bring in his definition of God as the personality-producing forces in the universe at the end of his socio-historical inquiry as a *Deus ex mente*. There is a seam, as it were, which can be felt in his writings as he leaves the well-elaborated historical section and tacks on the constructive part. One suspects that this seam is really a fault which would rupture under pressure. He juxtaposed his socio-historical inquiry and conceptual theism without letting the former play upon the latter and without reflecting self-consciously on the relationship between the two. To a less obvious extent this is true of E. S. Ames also.

Part of what I have been about in this study is an attempt to place conceptual theism (or, as I prefer, imaginative religious naturalism) within the context of a generous, radical empiricism.

Can one live (or die) for a working hypothesis? Will the language of inquiry draw the blood out of the language of devotion? It could. But that is a risk that must be taken. Without it one can confuse commitment with fanaticism. That way lies Jonestown and all of the Ayatollahs of the world. A working hypothesis, a model of God or the divine constructed in the language of inquiry, is a much needed moment in the ongoing reconstruction of the experiences of the transcendent.

CHAPTER FIVE

A DIALOGUE WITH ALTERNATIVE VISIONS

The final part of this presentation of the minimalist philosophy of this-wordly transcendence will contrast this view point and that of some other thinkers. Our purpose in this section is to provide a clarification of this neo-naturalist philosophy of this-wordly transcendence by contrasting it with other viewpoints and to attempt to give a reasoned defense of it by showing that it provides a more adequate grasp of and guide within the human situation. Thus this section is an attempt to provide clarification by contrast and to give a rationale for our viewpoint, to the extent that it can be done, by showing its relative adequacy as a piece of philosophical reflection compared with certain influential alternative viewpoints.

Three types of viewpoints will be considered. To the one side of minimalism Langdon Gilkey and the process thinkers Charles Hartshorne and Schubert Ogden are contemporary defenders of a more maximal and assured theism. On the other side Albert Camus and the *Humanist Manifestos* represent the humanistic alternative. Finally there is a group of thinkers whose positions in relation to minimalism are difficult to categorize but who are useful to examine for our twin purposes of clarifying and defending the minimalist option. This group includes John Dewey, Gordon Kaufman, and Mark C. Taylor.

My treatment of these writers, as well as of all the other thinkers we have commented on, is explicitly perspectival in intent. This is not an attempt to give an accurate and balanced delineation of the main features of their philosophies. Rather my attempt is to bring into focus those aspects of these philosophies which will be most significant for my purposes, namely, to clarify, to give a historical context, and to give a defense of my own viewpoint.

I. The Logic of Perfection: Hartshorne and Ogden

Both philosophy and theology have much to learn from process thought. Among its significant contributions to modern thought are the following: 1) It has held up an ideal of conceptual clarity. 2) It has shown how to move beyond many of the dilemmas of classical theism. 3) It has clarified (for a strong theism, in which I do not share) the ideas of: a)—the universality and reality of internal relationships between God and all beings; b)—both the sovereignty and tenderness of God; c)—the ontological supremacy and uniqueness of God; and d)—the significance of novelty, concreteness, and relationship.

However, two of the leading exponents of process thought, Charles Hartshorne and Schubert Ogden, have overstated their case, by claiming that certain statements about the existence and nature of God can be made with apodictic certainty. Given their conception of the importance of *a priori* reasoning, that is a serious weakness. (The question whether the valuable insights of process thought require such a claim of apodictic certainty lies outside the scope of this book.) Furthermore, process thought might be more appealing if it were not presented with such an air of extreme certainty, especially if such an extreme is unfounded.

In making this criticism I am taking neither a positivist nor a strict empiricist position. I am simply stating that the arguments do not prove their conclusions.

Charles Hartshorne has developed a variety of *a priori* arguments, related to the traditional ontological argument, which depend upon his treatment of the modal concept of necessity.

The basis of my criticism of Hartshorne's modal argument is that he fails to make a distinction between two types of modality. When asserting (or denying) propositions about the modal character of the existence of a being there are two modalities which can be discussed: the modality of the proposition and the modality of the existent. Suppose that someone wishes to assert that: "x exists necessarily." This is to assert that the existent, 'x', has the modality of necessity. This is the existential modality of necessity. In addition, the proposition itself can have a modality of necessity, of contingency, or of impossibility. Thus one could say that: "It is *possible* that 'x' exists *necessarily*." The proposition itself would be a contingent proposition about a necessarily existing being.[1] In this context "contingent" means "neither necessary nor impossible." It does not mean "contingent upon another event." The truth about the necessary aspect of God might be contingent in the former sense and this is my construal of the matter. To say it is contingent in the latter sense could be interpreted as a contradiction and Hartshorne would so interpret it.

There are logically, nine cases, which can be arranged in a table:

	necessary		x exists necessarily."
"It	is possible	that	x exists contingently."
	impossible		it is impossible for x to exist."

Using the symbol of '□' for the necessity operator and '◇' for the possibility operator, I introduce the following symbolism for the purpose of discussing propositions combining propositional and existential modality:

"□:□x" for "it is necessary that 'x exists necessarily'." (Note that this is not just one proposition with two modalities, but one with two types of modality.)

The disputed case would then be: "◇:□x," for "It is possible that 'x exists necessarily'."

Now Hartshorne recognizes only three basic modalities, necessity, contingency and impossibility:
"All modalities reduce to three:
Np, N~p, (~Np & ~N~P)."[2]
He does not recognize a distinction between the modality of an existent and the modality of a proposition about that existent.

> The Argument . . . works by exhaustion of the logically possible relations of ideas to things. Among these is the relation, "contingently unexemplified" in existence, also the relations: "necessarily exemplified," "impossible of exemplification," and finally "contingently exemplified."[3]

Furthermore, since Hartshorne recognizes no distinction between propositional and existential modality, he is left with the three basic modalities: necessity, contingency, and impossibility. In particular, Hartshorne would assert that the following three expressions are equivalent:
"It is necessary that x exists necessarily."
"It is necessary that x exists."
"x exists necessarily."

The structure of many of Hartshorne's arguments for the necessity of a Perfect Being can be symbolized by the following Modal Disjunctive Syllogism.[4]

(Premise 1) "□x v (◇x • ◇ ~ x) v ~◇x"

"Either 'It is necessary that x exists' or 'it is possible that x exists and it is possible that x does not exist' or 'it is not possible that x exists'."

(Premise 2) "~(◇x • ◇ ~x) • ~~◇x"

"It is not the case that: 'It is possible that x exists and it is possible that x does not exist' and furthermore it is not the case that: 'it is not possible that x exists'."

(Conclusion) "□x"

"It is necessary that x exists."

However, if we distinguish between propositional and existential modality, we must deny the first premise, since it does not exhaust all nine cases, (it being Hartshorne's intention to exhaust the modalities in his first premise.) Since there are nine cases, the conclusion ignores seven of the nine cases, including the disputed case that "It is possible that 'x exists necessarily'."

Hartshorne repeats his claim that Perfection (the existence of which is logically possible) cannot be merely contingent. The distinction between two types of modality is not addressed. Part of this is because he uses logical possibility in the exclusive sense of possibility exclusive of necessity.

Hartshorne attempts an argument against the distinction I view as crucial between propositional and existential modality.

> I question the validity of an ultimate distinction between logical and real possibility. Suppose that a law of nature forbids a certain logically conceivable thing. Is this thing then really and forever impossible? Only if there is no real possibility that the law should change. . . . I should reject as metaphysically invalid the notion of an eternal law of nature which excludes something logically possible. Such exclusion is proof enough that the law is contingent and not eternal.[5]

In reply to this argument we note that "an eternal law of nature" forbidding something to exist is not the only basis for rejecting existential possibility to the logically conceivable thing. A law of nature which holds good for the foreseeable future would also do the job, even if only for the foreseeable future. A statement of existential impossibility does not have to claim eternal validity.

A position similar to that taken here has been developed by John Hick.[6] Crucial to both of our analyses are the theses that: (1) "It is possible that a Perfect Being necessarily exists," ("◇:□x") is a meaningful assertion; and, (2) this assertion does not imply: "It is necessary that a Perfect Being necessarily exists." ("□:□x").

Hick refers to the modality expressed by assertion (1) as "hypothetical necessity" or "conditional necessity." This phrase seems contradictory. I suggest that propositional modality of possibility ('◇') could be referred to as "putative." Hence, "◇:□x," "It is possible that x exists necessarily," could be referred to as "putative necessity," thus removing the appearance of contradiction.

A second type of modal argument used by Hartshorne is based on the principle of Universal Existential Tolerance. This notion means that: (1) "the existence of perfection is compatible with any other sort of existence whatever," or, (2) "A 'predicate so general that any possible state of affairs would embody it' is necessarily embodied."[7]

Statement (2) sounds like the definite assertion of the truth of "Perfection exists." However, again Hartshorne overlooks the two levels of modality. Statement (2), when read within the light of what might be called "putative necessity," should read: "A predicate so general that any possible state of affairs *could* embody it *might be* embodied." If statement (2) had read, "A predicate so general that any possible state of affairs *does* embody it is necessarily embodied," then indeed this proposition about existential necessity would be necessary. However, statement (2) refers to a predicate such that any possible state of affairs *would* embody it, if such a predicate had existential status.

Again Hartshorne attempts to forestall criticism at this point.

> It may be objected that while the perfect could maintain itself, or exist, no matter what else existed, it does not follow that it does maintain itself or exist. But note that if nothing could conflict with the existence of perfection, then . . . perfection, by existing could prevent nothing else from existing, and therefore its non-existence could have no positive existence whatever.[8]

Again, universal compatibility means that *if* such a being exists, nothing would count against it. It does not mean that it does exist. I am not making the positivist claim that "Perfection exists" is an empty claim. I am rather claiming the "Perfection exists" has not been shown to have propositional necessity.

A third type of modal proof offered by Hartshorne is the Epistemic Proof. In stating it Hartshorne often directs this argument at what he considers to be the notion of hypothetical necessity. According to Hartshorne, critics will say:

> Yes, *if* there is a God, then all possibility is his potentiality, but only if. But (a) there is an 'if' only where there is a contrary possibility; and (b) the possibility of a Godless world is a possibility of something which God *could not* (logically could not) know, were it actual. And thus his power to know is being conceived as subject to limitation.[9]

That conception, of course, would be the conception of an idol, not God.

This is an intriguing argument. God knows all possibilities and since God cannot know God's possible non-existence, God's possible non-existence turns out not to be possible after all and thus there is no such thing as a hypothetical necessity. Again, we have the failure to distinguish propositional from existential contingency. Of course, God as a necessary being could not know the existential possibility of the divine non-existence. But perhaps we do not know anything more certain than the putative existence of such a necessary being. Hartshorne sets up an exclusive alternative: either God necessarily exists or else positivism is correct. However, so often when we meet an exclusive alternative, we must ask about a third approach. A logically derived exclusive alternative which seems air-tight, as in the present case, often calls for stepping back from the reasoning which sets up the dichotomy in the first place. If we do this we may find that there is a third case if the premises are undetermined. This third case is on a different logical level than Hartshorne's alternative. The alternative of "undetermined premises" or "unknown premises" is prior to Hartshorne's exclusive alternative of "God's necessary existence or positivism." Thus, when positivism is rejected, we still have two alternatives left: "existential necessity" or "propositional contingency." And, since propositional modality is different from existential modality, Hartshorne's epistemic proof does not eliminate propositional contingency.

One of Hartshorne's major principles is that of Modal Coincidence.

> Whatever world actually exists, God is thought of as having created it; whatever world might exist God is thought of as capable of creating it.

From this is derived the following attempted proof. Now if it is "possible" that God not exist, then his existence would be the actualization of a possibility not resting on God's own creative action.[10]
This is intimately related to the epistemic proof.

> Everything actual is accounted for in His actual knowing, as everything possible in His potential knowing.

In this discussion Hartshorne's reply to the criticism which Hick and I use is as follows:

> If then someone says, "Perhaps there is no being modally coincident with actuality and possibility in general," he seems to be saying, "If such a being were to exist, this would be because a certain possibility (that it might have failed to exist) had not been actualized, and another possibility, that it might exist, had been actualized."[11]

But then the modally coincident being, he continues, would not be modally coincident (which is absurd!), since there would be one possibility God could not possibly know, the alleged possibility of his own non-existence.

The point at issue is that for Hartshorne modal coincidence is conceived of primarily as existential modality, whereas the modality in the assertion, "Perhaps there is no being modally coincident with actuality and possibility in general" is propositional modality.

For an existential possibility to be actualized another possibility (its non-existence) has to lack actualization. But propositional possibility (contingency) involves indeterminacy, not an alternative possibility. Thus the translation sentence of "Perhaps there is no being modally coincident with actuality and possibility in general" which Hartshorne proposes in the last quotation should not be: "If such a being were to exist, this would be because a certain possibility had not been actualized and another possibility had been actualized." The translation should rather be: "If we were to assert that such a being exists, it would be because the reasons for so asserting would be clearer (or stronger) than they now appear." This does not imply the absurdity that the (existential) modally coincident is not modally coincident.

For Hartshorne there is a variety of *a priori* arguments, besides the modal argument, based on concepts not identified (at least initially) with deity or Worshipfulness. While he asserts that these arguments are all interdependent, we shall treat them separately.[12] Each of them manifests the general weakness of overstating its case, arguing in an explicitly definitive fashion with an argument that is weaker than the definitiveness claimed.

The first is a form of the design argument.

> Localized interaction cannot of itself make intelligible the possibility of any order and . . . without some order the concept of interaction itself lacks definite meaning, so that the denial of a strictly universal yet individual form of interaction would be the denial of any interaction at all.

This is an argument from localized interaction to order to a universal and individual form of interaction (the universal interaction of the Supremely Related Individual with all other individuals.) The crucial step is from order to the universal and individual form of interaction.

> Only universal interaction can secure universal order, or impose and maintain laws of nature cosmic in scope. . . . The alternative to God's existence is not an existing chaos but, rather, nothing conceivable.[13]

In other words, order needs to be "secured" or laws of nature need to be "imposed and maintained."

This argument, which could be called the "securing of order argument," is questionable on at least two counts: a) It does not require an extreme positivist criterion of meaningfulness to question the meaningfulness of the phrases "securing order" and "imposing and maintaining a law of nature." Granted that we have some notions of securing or imposing order (from potters to monarchs and office managers), what does the securing of a law of nature mean? There are different kinds of securing of order (marching bands, gardens and watches being different examples). But what sort of securing of order would the securing of a law of nature be? b) Furthermore, if the question of meaning could be answered, is the securing of order thesis true? Given that some types of order require securing, (marching bands, watches, and tidy attics), it does not follow that all order must be secured or imposed. Is it not reasonable to suggest that in some possible worlds (of which ours is one) some patterns of events are likely to last for a time? What is order except a pattern which has some temporal continuity (however brief and however changing)? Also, if such temporarily enduring patterns are likely to occur, why seek for an agent of imposition in all cases? To secure an intelligible explanation, why not look for internal factors of pattern-maintenance and external conditions of pattern-support (not imposition)? In short, isn't an ecologically oriented explanation as rational as an explanation oriented towards an agent of imposition?

The argument from design has a long list of critics. While it might be possible that these critics have made some major errors in reasoning (as Hartshorne demonstrates with some success for critics of the ontological argument), it is also possible that the critics are correct. At any rate, the argument that order needs an orderer is controversial and needs defending and Hartshorne has not done this. Watches require watchmakers, but all forms of order do not need an agent to secure the order. Thus the recognition that there is some degree of order in the world does not entail an ordering agent.

A third argument is a form of the cosmological argument.

> Since God alone is both contingent and necessary . . . a theistic proof might consist in showing that purely contingent existence is not self-sufficient or intelligible by itself, so that to deny God would be, absurdly enough, to reject any and every form of existence.[14]

The standard criticisms of this argument cannot be dismissed lightly. 1) What would it mean that a necessary being is the source of sufficiency and intelligibility? What does intelligibility mean? 2) Why is contingent being not self-sufficient or intelligible in itself? Why isn't the world just as adequate an expression for the ground and limit of intelligibility as is God? Why must intelligibility be *ab extra*? 3) Why is a contingent world plus its necessary creator any more intelligible than the total system of everything? One need not take a positivist, strict empiricist, or hard-line analytic approach to urge these questions.

Besides these arguments Hartshorne asserts that it is possible to base theistic proofs on such basic concepts as truth, beauty or goodness. Taken in their ultimate generality, these concepts "require divine valuation to make sense."[15] This is another example of Hartshorne's maximum/nothing dichotomy. Only contribution to the Supreme Experiencer makes sense of the pursuit of any value. Either there is a supreme experiencer of value or no value at all (which is absurd).

It may seem strange to hear Hartshorne accused of a dichotomy. He spends much time trying to move the available options from dichotomies to trichotomies, with his neo-classical, maximal theism supplying the third terms. However, the trichotomies are used to include neoclassical options and are steps in excluding classical theistic options. This leaves the final dichotomy of neoclassical theism or positivistic absurdity. Although the move to trichotomies is important, it is the final dichotomy, which I call the maximum/nothing dichotomy, coupled with the denial of the positivist alternative, which is crucial in Hartshorne's argument.

Again, why the dichotomy? Perhaps this world is an ambiguous mixture of realization and frustration. In such a world appropriate striving (and appropriate resignation) would make sense. It would call for courage.

Hartshorne has anticipated this objection:

> Living only for the finite vaguely foreseeable but limited human future, seems also irrational.[16]

This reply seems weak. Why is this irrational? Why is it irrational to go for all the gusto (and beauty and compassion) we can achieve? Hartshorne calls this subhuman. This seems another maximum or nothing move.

Hartshorne also refers to the "religious or 'global' proof."

> If an individual must have integrity in order to exist as an individual, and if the conscious form of integrity is worship, then . . . there is something irrational in choosing not to believe in God.[17]

The crucial assumption here is the thesis of the necessity of the integrity of the object of interest/love.[18]

Again, we may ask, 1) what does this mean? What would the integrity of the Supreme Object of interest or love be? Could we be aware of it enough to love or be interested? 2) Is integrity (even partly) a function of the worship and, thus, the decision of the subject? 3) How much integrity is needed or desirable? Once again, confronted with the "all or nothing" alternative, we may ask, why isn't partial integrity all that is attainable (and perhaps desirable)?

Schubert Ogden is another process thinker whose claims are set forth as following from conclusive arguments. Ogden argues from the necessity of an unconditioned meaning in life to God as the ground of this unconditioned meaning.[19]

Let us grant that God, conceived in neo-classical fashion, would make "the notion of a ground of ultimate confidence fully intelligible."[20] What is open to question, however, is the notion of the *necessity* of *unconditioned* meaning to life.

> Necessarily implied by any claim to moral truth whatever is the
> *unconditioned* meaningfulness of our life as subject to that claim.

By contrast, suppose a position like that of Alan Gewirth is taken:
every agent is logically committed, by the Principle of Generic Con-
sistency, to the acceptance of a moral principle which requires that
he ought at least to refrain from interfering with the same generic
features of action of his recipients (freedom and well-being) that he
claims, as his right, that they should refrain from interfering in
him.[21] This moral viewpoint does not imply the unconditioned
meaningfulness of life as subject to that claim. It does imply a concern for one's own well-being, but this does *not* require an unconditioned concern.

In another statement Ogden asserts:

> In whatever we say or do to witness the cause of man, we must beg
> the question of the ultimate meaningfulness of human life.[22]

Minimalism affirms that the possibility of a practically meaningful
life whose areas of meaning may be quite limited is a plausible and
liveable stance. The supremely meaningful life would be nice, but it
is not the only rational and pragmatic alternative, and that seriously weakens the attempted proof of Ogden's position.

Ogden asserts that we cannot ask the religious question without presupposing a ground of confidence.[23] Now granted that particular religious assertions may presuppose God, it does not follow
that God exists, since religious assertions *may* be pointless in a significant sense. This *is* a subject of debate.

Ogden draws an analogy between religious questions on the one
hand and moral and scientific questions on the other, attempting to
show that just as inquiry in the latter pair presupposes an unconditioned, so also does inquiry in the former.[24] However, Ogden is
wrong. We do *not* presuppose regularity in science, we seek to find
out *if* there is regularity. It may not be there. The hope that moti-
vates our search can sometimes be disappointed.

It seems as if we do presuppose an unconditioned in morals,

> that some course of action open to us ought to be adopted . . . a
> course . . . which promotes the maximum realization of all relevant
> interests.[25]

However, it might be that in a given situation there is no one course
of action that ought to be adopted. Consider a tragic moral dilemma. Perhaps we do hope for a choice which will promote a

maximum realization of interests, but again, a hope is not enough to establish an unconditioned presupposition. This hope may motivate our search, but to engage in the search does not entail that the hope will be fulfilled. Perhaps the debate can be clarified by discussing Ogden's treatment of the absurd hero of Camus.

> If all our actions are in principle absurd, the act of heroically re-sisting their absurdity must also be absurd. It, too, is *ex hypothesi* a totally meaningless response and can be supposed not a bit more fitting than the various attempts to flee from absurdity that Ca-mus so unsparingly condemns. Or, to take the other side of the di-lemma, insofar as resistance for the sake of man *is* a meaningful act—is somehow fitting as the alternatives to it are not—the ab-surdity of our existence cannot be as unrelieved as was originally alleged.[26]

I suggest that Ogden has again set up a dichotomy of extremes. His argument can be recast into a *Modus Tollens* form: if our exis-tence is unrelievedly absurd as Camus declares, then resistance is absurd. But, since Camus affirms the meaningfulness of heroic re-sistance, this denial of the consequent implies the denial of the an-tecedent. Thus, our existence is not unrelievedly absurd.

Two points can be made in reply. 1) The term "absurd" is am-biguous. On the one hand it could mean a *total lack* of meaning. Or it could mean a *lack of total* meaning. When Camus defines absur-dity he clearly indicates the latter meaning.

> I said that the world is absurd, but I was too hasty. This world in itself is not reasonable, that is all that can be said. But what is absurd is the confrontation of this irrational and the wild longing for clarity whose call echoes in the human heart. The absurd de-pends as much on man as on the world.[27]

It is not clear that the position of Camus requires the former mean-ing nor that he intends to include it. Thus the affirmations of the absurd hero of Camus do not contradict total lack of meaning. Rather the absurd hero recognizes the impossibility of fulfilling our nostalgia for unity, while searching for limited meaning.

2) The act of affirmation by the absurd hero is on a different logical and existential level than the recognition of absurdity. As a response to absurdity, the absurd hero's affirmations are second-level affirmations and thus are not contradicted by an apparent universality of meaningfulness at the first level. To search for

meaning in the face of the absurd is not contradicted by the pervasiveness of absurdity. The final sentence of *The Myth of Sisyphus*, "One must imagine Sisyphus happy," is not in contradiction with the body of the work but directly relates to the opening theme that suicide is the only serious philosophical problem.

The general criticism of Hartshorne and Ogden offered here has been that their conclusions do not achieve the apodictic certainty which they claim for them. 1) The modal arguments overlook the distinction between propositional and existential modality and hence, between putative necessity and existential necessity. 2) The ontological ultimate as a principle of explanation falls heir to all the criticisms of a transcendent principle of explanation: (a) the meaning of such a principle and also the sense in which it could explain anything is not clear and (b) how such a principle could escape the dilemma of vacuity or falsity is not clear. These criticisms are not adequately answered by Hartshorne and Ogden. 3) The argument to an unconditioned ground of meaningfulness not only is subject to the problem of the meaningfulness of a transcendent principle of explanation but in addition is buttressed by a disjunctive syllogism, employed by both Hartshorne and Ogden, the major premise of which can be stated as: "either there is unconditioned meaningfulness or no meaning at all." This maximum/nothing dichotomy rests on the assumption that partial meaningfulness is no meaning at all, hardly an indisputable starting point.

The options for philosophy of religion are not exhausted by a reliance on rational proofs on the one hand or the fideistic or positivistic rejection of rational proof on the other. There is a middle range of positions which employ strong but not conclusive arguments which need exploring. Such positions may involve room for such "subjective" factors as personal conviction, faith or temperament without rejecting a major role for reason. The use of reason in philosophical and religious thought need not be restricted to the search for apodictic certainty.

II. Theonomous Theism: Langdon Gilkey

One aspect of this study is the attempt to enrich religious naturalism by exploring the theocentric tradition which views human life from an ultimate viewpoint.[28] In the West this tradition includes Augustine, Luther, Calvin and the neo-orthodox and goes back to Jesus, Paul, and the prophets.[29] Specifically, I have been exploring Tillich, the Niebuhr brothers, and now Gilkey to see what religious naturalism can retrieve from this tradition. I seek to incorporate some of the insights of theocentric theology into a naturalistic framework.

Gilkey's project is to uncover an ultimate dimension in contemporary secular life. He does this not by analyzing explicit statements of secular self-understanding, since they reject or ignore ultimacy. Rather, he explores feelings and behavior in order to uncover a forgotten and unsymbolized horizon of ultimacy. He is guided by the theocentric tradition. Since this search is only a prolegomenon to theology, he seeks at this point merely to show the secular meaningfulness of God-language, not to claim its validity. This ultimate may be experienced either positively or negatively, as God or as a threatening emptiness, the Void.

I shall focus on the two books by Gilkey, *Naming the Whirlwind* and *Religion and the Scientific Future.*[30] I concentrate on four types of experience in which Gilkey finds this awareness of an ultimate horizon. These are the awareness of contingency, of relativity of meaning, of the ambiguity of freedom, and also certain elements in cognitive inquiry.

1. He suggests that we first become aware of ultimacy as a problem when we experience our contingency, when we cannot find an ultimate source to our life. Then an infinite Void at the depths threatens all we are and do. We feel emptiness and anxiety, perhaps despair. These feelings elicit strange behavior. We frantically look for something to fill up the emptiness and have a fanatical attachment to our answers. Hence an accurate picture of the human condition must use the categories of despair, meaninglessness, idolatry, the demonic and fanaticism. Like animals we act in order to survive, but unlike animals there is a drive toward ultimacy in this action.[31] A rival, the boss, the stock market, the latest news can become symbols of Fate, of an ultimate insecurity. The ultimacy of this threat gives the quest for survival and power its panicky and endless character with demonic possibilities. The search for job and financial security, status, office politics, career maneuverings, and professional jealousy all partake of this infinite dynamic.

Normally our security is socially supported. Our anxiety is compounded when we sense the finitude of our community and social fanaticism arises. The panic which comes from this sense of foreboding is one of the driving forces of historical life.

However, there are also signs of a positive creative power. There is a joy in life, a sense of vitality, of fulfillment at the use of our powers, a joy in community and personal intercourse. These common experiences buoy us up, make us glad to be alive and refuel our existence. These are religious, not just psychological experiences. They are experiences of being, of reality. There is ultimacy in these experiences since: a) being is not one of our values but is the basis of them all, b) this sense of reality is given to us, not created or controlled by us, and c) it appears within us as the ground of what we are, unlike finite things which appear over against us.

2. Ultimate meaninglessness is as deep a threat as the loss of existence. People need meaning in life, not just physical security. Meaning is the sense that our life and activities have or will someday have some sort of value, the sense that what we are and do is worthwhile. We need not be conscious of this feeling, but it is manifest in the energy which we pour into meaningful activities and in the loss of the sense of reality when we can find nothing constructive to do. We find that our purposes are as vulnerable as our being. There is a relativity to all our projects. The farm one generation builds, the families we nurture, the institutions and communities we help fashion, the books we write are all forgotten ere long. Who can even recall where a grandparent is buried?

The meanings which elicit our enthusiasm and powers are relative, but they must participate in a total system of meaning to overcome the threat of relativity.[32] Secularity understands this in practice, for it finds such total systems in the glory of one's career, nation or race, the myth of Progress, or the eschatologies of the revolutionaries. Each myth tends toward idolatry, and if made ultimate will result in destruction or despair.

When the ultimate context of meaning of a culture starts to crumble, the proximate meanings vanish. How silly to get excited over something relative and transient. Hence the demonic efforts of the privileged to protect at all costs the meaning which stems from their status.

The gift of a sense of the significance of what we do is unearned. Like the affirmation of existence, the sense of the meaning of life is given to us. You cannot say, "I shall enjoy my work" or "I shall have a new set of hopes." The love of something as worthful cannot be willed. As in the quest for ultimate security, there is common grace everywhere we experience the meaning and creativity of our particularity.

3. The third area in which ultimacy may be uncovered is that of freedom and autonomy. Every decision we make, every answer to the question, "Should I?," affirms a standard to evaluate the

alternatives. This norm has an ultimate or sacred character, for it is the foundation of the value of our existence and functions as an ultimate to which we give our lives and from which we expect to receive blessings. The sacred is now felt as an unconditional moral will which obligates and judges us.

Again we have the danger of idolatry and the demonic. Another ultimate appears, the tendency to give an unconditioned commitment to the well-being of oneself and one's group. We have a spiritual center such that if anything happens to it we fall to pieces, life means nothing. The center of such ultimate concern can vary: one's own power, career, family, group, but each sets up an idolatrous absolute. Such a center of concern is ultimate in that unconditioned loyalty, transcending other loyalties, is given to it. A person will do anything, sacrifice anything for it. Hence it functions as a god. Frequently this leads to the infinite expansion of the needs and desires of the self, which uses its rational and moral powers to justify this striving after its interests and security. The self is in bondage to its own well-being.

Often our idolatrous concerns lead us to act inhumanely. Thus greed, dishonesty, bias, ruthlessness and aggression stem from idolatry and the demonic. An analysis of freedom, this time as guilty freedom, leads to a judgment on our tendency to be unloving and to support injustice. The sacred is now opposed to us.

The sense of unworthiness and isolation which this experience of guilty freedom brings can be destructive, resulting in a feeling of unreality, loss of emotion, or bitterness. This sense leads to a search for self-acceptance and renewed community. We can seek relief in an unrealistic self-image or a finite community of acceptance, such as a friend, analyst, or group. But our efforts to prove our innocence are futile because others don't accept our doctored accounts of what happened. A finite community of acceptance is not the answer, for it shares in our conflicts and, if we receive acceptance from it, we lose our integrity and freedom.

Ultimacy appears in this third area because: 1) the need for acceptance is unconditional, 2) this acceptance recreates the self from beyond itself, and 3) the acceptance is unconditional in the knowledge of ourselves (for only an acceptance that knows us thoroughly is worth anything) and unconditional in its acceptance. What we need is not acceptance based on the assurance of our innocence but forgiveness of the guilt we know full well is there. Only the grace of the ground of life can heal without destroying our autonomy. Neither nature nor history contains such a power.[33]

4. A fourth area in which Gilkey finds ultimacy is in cognitive inquiry, epitomized by science. Here there are three points of ultimate intent: a) the passion to know, b) the global visions and theoretical structures presupposed by scientific inquiry, and c) the affirmation of what is judged to be true and the self-affirmation of the knower. In short, these points are motive, presupposition, and affirmation.

a. The passion to know can be called an *eros* towards knowledge. Scientific inquiry demands

> a determination to know ... patience, rigor, self-discipline, and hope—and all of these presuppose a deep passion to know. ... All scientific repugnance at prejudice, the closed mind, unexamined answers, and lack of rigor in facing uncomfortable truths, depends on this underlying eros to know.[34]

This eros has an element of ultimacy. The passion on which science depends must be an ultimate passion to find and adhere to the truth. It is an affirmation of the good of knowing for its own sake, an affirmation of the value of a set of cognitive standards. It is this commitment that sustains the search for an intelligibility not yet found. Such an affirmation is unconditioned. It involves an affirmation of a rationality which is there to be found even if I cannot demonstrate its existence, and a commitment to the ultimate value of that search and that achievement. Thus the first element of ultimacy in scientific inquiry involves the affirmation that knowing is possible and the commitment to scientific integrity, the disdain for anything but the beauty, order and simplicity of scientific explanation, and the refusal to affirm anything but what is veridically based on the evidence.

b. The second element of ultimacy in cognitive inquiry is that it requires a conditioned absolute, a fundamental theoretical structure which is believed to be true. For experience is intelligible only in relation to a method of inquiry, and data are determined as relevant only in relation to a theory about the data. For it is in terms of such a theoretical structure that the welter of facts is so ordered as to be manipulable, investigable, and intelligible. A conditioned ultimate, a vision of things which is held to be nonrelative, is presupposed in all knowing. Here again an aspect of ultimacy is present in scientific inquiry.

c. The third element of ultimacy in inquiry involves the virtually unconditioned grasp of what is judged to be true plus the self-affirmation of the knower as a knower. To begin with the virtually unconditioned grasp of what is judged to be true, a theory has conditions. If the conditions turn out to be the case, we say that our theory seems correct or probable. A rational judgment about a theory is thus made when, as far as can be determined, no important questions are left outstanding which would render the judgment vulnerable, when the judgment is virtually unconditioned and the proposition must be affirmed to be so. Here an "element of ultimacy in judgment enters: when the satisfaction of the conditions is seen and so the proposition is seen to be virtually unconditioned."[35]

The second element of ultimacy in judgment is

> that once having seen the unconditioned character of our judgment—that our theory "checks out" and that we can say "it is so"—*then* we cannot refuse to judge, nor can we remain in suspension. . . . In seeing, therefore, the unconditioned character of the judgment, we are compelled to affirm it. We do not then act as we *want;* we act as we *must,* that is, as rational beings. Our minds are bound by our own unconditional rational insight. . . . We must not only assent to the validity of the judgment but lay the claim of this truth . . . on the scientific community.[36]

Furthermore, there is the still deeper certainty that in this situation I know myself as a knower.

> Our hypotheses may be merely probable. . . . But our judgments concerning them are virtually unconditioned: not that what we affirm is *necessarily* so, but that we must and do assert that it *is* so because the conditions are fulfilled. And basic to this is the greater certainty of our self-affirmation as a knower: I know that I know when I judge. . . . All cannot be relative and tentative in inquiry: else we would never judge this to be the case, nor could we discriminate among hypotheses. . . . The process of inquiry cannot move forward unless it steps somewhere on firm ground, . . . the virtually unconditioned character of contingent judgments and our unconditioned affirmation therein of ourselves as knowers.[37]

These then are four areas in which Gilkey claims to have uncovered the forgotten dimension of ultimacy in our contemporary life. Although we cannot give here a full account of Gilkey's theory of language, we should sketch his idea of the value of religious discourse for common experience. For Gilkey words clarify and so give meaning to the felt character of a shared situation. By thus thematizing our experience words help give more precision and shareable form to our dim and inchoate experience. Secularism ignores the dimension of ultimacy, resulting in an impoverishment of the human spirit. Its myths and false ultimates are unchallenged and "its joys are left uncelebrated and so unexperienced, its terrors uncomprehended and so unconquered."[38]

We come now to the question of what naturalism, minimalist or otherwise, can make of all of this. It must first be recognized that a yearning for the ultimate is a key part of human experience and behavior. Gilkey is correct in this. His hermeneutic of our secular life rings true. His sketches of terror at the Void and of rejoicing in "common grace" are on target. His uncovering of ultimacy in our secular life brings into focus the presence of this hunger for absolutes in people who reject or ignore formal religion. Critics of religion often miss this point by claiming that this yearning for the infinite is a vestige of the primitive past or is created by organized religion. Institutional religion no more creates this yearning than do soap operas create a nostalgia for love.

Naturalism asserts that there is no ontological reality which satisfies this hunger for the unconditioned. There is no Ground or God which satisfies our yearning for the absolute any more than there is a heaven which satisfies our longing for immortality or a perfect love which satisfies our romantic yearnings. Given a survey of the available evidence, insights and arguments, religious naturalists can make a wager that there is no such ontologically supreme reality.

Gilkey seeks to provide a justification for a theistic, particularly a Christian, outlook on life. I find four types of rationale which he provides. Space permits only the briefest sketch of these and my replies. 1) Gilkey asserts a dichotomy between faith and despair or idolatry. But there is another possibility which this entire book seeks to delineate: resignation of all absolutes with openness to this-wordly transcendence and vulnerable commitment to penultimate values. 2) He asserts the need for religious language to thematize the experiences of ultimacy, as we just saw, and also freedom and destiny and Fate and bondage of the will. My reply is that an enriched naturalism can also symbolize these experiences. 3) He maintains that the justification of theological affirmations involves a revelatory illumination and personal validation. Such illumination and validation may be helpful, possibly necessary, for our basic affirmations. However, illumination and personal validation do not

provide sufficient rationale for these affirmations. 4) Gilkey argues
for God as the ground of the continuity of the temporal process.[39] As
I see it, such an argument is a *non sequitur*. The temporal process
does not need a ground for its continuity. If you don't describe it in
atomistic categories, the felt continuities within the stream of process will not be ruled out *a priori* and there will be no need to find
a ground to supply the missing continuity.

The problem for a naturalist's reflection on religion is to develop a way of thinking about ultimacy lest life be impoverished and
undisciplined at its depths. We need a theory of ultimacy which
will: (1) challenge false absolutes and our fanaticisms and frantic
searches for the infinite, (2) give rational support for our personal
efforts at renunciation of the ultimate, and (3) help us to comprehend the unease, even terror, at the loss of the positive Ultimate,
and yet to celebrate the temporary joys and partial victories which
are real and concrete.

The vision I suggest leads to a philosophy of critical openness. It
makes three challenges: (1) to be critically open to the gifts of life,
(2) to be critically committed to proximate ideals, and (3) to renounce the ultimate.

1. Gilkey is correct. There are experiences of what the tradition
calls "common grace" and we need to be open to them, although we
also need to be critical, lest we accept any foolish or dangerous gift.
Within the naturalistic framework such an experience may be conceived of as an awareness of a resource which is transcendent to the
situation as perceived. A cup of water, a reconciling word, a healing
medicine may be situationally transcendent resources, unexpected
and uncontrolled gifts to heal and renew. The challenge is to be critically receptive to these gifts.

2. We are called to responsibility to proximate ideals, causes,
institutions and persons. We must respond to such calls, although
we must be critical in such commitment lest we succumb to phony
or corrupt challenges or waste our efforts on trivial or overweening
demands. In short, we need to be ready to revise our values and ideals and to make our commitments with critical loyalty. Within the
naturalist framework such commitment is a revisionary process directed towards values transcendent as regulative ideas.

3. Gilkey is also correct that we constantly go after false absolutes. There can be terror and despair at glimpsing the Void and
this underlies much of the ennui and boredom, frantic activity and
escapism of our life. The approach of naturalism is to work through
the grief which comes from losing our ultimates, to work towards a

hard-won personal maturity. The loss of the absolutes, like the loss of parents, of loved ones, the betrayal of our first loves and hopes can end in cynicism or in grasping after false hopes. Or it can result in a maturity, sometimes painfully won, which gives up the hope of winning the ultimate, only to receive the small, but concretely real joys which belong to the finite. We can learn to appreciate the short-lived cherry blossoms.

These are the three challenges which the philosophy of openness makes: (1) critical openness to the gifts of life, (2) critical commitment to penultimate ideals, and (3) a mature renunciation of the ultimate.

Let us recapitulate these four areas of experience where Gilkey claims to uncover ultimacy and see what they look like from the viewpoint of a naturalism which also looks in the direction of ultimacy but finds no positive ultimate.

1. First there is the two-sided experience of contingency. On the one hand, Gilkey claims that when we really experience our finitude we either find an ultimate source of our existence or else we plunge into despair or into an endless panicky striving for ultimate security. On the other hand, when we experience the joys of life we are in touch with the unconditioned source of our existence. Such experiences point to the ultimate, Gilkey claims, because existence is the basis of all our values, not one among them, and also because they are given to us, we do not create or control them.

Naturalism, as I conceive it, can recognize, on the one hand, our despair and our endless striving for security. However, since there is no ultimate source of our being, we must face the Void honestly and summon, with appropriate help from our friends, what courage we can. We must give up the quest for ultimate security and engage in reasonable prudence, being ready to risk or even abandon security where it seems appropriate. We must situate ourselves with courage and prudence in the middle of Gilkey's triad of despair, fanatic striving and a glimpse of the positive Ultimate. This is a difficult, never finished task.

On the other hand, naturalism can join with Gilkey in openness to the gifts of joy in existence. However, neither as "given" nor as the "basis" of our other values are our positive experiences of existence signs of ultimacy. True, these gifts are largely not the result of our creation or control, but their givenness means that they come from beyond us. It does not mean they come from beyond everything. In the technical language of our minimal model, these gifts bringing joy are situationally, not ultimately, transcendent. Also, Gilkey claims that such joy in existence is of a different order than our other values since without existence these other values could not be. But this foundational quality of existence merely means it is the necessary condition of the realization of other values. It does not mean it derives from an ultimate source.

2. Gilkey's analysis of the second area of experience, meaningfulness and its threatened loss, is similar to his analysis of contingency. We search for a sense of worthwhileness to what we do, but this calls for an ultimate context of meaningfulness. On the one hand, relativity and transience threaten our meanings. Without such an ultimate context the proximate meanings vanish. On the other hand, the gift of a sense of the worth of what we do is unearned and thus points to an ultimate source.

Again naturalism can applaud Gilkey's analysis of human striving after ultimate meaningfulness. Once again we must face the issue of just how silly it is to be excited over proximate meanings. The answer is that we may be appropriately excited, ready even to sacrifice our life, but with a saving touch of irony, a realization that our passion is for proximate concerns. Again we must situate ourselves between despair, fanaticism, and an acceptance of a positive ultimate. Gilkey, along with many others, sees either all or nothing, either an ultimate context of significance or no significance at all. And modern man feels and acts out of a similar dichotomy. But the truth probably lies in avoiding the extremes, in an acceptance of the fragmentary but authentic worth of finite causes. The farms and schools we build will vanish, but our work for them has genuine albeit partial and temporary worth. With Gilkey I find much of our sense of worth unearned and unbidden. But this is a sign of our finiteness, not a sign of the ground of all finite meaning.

3. Next is the area of freedom. For Gilkey every choice affirms a norm of selfhood which has a sacred character since it is the foundation of the value of our existence. It is that to which we give our lives and from which we expect to receive blessings. The sacred here obligates and judges. Furthermore, to summarize Gilkey, freedom leads to an unconditioned concern for the well-being of one's self and one's group, leading to the infinite expansion of desires, bondage of the self, cruelty, in short, to idolatry and demonic behavior. In turn, guilty freedom results in a search for self-acceptance and renewed community. But another self or finite community is no answer. Others don't accept our efforts at self-justification, are guilty themselves, and our dependence on their acceptance threatens us. Only the ultimate ground of life can accept us unconditionally, with a thorough knowledge of ourselves, without destroying our autonomy.

Naturalism can agree that obligation and judgment are transcendent in the sense of pulling the self beyond its narrow confines. However, obligation and judgment are not transcendent in the sense of being rooted in ontological ultimacy. In addition we can appreciate Gilkey's analysis of guilty freedom which is far more profound than that of ordinary secular self-understanding. However, there is no ultimate acceptance. There may be partial forgiveness and fragmentary reconciliation. Such reconciliation is situationally transcendent, for it is not in our power to predict or to control and it might be strong enough to bring us back from the abyss of despondency or worse. We must learn to accept the absence of unconditional reconciliation. This requires real grief work and some of us may not achieve it or may hide from the depth of their evil. We must also accept fragmentary offers of forgiveness, which also is difficult. Indeed, the offers may not appear. We can hope, but not presume. In turn we must make our own offers of restoration, negotiating the line between self-abnegation and false pride, knowing that we all have fallen short. Who is sufficient for these things? None of us knows for sure.

4. Finally Gilkey claims to uncover three points of ultimate intent in cognitive inquiry, namely, motive, presupposition and affirmation. These are: (a) the *eros* to know, (b) global visions and theoretical structures presupposed by inquiry, and (c) the grasp of what is judged to be true and the self-affirmation of the knower. a) The *eros* to know is a passion involving the belief that knowing is possible and the commitment to the discipline of inquiry. This *eros* is unconditioned because the affirmations of the possibility and the intrinsic good of knowing, even when the possibility and the goodness cannot be shown, are unconditioned affirmations. b) The theoretical structure required to use any method or data is a conditioned ultimate, a particular vision held to be non-relative. c) When the conditions for a rational judgment about a theory turn out to be fulfilled, the judgment is virtually unconditioned, we are compelled as rational beings to affirm it and further we have an unconditional affirmation of ourselves as knowers which is the basis of all rational judgment.

Gilkey's analysis of science is valuable, challenging an extreme objectivism. These three elements of inquiry give an experiential root to God-language within the cultural enterprise of science and thus partially establish its meaningfulness. This does not show the validity of God-language, as Gilkey is quite aware. From minimalist naturalism these elements of motive, presupposition, and affirmation are best described as having ultimate intent, but as not being grounded in an ontological ultimate. They point to certainty in the midst of relativity, particularity and tentativeness. They are finite footprints on the path of inquiry, not traces of an ontological ultimate.

In short, what naturalism can learn from Gilkey is that our yearning for the ultimate is present in both our feelings and our behavior. We must learn to face, with a seriousness often lacking in naturalism, this striving after the ultimate, our anxiety of not finding it, and our demonic and idolatrous attempts to secure it. Although naturalism cannot accept his vision of a positive ultimate, he has shown that this striving is a powerful component of normal human existence and that we must come to terms with it.

III. A Profound Secularism: Albert Camus

Another recent thinker with interesting parallels with our minimalist approach is Albert Camus. His *Myth of Sisyphus* is an exploration of the meaning of life without an ontological ultimate. He has explored this problem in a thoughtful and provocative way, raising questions about the meaning of life parallel to those of Hartshorne, Ogden and Gilkey, yet answering them with ontological modesty.

Camus is known as a thinker and novelist of absurdity and alienation, of lack of purpose and coherence in the world. For him people must be dependent on themselves to wrest what value can be had in life. He does not spend much time arguing against the theistic position, but rather rejects its existential stance as an attempt to escape from the absurdity of life. In other words Camus reflects on what it means to live without appeal, without appeal to a God who will judge men accurately and set things right. Camus is concerned with studying the effects of both living with and without belief. He is an example of self-conscious secularity, of a secular thinker who deliberates seriously about the central topics of human existence.

For Camus the sense of the absurd is formed by the conjunction of three factors: 1) man's desire or nostalgia for unity and rationality, an appetite for the absolute; 2) the disunity and irrationality of the world; and 3) the hiatus between these two. Without the nostalgia for ultimate coherence, the lack of ultimate coherence would not be absurd.[40]

At this point I am in fundamental agreement with Camus. There is a desire for ultimate coherence. This is manifested paradigmatically in the belief in God, God's rule of the world, and an existence after death as the consummation or unveiling of this unity. However, the ontological reticence of our minimalism affirms that this ultimate coherence is, if not illusory (such a statement would not be reticent and modest!), at least not to be affirmed with enough confidence as to be a major motif of one's life.

I take it that this yearning for coherence is obvious. Oliver Wendell Holmes, Jr. called it "a demand for the superlative." Indeed,

> it is not enough for the knight of romance that you agree that his lady is a very nice girl—if you do not admit that she is the best that God ever made or will make, you must fight. . . . This demand is at the bottom of the philosopher's effort to prove that truth is absolute and of the jurist's search for criteria of universal validity.[41]

Further, I have made my case for the lack of an ultimate coherence or, more modestly, for the lack of grounds for affirming this ultimate coherence in Chapter One.

It is very important to realize at this point that Camus does not deny meaning or coherence to life. He is rejecting ultimate coherence. Life is meaningful, but its meaning and coherence are local and transitory and must be fought for and won. The absurdity is not an absolute meaninglessness, as I interpret Camus. Rather the absurd means not totally rational, not totally coherent.

If my reading of Camus is correct, then there is a fundamental agreement between Camus and our minimalism. Meaning and coherence are partial, temporary and local, vulnerable and ambivalent. This means that the minimalist position, like that of Camus (on our interpretation) rejects the false dichotomy of Gilkey, Hartshorne, and Ogden. Total meaning guaranteed by a Kantian-like Guarantor of meaning and no meaning at all are not the only alternatives. Fragmentary and vulnerable meaning is also possible.

To be sure, there are some differences between Camus and this position of openness to situational transcendence and continuing challenge. The differences lie precisely at these points of openness to minimally transcendent resource and challenge.

The first major point of divergence is that Camus does not explicitly stress openness to situationally transcendent resources, at least when discussing the absurd. There is a real sense in which for

Camus meaning must be achieved, must be fought for and won, if I read him correctly. As I understand life, however, much of the time meaning may be received. This is not a passive reception, but a co-operation, a transaction between the qualities in the local and temporary yet wider than presently perceived situation and the self. The difference here is partly the difference between an outlook with freedom and choice at the center and one with transaction or interaction at the center. In part this is the difference between a post-Cartesian, post-Kantian continental dualism and American process or naturalistic contextualism.

Thus the first major point of divergence between Camus and the minimalist philosophy is that Camus does not explicate openness to situationally transcendent resources. However, this must be said with caution, since nature plays a role in Camus similar to that of situationally transcendent healing resources in our minimalism. There is a therapeutic role to nature in some of the closing essays in *The Myth of Sisyphus*. Then there is the ending of Camus' novel *The Stranger*.[42] Awaiting execution, the main character, Meersault, opens himself to the world. And the universe almost feels brotherly as he lays his heart open to the benign indifference of the universe. This is almost like the feeling of common grace in Gilkey. Whatever one may think of the ending of the novel, the comment that there is no openness to situationally transcendent resources in Camus must be made with caution in the light of the therapeutic role of nature in Camus.

The second major point of divergence between Camus and the minimalist philosophy is that Camus has no continuing axiological challenge, no prophetic protest or lure capable of a transvaluation of values, at least in *The Myth of Sisyphus*. When he wrote *The Rebel*, however, there was a sense of continuing prophetic challenge, as we shall see below. However, in *The Myth of Sisyphus*, there is no real sense of the worth of another person's life, for example, which could challenge my own scale of values.

Camus affirms three characteristics of living out the absurd experience: revolt, freedom and passion. Revolt affirms a value of one's life. Freedom is brought to light by the absurd. Man no longer lives in relation to larger schemes of meaning or vocation of God. This is freedom. Passion is the desire to exhaust the series of present moments. There are no preferences, no scale of values. One is concerned, not for the best life, but for the most life.

At this point there is a shift of focus when moving from Camus to the minimalist vision of religious transcendence. I grant that meaning is often felt in revolt. But there is also meaning, fragmentary and vulnerable to be sure, often to be found in transactions which have more of a note of mutuality, even of receiving, than is found in revolt. Further, given the reality of local coherence, if we don't live in terms of overall schemas of meaning, we do have fragmentary schemas. These call, not just for freedom, but also for commitment and loyalty. There can be genuine loyalty to transitory and vulnerable meanings. Freedom can be a dimension of such commitment. Finally, there are value preferences. Discernment of worth and its challenge shows that some things are worth more than others. Indeed, sometimes length of life is not the supreme good. There are things worth dying for (although this is a dangerous judgment, constantly skirting the pathological).

The position Camus worked out in *The Myth of Sisyphus* was modified in *The Rebel*.[43] From this perspective Camus finds that the concept of the absurd in *The Myth of Sisyphus* did not yield a right or wrong as far as murder. In the earlier work we are free to stoke the fires of the slave camp crematory or to care for lepers. It is a matter of indifference. Now, in *The Rebel*, Camus finds that we are faced with the problem of murder. Murder has become justified in the world by national ideologies. We have slave camps under the flag of the free, crime wearing the apparel of innocence.

In his new approach Camus says that if we follow out the absurdist position of the earlier book we will come to affirm the solidarity of human life, a genuine preference of values. In the earlier writing Camus had repudiated suicide and affirmed that human life was good. Now Camus recognizes that this means that other people also have the right to live. Now he affirms that rebellion is the affirmation of value in the face of valuelessness. Rebellion is a "yes" to the value of the rebel. If one prefers the risk of death to the negation of one's rights, then one holds that these rights are even more important than himself. Rebellion thus affirms the solidarity of mankind. I revolt. Therefore we are. This note of solidarity is brought out quite strongly in Camus' magnificent novel, *The Plague*.[44]

This recognition of values more important than life is a parallel to the continuing challenge of transcending good in our minimalist understanding, especially when seen as an affirmation of the solidarity of humanity.

A further note of continuing challenge comes in the distinction Camus makes between rebellion and revolution. For Camus, revolution is rebellion gone wrong. Revolution follows the appetite for absolutes. It attempts to bring human history into accord with a static conception of the ideal which has become absolutized. Revolution negates the solidarity of man which rebellion affirms. It negates this solidarity through violence and deceit. The revolutionary ends by becoming either an oppressor, a policeman and bureaucrat, or else by returning to the sense of human solidarity.

In *The Rebel* Camus has a brief meditation on Kaliayev and "the fastidious assassins" whom he takes as models of rebellion that avoids the errors of revolution. They placed value above both the oppressor and themselves. They believed that one could kill or assassinate a tyrant only in extraordinary circumstances and that then one must accept the sentence of death for oneself.

Revolution absolutizes. This is the nostalgia for unity again. Rebellion affirms that we are. Revolution affirms that we shall be, after the others have been killed. Given the preference of Camus for rebellion, he goes on to say that murder thus must only be a desperate exception. It is a limit which, if one reaches it, requires that one must oneself die. Rebellion does not legitimize murder. The only proper stance is to rediscover a sense of limits and of moderation.

This sense of Camus that not only oppression must be fought but that also the fight against oppression by revolutionary zeal must be challenged has definite echoes of continuing challenge in the minimal model. Not only is his rejection of absolutizing and the nostalgia for unity similar to our renunciation of ontological absolutes, there is also the sense that a movement in the right direction (rebellion) can go wrong (revolution) and itself stands in constant need of examination and continual challenge. Even our apparent good is not unambiguously good. The sense of limits and moderation has definite echoes in our concept of critical loyalty to temporary coherence.

Thus we find definite echoes of our minimalist stance of openness to situationally transcendent resources and challenge in Camus, especially when we include some of the insights of *The Rebel*.

IV. Humanism: The Humanist Manifestos

Religious naturalism, especially in its ontologically minimal version, is a mediating position and, as such, it will appear to be hard to distinguish from positions on one side by those who stand on the other side. Religious persons, persons with a traditional orientation, may find it hard to distinguish this philosophy from Humanism. An examination of the *Humanist Manifestos I* and *II* will be a good way to bring this issue into focus.[45] The differences will be subtle, and partly a matter of attitude, except at one crucial and revealing point. That point is our respective understandings of the nature of religion, namely whether it is anything more than the dedication to the pursuit of ideals. The *Manifestos* display what I call their extreme Pelagian approach to religion. This one point of theoretical difference reveals, I claim, a major difference of attitude, of style of existence, which underlies all of the other apparently minor and subtle points of divergence.

The first point of difference is in our respective understandings of religion. From the minimalist perspective, the *Humanist Manifestos* reveal a major deficiency in their descriptions of religion and likewise in their attitude toward the genuine or proper function of religion, in other words, what a religious humanism would be. This major deficiency is that the manifestos, like the Columbia naturalists, see religion as the pursuit of ideals and not also as openness to resources. This extreme Pelagian approach overlooks completely what I refer to as "the real aspect of transcendence." An examination of the key passages treating of religion will reveal this deficiency. *Humanist Manifesto I* is indicative.

> Religions have always been means for realizing the highest values in life. Their end has been accomplished through the interpretation of the total environing situation (theology or world view), the sense of values resulting therefrom (goal or ideal), and the technique (cult) established for realizing the satisfactory life.[46]

Note that the means of realizing the highest values are world view, ideal and cult, with no mention of a reality or realities to help in realizing these values. That there is no reality to help us is, of course, the essence of humanism (in the sense that we are using the word).[47] The deficiency in the *Manifestos* is both theoretical (half of religion is left out, the half which responds to transforming resources) and practical. The discrimination of situationally transcendent resources, of unmanipulable and unforeseen realities which heal, is unthematized and thus discriminated and nurtured in practice only with difficulty. This is a very truncated style of existence.

The crux of the difference between *The Humanist Manifestos* and the philosophy of openness to transcendence minimally concieved is right here. The minimalist approach does not deny these realities. It reconceives them. It encourages the nurture of the attitude of openness and the sensitive discrimination of them. This brand of religious naturalism offers an analysis of and affirmation of cooperating or transactional grace, minimally conceived.

Confirmation of our interpretation of the first manifesto lies in these further passages.

> Religion consists of those actions, purposes, and experiences which are humanly significant. . . .
>
> Religious humanism considers the complete realization of human personality to be the end of man's life and seeks its development and fulfillment in the here and now. . . .
>
> In place of the old attitudes involved in worship and prayer the humanist finds his religious emotions expressed in a heightened sense of personal life and in a cooperative effort to promote social well-being.[48]

This same motif is apparent in the second manifesto. The preface to *Humanist Manifesto II* finds the positive aspect of humanism to be the pursuit of ethical ideals.

> Views that merely reject theism are not equivalent to humanism. They lack commitment to the positive belief in the possibilities of human progress and to the values central to it. . . . Humanism is an ethical process through which we all can move.[49]

Another way of putting this is that humanism is not just the rejection of theism but includes a positive commitment to progress, an ethical process.[50]

A second point of difference between minimalist religious naturalism and the *Humanist Manifestos* is that it is clear that the *Manifestos* reject any reinterpretation of traditional religions.

> Promises of immortal salvation or fear of eternal damnation are both illusory and harmful. They distract humans from present concerns, from self-actualization, and from rectifying social injustices.[51]

This is a different stance than the minimalism adopted here. The exploration of the monotheistic traditions in order to discover the triadic schema underlying the minimal model and also the exploration of experience to uncover experiences of situationally transcendent resources and awareness of continually challenging ideals is self-consciously rooted in traditional religions, especially the notions of grace or spirit and the prophetic protest. However, the minimalist reconception of them and our use of the language of inquiry is a radical departure from the traditions and does not "perpetuate old dependencies and escapisms" nor could this "easily become obscurantist." Perhaps this is because minimalism is more reconception than reinterpretation.

In the third place, related to the neglect of situationally transcendent resources is the attitude of the *Manifestos* toward human capabilities. In the concluding words of the first *Manifesto:*

> Man is at last becoming aware that he alone is responsible for the realization of the world of his dreams, that he has within himself the power for its achievement. He must set intelligence and will to the task.[52]

In the second *Manifesto* there is a more ambiguous attitude toward these capacities, made clear in the attention given to technology and science. On the one hand there is a decided optimism about technology when used wisely.

> Using technology wisely, we can control our environment, conquer poverty, markedly reduce disease, extend our life-span, significantly modify our behavior, alter the course of human evolution and cultural development, unlock vast new powers, and provide humankind with unparalleled opportunity for achieving an abundant and meaningful life.[53]

However, there is a recognition of the danger in the unwise use of technology.

> The future is, however, filled with dangers. In learning to apply the scientific method to nature and human life, we have opened the door to ecological damage, overpopulation, dehumanizing institutions, totalitarian repression, and nuclear and biochemical disaster.[54]
>
> Reason and intelligence are the most effective instruments that humankind possesses. . . . But reason must be tempered by humility, since no group has a monopoly of wisdom or virtue. Nor is there any guarantee that all problems can be solved or all questions answered.[55]

This approach is sane and balanced. However, there is an underlying trust in human powers that I don't think is quite cautious enough. The attitude here toward technology and science is more ambiguous and vacillating than the steadily ambivalent stance which I think is needed. The underlying premise is that we can save ourselves.

> We can discover no divine purpose or providence for the human species. While there is much that we do not know, humans are responsible for what we are or will become. No deity will save us; we must save ourselves.

> We further urge the use of reason and compassion to produce the kind of world we want—a world in which peace, prosperity, freedom, and happiness are widely shared. Let us not abandon that vision in despair or cowardice. We are responsible for what we are or will be.[56]

There is something very healthy and needed about this emphasis on responsibility. Yet I can't help thinking that it lacks a sensitivity to non-human worth, a caution and tentativeness about how our best plans can be dangerous and are rooted in self-assertiveness. The message given by the second *Manifesto* is so desperately needed today that one hesitates to question it. Yet I think that the notes of caution and of needing to be more open are needed.

The fourth point of divergence between the *Manifestos* and the minimalist vision of transcendence is that there is a decided emphasis on the value of humanity in these *Manifestos*.

> Obviously humanism does not deny the possibility of realities as yet undiscovered, but it does insist that the way to determine the existence and value of any and all realities is by means of intelligent inquiry and by the assessment of their relation to human needs. . . .

> Believing that religion must work increasingly for joy in living, religious humanists aim to foster the creative in man and to encourage achievements that add to the satisfactions of life.[57]

Our minimalism could hardly quarrel with these ideals. However, there are two points of differing emphasis. In the first place the philosophy of openness makes sensitive discernment of worth the opening point in ethical discussion. The point is not just the fulfillment of human potential, worthy as that is. The point is that there are real dimensions of worth in our experience to which we need to respond. The shift, if one may put it this way, is from fulfillment to responsiveness. A second difference is that the minimal model of transcendence emphasizes continual challenge from some ideals, the possibility of a real transvaluation of values. The prophetic protest even against our values and ideals needs to be lifted up, and this note I find lacking in the *Manifestos*.

Perhaps this is placing an undue weight on a mere matter of emphasis. Nevertheless I think that there is something here. The difference is clear when we look at the second Manifesto.

> We affirm that moral values derive their source from human experience. Ethics is *autonomous* and *situational*, needing no theological or ideological sanction. Ethics stems from human need and interest. To deny this distorts the whole basis of life. Human life has meaning because we create and develop our futures. Happiness and the creative realization of human needs and desires, individually and in shared enjoyment, are continuous themes of humanism. We strive for the good life, here and now. The goal is to pursue life's enrichment despite debasing forces of vulgarization, commercialization, bureaucratization, and dehumanization.
>
> The *preciousness and dignity of the individual person* is a central humanist value. Individuals should be encouraged to realize their own creative talents and desires. . . . The possibilities of individual *freedom of choice* exist in human life and should be increased.[58]

We can hardly disagree with these concerns for human need and the value of the individual. However, there is no note of a need for the transformation of values or of challenge to the choices of the individual.

A minor but perhaps significant point is that the *Humanist Manifesto II* recognizes "an individual's right to die with dignity, euthanasia, and the right to suicide."[59] What is worth pausing over here is that euthanasia is spoken of without a cautionary note concerning its abuses. Further, the language speaks not of a right to refuse treatment, but of a right to suicide. The right to die with dignity had already been spoken of. Without contextual language providing qualifications, this discussion seems to negate the interrelatedness of much personal life and to overlook interpersonal responsibility. This lack of qualification is disturbing.

Perhaps one should not place too much emphasis on isolated phrases. Both *Manifestos* explicitly indicate that signers need not agree with the totality of the documents. However, there needs to be a greater recognition of situationally transcendent growth-enhancing and healing resources in our experience, of the dangers in our plans and projects, and of the need to continually challenge our values and ideals. The Manifestos could be construed as including these themes, but I find them not central to their articulated focus.

Put briefly, the major difference between minimalism and the affirmation of God by Hartshorne, Ogden, and Gilkey is the difference between ontological reticence and the full affirmation of God conceived as an ontological ultimate. Given the difficulty of supporting such a complete affirmation of a maximal ontological ultimate and given the human mind's propensity to error and wish-fulfillment, minimalism seems the appropriate approach. Further, all three of these thinkers rely at a crucial point on a false dichotomy: either there is the ultimate guarantor of meaningfulness or else life is meaningless. The dichotomy overlooks the real possibility and existential viability of the pursuit of partial and transitory meaning. They ignore the intrinsic meaningfulness of the pursuit of truth, beauty, human potential, a just social order and other values worth struggling and perhaps even dying for.

On the other hand the chief difference between minimalism and the viewpoints of Camus and the *Humanist Manifestos* is that neither fully advocates an openness to situationally transcendent resources or to continuing challenging ideals. In their rejection of God they seem to have overlooked the real presence of divine qualities in the world. They have not fully articulated the situationally transcendent resources of healing and recreation, the unforeseen and unmanipulable gifts of life.

It is because the minimal philosophy of transcendence thematizes and encourages openness to situationally transcendent resources and penultimate yet continually challenging ideals that its relative adequacy is here advocated.

There are three recent thinkers who, like myself, can hardly be classed as either theists or humanists. I have, on a number of occasions, been asked to clarify my relationship with them. These three are John Dewey, Gordon Kaufman and Mark C. Taylor.

V. The Religious Quality of Experience: John Dewey

The religious naturalism developed here is very close to that of John Dewey. The differences between Dewey's notion of the religious quality of experience and my minimalist vision of situationally transcendent resource and continually challenging demand need to be explored. I shall focus on three themes: the reconstruction of experience, the sense of the whole, and God as the imaginative unity of ideals.

1. Reconstruction of Experience.

The generalization that all life is change and development together with the prescriptive principle that life should be changed intelligently, we may refer to as the reconstruction of experience.

The proper function of ideals in this reconstruction is to criticize and suggest change, to stimulate and guide inquiry. For example, "democracy . . . (as) the idea of community life itself . . . is not a fact and never will be. It is an ideal in the only intelligible sense of an ideal: namely the tendency and movement of some thing which exists carried to its final limit, viewed as completed, perfected."[60]

What is the relation between Dewey's conception of ideals and my notion of the ideal aspect of transcendence? Dewey is critical of ideals when conceived of as unattainable, static, vague and supplemented by a priori unexamined formulas. The proper function of ideals in the reconstruction of experience is to criticize and suggest change, to stimulate and guide inquiry. With this I agree. However, it would seem as if Dewey would reject my notion of continually challenging ideals since they are unattainable. However, note carefully. "Democracy . . . (as) the idea of community life itself . . . is not a fact and never will be," and yet it performs a useful critical function. This is very similar to my notion of a continually challenging ideal.

One major difference in our notion of ideals is subtle but important. Both Dewey and I urge us to be ready to undergo continuous reconstruction of our ideals and values. However, Dewey did not emphasize sufficiently the finiteness and self-deception of human intelligence. I think that we need an even more radical willingness to undergo major change in our ideals and values. This openness to radical reorientation, this sense of the limitations and potential perverseness of even our intelligence and our democratic social values Dewey would assent to, but would not stress as a continual theme of his thought and practice. This difference appears more clearly when the theocentric emphasis of a Tillich, the Niebuhr brothers, Gilkey, or even Wieman is placed next to Dewey. There is a difference between Dewey's reconstruction of experience by intelligent cooperative inquiry and reconstruction by the experience of transcendent ideals. The notion of ideal transcendence is our naturalistic appropriation of the prophetic principle.

Dewey does not stress the self-delusions of the inquiring mind the way a Niebuhr or a Gilkey would. He knows about rationalizations. And his notion of the self-corrective nature of scientific, democratic thought seeks to correct them. Yet he did not sufficiently feel the danger of self-delusion in the method of intelligence, in cooperative scientific inquiry.

A second difference is in the focus of our attention. Dewey wished to place an equal balance on the self and its environment. Yet his emphasis seems to be somewhat manipulative in outlook. Dewey is not the crude philosopher of American activism as portrayed by Santayana. Yet the term "reconstruction" encourages, despite Dewey's intentions, a style of careless forging ahead with the latest scheme. Also Dewey's key phrase, "development," invokes images of bulldozers and poorly designed buildings. We can't blame Dewey for all of the connotations of words, yet there is in his outlook not enough of a sense of caution and openness.

Dewey's stress is on active reconstruction, not openness. Dewey was a great teacher of teachers. What he failed to stress sufficiently was teachableness. Dewey needed to reflect more on receptiveness.

2. The Sense of the Whole.

Dewey would sometimes speak of a sense of the whole.

> In a genuine sense every act is already possessed of infinite import. . . . The boundaries of our garden plot join to the world of our neighbors and our neighbor's neighbors. That small effort which we can put forth is in turn connected with an infinity of events that sustain and support it. . . . It is the office of art and religion to evoke such appreciations and intimations; to enhance and steady them till they are wrought into the texture of our lives.[61]

It is significant that Dewey chose a series of gardens as his image of the sense of the whole. For Dewey a garden represents work, a reconstruction of the world. For him the meaning of the whole is tied up with the significance of work, of the activity of the self.

For Gilkey the sense of the whole is not gained by imaginatively extending one's work to include all human work. Rather, the longing for a sense of the whole is a longing for unconditioned meaning. When Gilkey uses an agricultural image, it is that of a farm which is decaying. For him, unless our sense of meaning can be rooted in

that which transcends our gardens and farms, we will either fanatically defend them or else the nerve of effort will be cut and we will
be lost in boredom or terror.

I share with Gilkey as against Dewey a sense of the potential
loss of our gardens, indeed of all gardens. Hence, we cannot easily
find a sense of worth by imagining all of the gardens. Besides, we
cannot always work in our gardens. For a minimalist philosophy as
I am trying to develop it, we can discern or speak meaningfully of no
positive ontological ultimate in the way that Gilkey can. We need to
develop a sense of the limited significance of our being, doing, and
having. We can see the garden next door and envisage several beyond that. This will give added meaning to labor in our own garden.
But we must also realize that it may become a shopping center or
slum tomorrow. Thus we must moderate our aggressiveness and our
defensiveness and, with a touch of ironic humor, speak to the temp-
tations of despair.

What a life-style of openness can help provide is a readiness to
receive functionally transcendent resources and challenges for our
life at hand, including the gardens we tend.

3. God as the Imaginative Unity of Ideals.

Dewey's first presentation of the meaning of the term "God" in
A Common Faith is that the word

> denotes the unity of all ideal ends arousing us to desire and ac-
> tions . . . the ideal ends that at a given time and place one acknowl-
> edges as having authority over his volition and emotion, the values
> to which one is supremely devoted, as far as these ends, through
> imagination, take on unity.[62]

This is very close to our minimal model. Both have an emphasis on
ideals to which one is supremely devoted, the acknowledgement of
the plurality of these ends, with unity supplied through the imagination, and the contrast with the ontologically supreme Being of
traditional theism. Further, Dewey and I agree that imagination,
which provides the unification to the plural elements, is not illusory, but a power of entertaining possibilities in such a way as to
have authority over us, to have power to convict us. I think that I
would broaden the texture of what unifies these ideals by including
the unifying function of language and of our abstractive powers, an
inclusion with which Dewey would readily agree.

It seems as if Dewey stressed the ideal aspect of transcendence and overlooked the real aspect. However, this definition by Dewey is only a first approximation. A more important difference is that in Dewey's definition there is lacking the radical, possibly revolutionary nature of the ideals. For our values may need reevaluation. Our best needs to stand under judgment. It may be that the ends to which we are supremely devoted are narrow, totalitarian or destructive. To be sure Dewey would urge us to grow and reconstruct our evaluations through intelligent, cooperative inquiry. However, there is lacking that note of caution and recognition of self-deception which theonomous theologians like Gilkey urge upon us and which I have tried to assimilate on a naturalistic basis.

In developing his analysis of the term "God," Dewey comes close to what I call the real aspect of transcendence.

> The view I have advanced is sometimes treated as if the identification of the divine with ideal ends left the ideal wholly without roots in existence and without support from existence. . . . On the contrary what I have been criticizing is the *identification* of the ideal with a particular Being . . . and what I have tried to show is that the ideal itself has its roots in natural conditions; it emerges when the imagination idealizes existence by laying hold of the possibilities offered to thought and action.[63]

This talk of the roots of the ideal in natural conditions parallels my notion of the real aspect of the transcendent. However, Dewey's discussion is sketchy and comes as an afterthought. A reading of *A Common Faith* suggests that his intention in defining the object of the religious attitude is the inclusive unity of ideal ends. The discussion of the anchoring of these ideals in existence comes as an answer to an objection. On this reading Dewey fails to give proper emphasis to the real as well as the ideal aspects of this-worldly transcendence.

A further distinction between Dewey and myself is that for him these roots of the ideal seem to be conditions of their feasibility. I understand the real aspect of transcendence to be actual forces of creation and renewal. Hence my concern is with openness to these processes, not with understanding and controlling them. I encourage empirical study and methodical manipulation (usually), but I also encourage a stance of openness and receptivity.

Dewey and I both find the word "God" to be optional and prefer the term "the divine." For Dewey, "the 'divine' is thus a term of human choice and aspiration."[64] I would grant the human element, but wish to emphasize the often compelling and overpowering nature of the axiologically transcendent and of situationally transcendent resources of renewal. I would say that the "divine" is a term of human recognition and acknowledgement.

A final point of similarity is that Dewey grants the selective function of the terms "God" and "divine."

> Whatever the name, the meaning is selective. For it involves no miscellaneous worship of everything in general. It selects those factors in experience that generate and support our idea of good as an end to be striven for. It excludes a multitude of forces that at any given time are irrelevant to this function.[65]

I generally agree but would rather say:

> It selects those factors in experience that generate and support *and transform* our idea of good *and that provide situationally transcendent resources of renewal.*

VI. Theology as Imaginative Construction: Gordon Kaufman

Recently Gordon Kaufman has been elaborating a notion of God which has certain parallels with the approach outlined here. Giving concreteness to his notion that "God" is an imaginative construct for the ultimate point of reference, Kaufman at times identifies God with the cosmic forces working toward humanization or, in his recent move to be less anthropocentric, the cosmic forces of creation.[66]

Kaufman argues that our ideas of God are imaginative constructs.

> All speech to and about God, and all 'experience of God', is made possible by and is a function of the constructive powers of the imagination.[67]

Kaufman defines God as the "ultimate point of reference to which all action, consciousness and reflection can lead." No reflection, no devotion, no action can intend a reality "beyond" God. "God" is a limiting idea, "the idea of that beyond which we cannot go either in experience, thought or imagination."[68]

The image/concept of God involves the notion of a "personal/ agential" being. Kaufman sees a continuum from highly mythical and symbolic images of God (God as a personal being, for example) to abstract notions such as "the cosmic ground for our humanity." Kaufman holds that "the mythic and the metaphysical dimensions of the image/concept of God must be held together."[69] To this end images from the whole continuum must be used.

Kaufman's identification of God with the cosmic forces working toward humanization is very fascinating. The parallel with both Shailer Mathews and the minimalist model proposed in chapter one is remarkable.

> 'God' is a symbol that gathers up into itself and focuses for us all those cosmic forces working toward the fully humane existence for which we long.

> God symbolizes that in the ongoing evolutionary-historical process which grounds our being as distinctively human and which draws (or drives) us on toward authentic human fulfillment.[70]

Now the symbol of God is clearly a personifying symbol.

> Such a personification has a considerable advantage for some purposes over abstract concepts such as "cosmic forces" or "foundation for our humanity in the ultimate nature of things": the symbol "God" is concrete and definite, a sharply defined image, and as such it can readily become the central focus for devotion and service.[71]

We should note that he quickly glides from the plurality of "cosmic forces" in his metaphysical referent to the personified symbol of "god." Like Wieman, his concern for the religious power of the symbol of God is dominant.

This, I trust, is a brief but fair picture of Kaufman's reconstruction of the image/concept of God. It lacks reference to what Kaufman calls the other theological categories, humanity, the world, and Christ, but I think it will suffice for our present purposes.

The similarities between the minimalist model of transcendence and that of Kaufman are partly those of the similarities between a historicist Kantianism and a pragmatic analysis of the concept of God which owes much to H. Richard Niebuhr and Tillich. For both views "God" is an imaginative construct, an image/

concept with reference to real forces at work and with powerful pragmatic import.

The distinction drawn by Kaufman between the relativizing and the humanizing function of the symbol of God is similar to my distinction between the ideal and the real aspects of transcendence. However, there is a unity to Kaufman's notion of God as "Supreme Relativizer" which goes beyond the concept of ideal transcendence in my minimal model. The metaphysical modesty which undergirds my outlook challenges this notion of a single Relativizer. To use fairly precise language, I am developing a working model, not of God, but of the divine or sacred qualities or dimensions of experience.

A second difference is that Kaufman's notion of God as "Supreme Humanizer" also has a unity which differs from my notion of many experiences of real transcendence. These experiences of real transcendent powers are all experiences of enhancement or nurturing of our humaneness, but again, Kaufman has imported a unity into these experiences, a unity which is closer to traditional theism but which oversteps the bounds of legitimate ontological reticence.

A third point of differentiation between the models of Kaufman and myself is that in specifying the referent of the term "God" or "the divine," I do not make the cosmic-evolutionary sweep of the humanizing process the primary focus of attention. I have a sympathy with Kaufman here. Nevertheless, my focus is less on the total evolutionary process than on specific experiences of situationally transcendent qualities or forces. Recognition of the cosmic process is more of an intellectual construct, an inference from the data of science. On the other hand, the experiences of transcendence are concrete, real and insistent. I feel closer to Meland's comment that these experiences can at times be terribly real than I do to the cosmic vision of Smuts, Alexander or Mathews (however much sympathy I have for this vision). My model of the divine is not based on a world view generalized from evolutionary theory. It does not reject such a world view, but it is more closely tied to specific experiences of unexpected and unmanageable resources and healing.

Like Kaufman I find an imaginative or symbolic unity to the many this-worldly transcendent forces and values. Nonetheless, the forces of humanization or creation (the real aspect of transcendence) have a generic similarity only and the continually challenging norms and values (the ideal aspect of transcendence) have unity only as a regulative idea, a living hope. The imaginative unity of devotional and liturgical language needs to be purified (even while it enriches) the more precise language of theoretical, reflective inquiry.

VII. A/Theology: Mark C. Taylor

Recently Mark C. Taylor has been developing what he calls an "A/theology," in which he attempts to think about religious issues after the "death of God." At first glance it might seem that there would be similarity between this view and a minimalism which seeks to think religiously without the God of classical or revised theism. However, Taylor seems to have taken as his starting point the position of Dostoevsky's Ivan Karamozov that without God everything is permitted. The trouble is that Taylor does not seem to have examined the dichotomy involved here: either God exists or else everything is permitted. Without God as traditionally conceived is, indeed, everything permitted?

In his postmodern a/theology, Taylor's argument assumes a dichotomy between the ontotheological perspective, from Augustine to Hegel, and a postmodern viewpoint which moves to the opposite extreme. Since Taylor deconstructs the former notion, he is left with the opposite alternative. As often happens with dichotomies, this one turns out to be false. More choices are available than the two considered. There is for example, an entire range of options clustered around both the process viewpoints and the related positions of radical empiricism. It is surprising that Taylor does not consider these options, since he delineates a process-relational view in chapters 3 and 4 of *Deconstructing Theology*.[72] My critique is that there are alternatives to both the ontotheological tradition which he rightly rejects and the extreme a/theological view which he espouses.

Taylor starts with a rejection of classical theism. He identifies the God of classical theism as the transcendent and eternal First Cause.

> According to the tenets of classical theism, God, who is One, is the supreme Creator, who, through the mediation of His divine Logos, brings the world into being and providentially directs its course. This Primal Origin (First Cause or *Arche*) is also the Ultimate End (Final Goal or *Telos*) of the world. Utterly transcendent and thoroughly eternal, God is represented as totally present to Himself [*sic*]. He is, in fact, the omnipresent fount, source, ground, and uncaused cause of presence itself.[73]

Taylor's world view is based on the contrast he perceives between the traditional ontotheology of classical theism and postmodern writing with infinite possibilities of meaning. This contrast starts to become clear as he writes of the death of God.

> The main contours of deconstructive a/theology begin to emerge with the realization of the necessary interrelation between the death of God and christology. Radical christology is *thoroughly* incarnational . . . The death of God is the sacrifice of the transcendent Author/Creator/Master who governs from afar. Incarnation *irrevocably* erases the disembodied logos and inscribes a word that becomes the script enacted in the infinite play of interpretation.[74]

> 'Logos is a son. . . . Without his father, he would be nothing but, in fact, writing.' . . . By enacting the death of the transcendent(al) Father/signified, the word becomes the wayward, rebellious, errant 'son.'[75]

Taylor bases his view of traditional ontotheology on what he sees as the main Christian dualism or dyad which results in the suppression of one term of the dyad by the other.

> Most of the Christian theological network rests on a dyadic foundation that sets seemingly exclusive opposites over against each other. Furthermore, these paired opposites form a hierarchy in which one term governs, rules, dominates, or represses the other. For example, God governs the world, eternity and permanence are more valuable than time and change, presence is preferable to absence, spirit more worthy than body, etc. The grounding principle of this exclusive network is an abstract notion of identity, difference, and non-contradiction.[76]

Taylor seeks to contrast this dyadic hierarchy (the ontotheological) with a free-playing, multivalent erring (the a/theological). The problem with Taylor's view is that there are a great many religious options available besides the ontotheological and a/theological dichotomy. We can follow this in the four notions developed in his *Erring*.

Taylor's first dichotomy is between God as the absolute Author/Creator/Master of ontotheology and the God incarnate of a/theology inscribed in writing which errs in an unending play of interpretations that marks the death of God in an eternal kenosis.[77] Other options which he overlooks include God as the ever-responsive and ever-sensitive companion of much process theology and as the sensitive nature within nature of Bernard Meland. Such a god would not be the absolute, isolated Master but would also not be marked by unfettered play, since the past character of God would provide a stable factor in the ongoing divine life. (This is William Dean's point in *History Making History*.[78]) For our purposes we may add that Taylor also overlooks the possibility of a religious naturalism such as that of John Dewey, Henry Nelson Wieman, Mordecai Kaplan, or Samuel Alexander. And of course, he did not envision the type of religious naturalism represented by the minimalism developed in this book.

Taylor's second dichotomy is between the sovereign self in the image of the self-identical, self-conscious, absolute God as Master and the notion of the self as an erratic trace, a generous communicant, able to take delight without possessiveness.[79] However, Taylor overlooks the variety of process-relational views of selfhood already developed, from Mead to Neville, which can do much of what he is groping for.[80]

Taylor's third dichotomy is between history as a linear, logocentric, imaginative construction on the one hand, an attempt to deny death and overcome the despair of the unhappy conscience over the opposition between "reality" and "ideality" and on the other hand history as an endless erring, willing to affirm the real and breaking the power of the ideal, a purposeless erring which breaks the psychology of mastery and the economy of domination by spending generously. Erring is beyond good and evil, affirming the stance of carnival.[81] Again, Taylor overlooks the historicism of Dean and others rooted in the early Chicago School which offers a non-logocentric of view of history, recognizes the presence of interpretation in the construction of history, affirms a developing purpose, recognizes the reality of evil, having appropriate generosity, with changing and relative but real convictions about good and evil, and with community, not carnival, as its basic social metaphor.[82]

Taylor's fourth dichotomy appears in his theory of meaning. Taylor rejects "the book" as an ordered, logocentric totality, the author of which limits the proliferation of meanings, and truth as unified, singular, simple and abiding. The alternative is "writing" as incessant erring, forever vague, without a foundation to anchor its proper meaning. Interpretation does not discover the correct meaning, but forever produces new ones.[83] Once again there is at least one major view which Taylor ignores. The pragmatic view sees meaning as plural but not infinite, the process of inquiry not as erring but as developing criteria of adequacy without needing secure foundations, and interpretation as productive yet constrained by past links in the chain of interpretations.[84] Related to the pragmatic is a radical empiricist use of sensitive discernment which also takes us beyond the dichotomy of objectivity and subjectivity, offering another option in addition to Taylor's alternative of a correct meaning anchored in a logocentric foundationalism and an infinite play of meanings. The conclusions of such inquiry will have neither apodictic certainty nor be infinite erring, but rather tentative and minimal convictions, provisional and yet truths seen clearly enough and held strongly enough to live and to die by.

The overall difficulty I have with Taylor is that he ignores most of the viable options in present-day religious thinking. He dismisses a traditional view of God, with which many of us have problems anyway, identifies this with both rationality and suppression, and then goes on to the opposite extreme of apparent irrationality and arbitrariness. Both poles of this dichotomy are unattractive. Taylor neglects a whole range of options, including religious naturalism. It is precisely religious naturalism, it is argued in this book, that can support the relative adequacy of cautious inquiry and a life-style of structured freedom.

One more point can be made about Taylor. He defangs any prophetic protest. Using Hegel's notion of the unhappy consciousness, he sees ideals as causing estrangement.

> The perceived estrangement of 'reality' and 'ideality' creates the suffering of the historical agent. . . . The unhappy subject is forced to acknowledge the undeniable transcendence of the 'ought'. Insofar as history is suspended between 'is' and 'ought', it *falls* within the domain of the law.[85]

In particular, he affirms that axiological transcendence results in perpetual discontent and furthermore is a sign of a hatred of all that perishes.

> The quest for truth represents a futile effort to escape the world of appearances and to discover (or uncover) the fugitive transcendental signified. In spite of protests to the contrary, this pursuit is never disinterested. 'The will to truth' simultaneously expresses 'hatred for all that perishes, changes, varies' and gives voice to a longing 'for a world of the constant'.[86]

This is to accept Nietzche's view too uncritically. A will to truth is not necessarily a hatred of the perishing. It is a longing to understand the perishing, the changing, and the varying in order to understand and perhaps to love them more adequately and more fully. The will to truth need not be Nietzsche's image of Platonic transcendence of the finite. It can be rather a love of the perishing, changing, and varying which seeks to transcend, not the finite, but our erroneous understandings of it.

Here again, for Taylor it seems that you either love everything or hate everything. But are there not some things worth transforming? Are ignorance, prejudice, disease, and hatred worth contending with? While being this-worldly, must we wallow in everything? To love the finite does not mean to accept it without change. That way lie the worst excesses of Hindu civilization, as Aurobindo clearly saw.[87] If suppression needs to be removed, as Taylor thinks, then that is one thing that is unacceptable. Therefore we cannot simply accept the finite. Let us grant that there has been much suppression, including suppression by nice Christians or by nice liberal people. The cure, however, is not to accept anything. Between toleration of everything, including evil, and the rejection of all things except one's parochial notions, there lies a vast range of options where we must exercise responsible decisions.

Having removed a sense of the transcendent, Taylor wishes to affirm the finite.

> While the affirmation of the perfection of the end entails the denial of everything that falls short of the *telos,* the denial of the completion of the end opens the possibility of affirming what previously had seemed inadequate and insufficient.[88]

> When desire forsakes the prospect of complete satisfaction, it opens the possibility of delight.

> Delight is the inversion of satisfaction. Satisfaction is possessive—to seek satisfaction is to strive for the fulfillment that seems to result from the appropriation of otherness. Delight, by contrast, is non-possessive. . . . In delight, one does not seek to master, does not cultivate the useful, and does not long to consume.[89]

Minimalism surely agrees in loving the cherry blossoms without possessiveness. But such delight must join with a determined struggle. The Bhagavad Gita was close to the truth. We must struggle for the right and good as we understand our duty, without absolutizing our understandings. We must at the same time learn to renounce our possessiveness. What I find lacking in Taylor is any sense of struggle, any sense of standards, even non-absolute standards.[90]

Conclusion: A Secularity of Openness

There are two types of secular existence: the self-assured and the alienated. Having lost a transcendent source of meaning, the secular world tends either to absolutize one partial source of meaning or else finds no meaning at all. And having lost a transcendent source of judgment, secularity has no perspective from which to criticize its attachment to relative meanings. Having lost its Archimedean point, the secular world tends to be caught between a self-satisfaction tending towards fanaticism and an alienation tending towards despair. In short, secularity is in a state of closure to transcendent sources of criticism and renewal.

The recovery of openness to situational transcendence and continuing challenge within the secular could clear the way for the rehumanization of our existence by resources of criticism and renewal. A perspective of continuing criticism helps to avoid idolatry. A situationally transcendent source of healing helps to avoid meaninglessness. Their recovery would give rise to the secularity of openness.

Openness is the recognition and reception of continuing criticism and situationally transcendent renewal. It includes appreciation for past benefit, receptivity to present succor, and hope for future resource. It includes an awareness of one's shortcomings and a commitment to one's responsibilities. Openness to extraordinary processes of judgment and renewal would pave the way for these forces to work more fruitfully. Expectancy and receptivity to untapped resources and unrecognized demands is the antidote to complacency and cynicism. These processes are a jolt to self-assured secularity and reconciliation to alienated secular existence.

In situational transcendence the source of experienced support and demand comes from outside of the perceived situation of the self. It is unexpected and superior in power, worth, and claim to any resource or demand perceived from within the situation.

Moments of defeat can bring despair and moments of triumph can bring complacency. Both of these types of extremity can be met with openness to transcendence. Despair can be met with hope, an outlook of expectancy for situationally transcendent resources. Complacency can be answered with an awareness of larger obligations.

The experience of transcendence can also bring courage in the midst of the awareness of finitude. Otherwise the radical contingency of existence can be ignored, leading to existential shallowness, or can be faced with despair or with an aggressive clutching at life. The courage to overcome the anxiety of finitude, to accept the stubborn givenness of existence and the relative and ultimate threats to this existence, comes from an attitude of openness to transcendence, an attitude which accepts the givenness of life with gratitude, as a gift and an opportunity.

Finally, action in situations of crisis is fraught with risk. Openness to situationally transcendent resources of courage can yield the courage to act in the opportune moment.

In continuing challenge the beckoning standard differs from conventionally accepted norms. The continuing demand lies in the goal and in the need for discipline or self-correction. Such continuing challenge is especially needed in inquiry after truth, in the creation of beauty, in the pursuit of authentic humanity in our moral life, and in the struggle for the realization of social values.

Openness to continuing challenge is the personal or cultural attitude which responds to such continuing challenge. Openness to continuing challenge means an openness to continual criticism, including criticism of one's own achievements, values, and hopes. It is a self-critical attitude, an attitude which refuses to remain satisfied with any concrete achievement. It wrestles against all idolatries, including those of one's own self and people.

Openness to continuing challenge embodies the principle of permanent self-correction, the perpetual questioning of the attained fruit of the pursuit of meaning, together with the belief that significant attainment is possible. It is an attitude which criticizes both establishment and protest and which hunts for resources and renewal in both the new and the traditional. This is an attitude which can be committed to a cause without being fanatical, can be loyal and yet critical. It is a lure to the pursuit of meaning and a prod against complacent self-satisfaction when any meaning has been attained. It is receptive to the continually challenging transcendent, which is an unattainable but ever-attracting goal.

Openness to continuous challenge in the search for value is an alternative to the fanatic assumption that the absolute has been achieved and the cynical assumption that the search is fruitless. As such it is a hallmark of a life of openness.

Who is sufficient for a life of openness to transcendent resources and continuing challenge? No one can presume. We can, however, walk in the hope that these resources will sensitize and strengthen us yet more.

NOTES

Introduction

1. Paul Tillich, *Theology of Culture* (New York: Oxford University Press, 1959), p. 43; Paul Tillich, *The Religious Situation,* trans. by H. Richard Niebuhr (New York: Meridian Books, Inc., 1932), pp. 42–48; Paul Tillich, *The Courage to Be* (New Haven: Yale University Press, 1952), pp. 139–142.

2. William Butler Yeats, "The Second Coming," A. J. M. Smith, *Seven Centuries of Verse: English and American* (New York: Charles Scribner's Sons, 1947), p. 531. Langdon Gilkey has given a penetrating analysis of the secular mood. I would place three of Gilkey's characteristics of the secular mood, contingency, relativity, and temporality, into the alienated type in their more negative forms of loss of purpose, determinism, and transience. His fourth mark, autonomy, would fit into the self-assured type. Cp. Langdon Gilkey, *Naming the Whirlwind: The Renewal of God-Language* (Indianapolis: The Bobbs-Merrill Company, 1969), p. 47.

3. H. Richard Niebuhr, *Radical Monotheism and Western Culture* (New York: Harper & Brothers, Publishers, 1960), pp. 49–63; Paul Tillich, *Systematic Theology,* I (Chicago: The University of Chicago Press, 1951), pp. 84–85.

4. A major difference between myself and Langdon Gilkey is that I attempt to use religious language to uncover secular experiences of transcendence, while Gilkey is concerned to uncover secular experiences of transcendence in order to renew religious language. See Gilkey, *Naming the Whirlwind,* Part II and his *Religion and the Scientific Future: Reflections on Myth, Science, and Theology* (New York: Harper & Row, Publishers, 1970), pp. 35–64.

5. Henry Nelson Wieman, *Religious Experience and Scientific Method* (New York: The Macmillan Company, 1926), pp. 9–10.

Chapter One. A Model of Divine Immanence

1. For Santayana's distinction between piety and spirituality, see George Santayana, *The Life of Reason: or The Phases of Human Progress,* revised one-volume edition with Daniel Cory (New York: Charles Scribner's Sons, 1953), pp. 258, 264. I am indebted to Marvin Shaw for pointing out the parallel with Santayana.

2. Bernard M. Loomer, "Empirical Theology within Process Thought," in Bernard E. Meland, *The Future of Empirical Theology* (Chicago: The University of Chicago, Press, 1969), p. 151.

3. Whether our minimal model would satisfy John Cobb's formal definition of God as "a unitary actuality supremely worthy of worship and commitment" depends on how "unitary" and "supremely worthy" are interpreted. I think it could satisfy this definition, although the two crucial terms are stretched close to their reasonable limits. John B. Cobb, Jr., *God and the World* (Philadelphia: The Westminster Press, 1969), p. 20. A previous version of this minimalist model was published as "A Minimal Model of Transcendence" in the *American Journal of Theology and Philosophy,* Vol. 8, No. 3 (September, 1987), pp. 121–135.

4. Bernard Loomer, *The Size of God: The Theology of Bernard Loomer in Context,* ed. by William Dean and Larry Axel (Macon, GA: Mercer University Press, 1987), pp. 41–42; Bernard M. Loomer, "The Size of God," *American Journal of Theology and Philosophy,* Vol. 8, Nos. 1 & 2, Jan. & May, 1987, pp. 41–42.

5. J. Harley Chapman, *Jung's Three Theories of Religious Experience* (Lewiston: The Edwin Mellen Press, 1988), pp. 85, 88–89, 125).

6. See Martin Buber's criticism of Tillich's attempted substitutes for the word "God" as an "abstract facade" and Tillich's own appreciation of this criticism. F. Forrester Church: *The Essential Tillich: An Anthology of the Writings of Paul Tillich* (New York: Macmillan Publishing Company, 1987), p. 229.

7. H. Richard Niebuhr, *Radical Monotheism and Western Culture: with Supplementary Essays* (New York: Harper & Brothers, Publishers, 1960), pp. 16–18.

8. Rudolf Otto, *The Idea of the Holy: An Inquiry into the Non-rational Factor in the Idea of the Divine and its Relation to the Rational,* trans. by John W. Harvey (New York: Oxford University Press, 1958), pp. 12–40; Herbert H. Farmer, *Revelation and Religion: Studies in the Theological Interpretation of Religious Types* (London: Nisbet & Co. Ltd., 1954), pp. 60–65, 79; H. Richard Niebuhr, *Radical Monotheism and Western Culture,* pp. 16–23.

9. William James, *The Varieties of Religious Experience* (New York: Collier Books, 1961), p. 377.

10. Ibid., p. 390.

11. John E. Smith, "The Structure of Religion," *Religious Studies*, I, No. 1 (October 1965), pp. 63–73; cp. *Experience and God* (New York: Oxford University Press, 1968), pp. 164–167; Josiah Royce, *The Problem of Christianity*, Vol. I (New York: The Macmillan Company, 1913), p. 44; William James, *A Pluralistic Universe* (London: Longmans, Green and Co., 1942), pp. 303–305.

12. T. Patrick Burke, *The Fragile Universe: An Essay in the Philosophy of Religions* (New York: Barnes & Noble, 1979), p. 48; Frederick J. Streng, *Understanding Religious Man*, (Belmont, CA: Dickenson Publishing Company, Inc., 1969), p. 4.

13. J. Harley Chapman, *Jung's Three Theories of Religious Experience*, p. 145; Robert C. Neville, *God the Creator: On the Transcendence and Presence of God* (Chicago: The University of Chicago Press, 1968). As Whitehead put it, "philosophy . . . cannot be proved." *Modes of Thought* (New York: The Macmillan Company, 1938), p. 67. Stephen Pepper's way of stating this is that a World Hypothesis cannot be proved true, since the World Hypothesis itself determines the procedure of affirming truth. Stephen C. Pepper, *World Hypotheses: A Study in Evidence* (Berkeley University of California Press, 1961), pp. 342–347. Herbert Feigl made a distinction between validation and vindication. An assertion can be validated in terms of criteria of knowledge, but these criteria themselves cannot be validated, but only vindicated. Herbert Feigl, "Validation and Vindication: An Analysis of the Nature and Limits of Ethical Arguments," in *Readings in Ethical Theory*, ed. by Wilfred Sellers and John Hospers (New York: Appleton-Century Crofts, Inc., 1952), p. 674. Probably our sense that a philosophy cannot be proven has been strengthened by our sense of the history of philosophy. According to Dilthey, "the coming of an historical awareness . . . destroys forever the belief in the absolute validity of any one philosophy." Wilhelm Dilthey, *Dilthey's Philosophy of Existence: Introduction to Weltanschauungslehre*, trans. by William Kluback and Martin Weinbaum (New York: Bookman Associates, 1957), p. 20. Cp. p. 30. What I wish to suggest is that while a philosophy, specifically an ontological position cannot be proved, a case can be made for it.

14. Douglas Clyde Macintosh, *Theology as an Empirical Science* (New York: The Macmillan Company, 1919), pp. 162, 201. Cp. pp. 140, 177, 181. See also his discussion of God's aseity and his assertion that "God can adequately control the universe."

15. Henry Nelson Wieman, *The Source of Human Good*, (Carbondale: Southern Illinois University Press, 1946), pp. 65, 79.

16. Among other places, see Charles Hartshorne, *The Logic of Perfection and Other Essays in Neo-classical Metaphysics* (LaSalle, IL.: Open Court Publishing Company, 1962), pp. 41, 50–51, 70–73.

17. Thomas Aquinas, *Introduction to Saint Thomas Aquinas,* edited by Anton C. Pegis (New York: The Modern Library, 1948), pp. 25–26.

18. Josiah Royce, *The Religious Aspect of Philosophy: A Critique of the Bases of Conduct and of Faith* (New York: Harper & Brothers, Publishers, 1885), chapter 11, esp. pp. 423, 427, 431–433. Kant employs a moral version of this "necessary presupposition argument." The concept of God functions in this argument as a guarantee of the unity between happiness and morality. Now, assuming the need for such a unity (which is open to question), this unity can be affirmed without postulating a cause of this unity and calling it "God." Immanuel Kant, *Critique of Practical Reason,* trans. by Lewis White Beck (New York: The Liberal Arts Press, 1956), p. 129. Tillich uses a variation of this argument. For Tillich, God is the presupposition of the question of God. As the unconditioned element in all of man's spiritual functions, God is the necessary presupposition of knowledge, morality, and all of man's search for meaning. However, as I try to make clear elsewhere, what Tillich refers to as the unconditional element in the search for meaning can be thought of without reference to God or to a ground of being simply by postulating the meaningfulness of the pursuit of meaning and the possibility of approximating closer to its goal. The goal is, in Kantian terms, a regulative rather than a constitutive idea. Paul Tillich, *Systematic Theology,* Vol. I (Chicago: The University of Chicago Press, 1951), pp. 204–210; *The Theology of Culture* (New York: Oxford University Press, 1959), pp. 22–25.

19. Frederich Schleiermacher, *On Religion: Speeches to its Cultured Despisers,* trans. by John Oman (New York: Harper & Brothers, Publishers, 1958), p. 36; *The Christian Faith,* ed. and trans. by H. R. Mackintosh and J. S. Stewart (Edinburgh: T. & T. Clark, 1928), pp. 5, 12.

20. Tillich, *The Theology of Culture,* p. 23.

21. This idea of a concept unifying reason but at its boundary derives from Kant. For a discussion of God as the Ideal of Pure Reason and the idea of a First Cause and its denial as an antinomy of reason see his *Critique of Pure Reason,* trans. by Norman Kemp Smith (London: Macmillan & Co., Ltd., 1958), pp. 315–327, 396–402, 485–531. For the regulative employment of Ideas, see pp. 532–549. Toulmin's concept of a limiting concept is also at work here. Stephen Edelston Toulmin, *An Examination of the Place of Reason in Ethics* (Cambridge: Cambridge University Press, 1960), pp. 202–221.

22. William James comes close to Pascal by asserting that: "Our passional nature not only lawfully may, but must, decide an option between

propositions, whenever it is a genuine option that cannot by its nature be decided on intellectual grounds." William James, *The Will To Believe and Other Essays in Popular Philosophy* (New York: Dover Publications, Inc., 1956), p. 11. I suggest that this approach is lacking in intellectual integrity and could easily set a pattern for thinking in other areas where it could prove very dangerous. Our proneness to wish-fulfillment needs no encouragement.

23. I am indebted to Bernard Meland's discussion of occasions of awareness of spirit in moments of extremity. Meland's notion of the transcendent differs, of course, from the minimalist position articulated here, but his analysis of the experience of renewal is helpful. Cp. Bernard Meland, *Realities of Faith*, (New York: Oxford University Press, 1962), pp. 223–227, 230, 235, 241–242; *Higher Education and the Human Spirit* (Chicago: The University of Chicago Press, 1953), pp. 162–165, 180; *Faith and Culture*, pp. 171–173, 181; Marvin C. Shaw, *The Paradox of Intention: Reaching the Goal by Giving Up the Attempt to Reach It*, (Atlanta: Scholars Press, 1988), esp. chapters 1, 10, 11, 12.

24. Meland, *Realities of Faith*, p. 235.

25. Bernard Meland, *Faith and Culture*, (London: George Allen and Unwin, Ltd., 1955), pp. 168–169.

26. Meland, *Realities of Faith*, p. 235; cp. pp. 235–236.

27. Meland, *Higher Education and the Human Spirit*, p. 180.

28. Albert Camus, *The Myth of Sisyphus and other Essays*, trans. by Justin O'Brien (New York: Random House, Inc., 1955), pp. 9–12. I have been profoundly influenced by Tillich's treatment of anxiety and finitude. Cp. Paul Tillich, *The Courage to Be*, (New Haven: Yale University Press, 1952), pp. 175–176; *Love, Power and Justice: Ontological Analyses and Ethical Applications* (New York: Oxford University Press, 1954), pp. 39, 110–111.

29. H. Richard Niebuhr, *The Responsible Self: An Essay in Christian Moral Philosophy*, (New York: Harper & Row, Publishers, 1963), pp. 109–126.

30. Ibid., p. 112.

31. A complete discussion of this topic would involve the distinction between pathological and ontological anxiety somewhat after the fashion of Paul Tillich. Martin Heidegger, *Being and Time*, trans. by John Macquarrie and Edward Robinson, (New York: Harper & Brothers, 1962), pp. 296–299, 352–358, 396–400.

32. Paul Tillich, *Systematic Theology*, III, (Chicago: The University of Chicago, 1963), pp. 262–265.

33. Immanuel Kant, *Critique of Pure Reason,* trans. by Norman Kemp Smith (London: Macmillan and Co., Ltd., 1958), pp. 532–549.

Chapter Two. *Historical Context*

1. David Hume, *Dialogues Concerning Natural Religion,* in *The English Philosophers from Bacon to Mill,* ed. by Edwin A. Burtt (New York: The Modern Library, 1939), p. 718.

2. Hume, p. 720.

3. Hume, p. 727.

4. Hume, p. 745.

5. John Stuart Mill, *Three Essays on Religion* (New York: AMS Press, Inc., 1874, 1970), pp. 125–257.

6. Mill, p. 176.

7. Mill, p. 181.

8. Mill, p. 192.

9. Mill, p. 194.

10. Mill, pp. 186–187.

11. Mill, pp. 194–195.

12. Mill, pp. 128–129.

13. Mill, pp. 174–175.

14. William James, *A Pluralistic Universe* (London: Longmans, Green and Co., 1942), pp. 309–310.

15. Ibid., p. 315.

16. Ibid., p. 292.

17. Ibid., p. 309. See Bernard Meland, *The Realities of Faith: The Revolution in Cultural Forms* (New York: Oxford University Press, 1962), p. 183.

18. James, *A Pluralistic Universe,* p. 310–311.

19. James, *Varieties of Religious Experience,* p. 407.

20. James, *A Pluralistic Universe,* p. 311.

21. Ibid., p. 321; cp. pp. 322–325.

22. Ibid., p. 318.

23. Ibid., p. 329.

24. Alfred North Whitehead, *Modes of Thought*, (New York: The Macmillan Company, 1938), chap. 6.

25. Alfred North Whitehead, *Process and Reality*, ed. by David Ray Griffin and Donald W. Sherburne (New York: The Free Press, 1979), pp. 4, 13.

26. William Dean, *American Religious Empiricism* (Albany: State University of New York Press, 1986), chapter 1; Nancy Frankenberry, *Religion and Radical Empiricism* (Albany: State University of New York Press, 1987), pp. 89–93, 130–133; Bernard Meland, *Faith and Culture* (London: George Allen and Unwin, Ltd., 1955), pp. 115, 118–119; Bernard Meland, *Higher Education and the Human Spirit* (Chicago: The University of Chicago Press, 1953), pp. 62–63; Bernard Meland, *Realities of Faith* (New York: Oxford University Press, 1962), pp. 93–94, 122, 162; Bernard Meland, "The Structure of Christian Faith," *Religion in Life*, Vol. XXXVII, No. 4, Winter 1968, pp. 560–561.

27. Charles Hartshorne, *The Logic of Perfection and Other Essays in Neoclassical Metaphysics* (LaSalle, IL: Open Court Publishing Company, 1962), pp. 4–5.

28. Bernard Meland, "Analogy and Myth in Postliberal Theology," *Process Philosophy and Christian Thought*, edited by Delwin Brown et al. (Indianapolis: The Bobbs-Merrill Company, Inc., 1971), p. 162.

29. Shailer Mathews, *The Growth of the Idea of God* (New York: The Macmillan Company, 1931), p. 226.

30. Clark Williamson has been very critical of the easy alliance between modernism and middle-class, liberal values. See his contribution to *Mainstream Protestantism: Disciples Relation to American Culture 1880–1989*, edited by D. Newell Williams (Grand Rapids: William D. Eerdmans Publishers, 1991).

31. Edward S. Ames, *Religion* (New York: Henry Holt and Company, Inc., 1929), pp. 154, 157.

32. Ibid., p. 178.

33. Ibid., p. 180.

34. Ibid., pp. 180–181.

35. Gerald Birney Smith, "Is Theism Essential to Religion?," *The Journal of Religion*, Vol. V, No. 4 (1925), pp. 356–377. In this book I have appropriated the mature Smith. For a more balanced account of Smith drawing on a wide variety of sources, see Creighton Peden's excellent study,

The Chicago School: Voices in Liberal Religious Thought (Bristol, IN: Wyndham Hall Press, 1987), pp. 44–56.

36. Bernard Eugene Meland, *The Realities of Faith: The Revolution in Cultural Forms* (New York: Oxford University Press, 1962), p. 93.

37. Ibid., 64, 97, 100, 107, 114–115, 163, 207; Bernard Eugene Meland, *The Secularization of Modern Cultures* (New York: Oxford University Press, 1966), pp. 48, 69, 117, 137, 160.

38. Meland, *The Realities of Faith*, pp. 163–164. Cp. 116, 122, 351.

39. Alfred North Whitehead, *Process and Reality: An Essay in Cosmology* (New York: The Macmillan Company, 1929), p. 6. This quotation is from the earlier edition of *Process and Reality* used by Meland in *The Realities of Faith*, p. 158. Cp. Meland, *Higher Education and the Human Spirit*, p. 97; Bernard Meland, *Seeds of Redemption* (New York: The Macmillan Company, 1947), pp. 155–162.

40. Meland, *The Realities of Faith*, p. 159. Cp. p. 162.

41. Bernard Meland, *Faith and Culture* (London: George Allen and Unwin, Ltd., 1955), p. 195.

42. Alfred North Whitehead, *Dialogues of Alfred North Whitehead*, ed. by Lucian Price (Mentor Books, 1956), p. 277, quoted in Meland, *The Realities of Faith*, pp. 145–146.

43. Bernard E. Meland, *Fallible Forms and Symbols: Discourses of Method in a Theology of Culture* (Philadelphia: Fortress Press, 1976), pp. 21–58; William Dean, *American Religious Empiricism*, pp. 15–17. Of the recent essays by Bernard Meland, the essays in Parts II and III are very suggestive for the approach used in this philosophy. See Bernard Eugene Meland, *Essays in Constructive Theology: A Process Perspective*, ed. by Perry LeFevre (Chicago: Exploration Press, 1988), pp. 59–208. I am omitting all reference to the comments of Meland on the Dewey-Wieman debate on the issue of the unity/plurality of the divine and to Meland's own early contribution to this issue. For Meland's contribution to the Dewey-Wieman debate, see Bernard E. Meland, "Is God Many or One?," *The Christian Century*, L (May 31, 1933), pp. 725–726; Bernard E. Meland, "Toward a Valid View of God," *Harvard Theological Review*, 24 (1931), pp. 549–557.

44. Douglas Clyde Macintosh, *Theology as an Empirical Science* (New York: The Macmillan Company, 1919), pp. 41, 44.

45. Ibid., p. 161.

46. Ibid., pp. 180, 182, 184.

47. Edgar Sheffield Brightman, *The Problem of God* (New York: The Abingdon Press, 1930, pp. 183, 189, 192.) See also Edgar Sheffield Brightman, *A Philosophy of Religion* (New York: Prentice-Hall, Inc., 1940), pp. 286–341.

48. Ibid., p. 181. As a matter of autobiography I am not sure how much I owe to Brightman. Musings on Brightman did reinforce my own line of thought that a finite God might be a fruitful concept to pursue. Like Brightman I also drew inspiration from William James, John Stuart Mill, and, in a paradoxical sense, from Kant's treatment of the teleological proof. The Minimal Model is, of course, far more radical than Brightman's limited deity. I did not study Brightman in any detail until the mid-1970s.

49. Ibid., p. 113.

50. Ibid., pp. 116, 118.

51. Ibid., p. 184.

52. Ibid., p. 189, 193. Cp. pp. 188–189.

53. Ibid., p. 191.

54. Ibid., p. 137.

55. Philip Henry Phenix, *Intelligible Religion* (New York: Harper & Brothers, 1954), pp. 81–83, 89.

56. Ibid., p. 37.

57. Ibid., pp. 87–88.

58. Ibid., pp. 99–100.

59. Phenix, *Intelligible Religion*, pp. 103–109; Shailer Mathews in *Religious Life*, ed. by E. Sapir, Vol. 11 of *Man and his World*, ed. by Baker Brownell (New York: D. Van Nostrand Company, Inc., 1929), p. 54.

60. Immanuel Kant, *Critique of Pure Reason*, trans. by Norman Kemp Smith, (London: Macmillan & Co., Ltd., 1958), pp. 315–327, 396–402, 485–531 for a discussion of God as the Ideal of Pure Reason and the Antinomy of the idea of a first cause.

61. Immanuel Kant, *Critique of Practical Reason*, trans. by Lewis White Beck (New York: The Liberal Arts Press, 1956), p. 129.

62. The ontological restraint advocated in this book allows for the possibility of hope in life after death. Otherwise we claim to know too much. However, such a hope is not a major directive of life nor a pragmatically significant belief. We cannot accept James' right to believe, although I can hear Bernard Meland over my shoulder urging caution against the apparent certainty of my reticence.

63. Bernard Meland, *Faith and Culture*, pp. 28–33.

64. Kant, *Critique of Pure Reason*, pp. 532–549.

65. Paul Ricoeur, *The Conflict of Interpretations: Essays in Hermeneutics*, ed. by Don Ihde (Evanston: Northwestern University Press, 1974).

66. Paul Ricoeur, "Biblical Hermeneutics" in *Semeia: An Experimental Journal for Biblical Criticism*, IV (1975); Paul Ricoeur, *Essays on Biblical Interpretation*, ed. by Lewis S. Mudge (Philadelphia: Fortress Press, 1980); Paul Ricoeur, "Listening to the Parables of Jesus," in *The Philosophy of Paul Ricoeur: An Anthology of his Work*, ed. by Charles E. Reagan and David Stewart (Boston: Beacon Press, 1978), Paul Ricoeur, *The Symbolism of Evil*, trans. by Emerson Buchanan (Boston: Beacon Press, 1967).

67. Don Ihde, "Editor's Introduction," in Paul Ricoeur, *The Conflict of Interpretations*, p. xx; Paul Ricoeur, *The Symbolism of Evil*, p. 351.

68. Paul Ricoeur, *The Conflict of Interpretations*, pp. 412, 440.

69. Don Ihde speaks of faith being displaced by hope (ibid. p. xx), but perhaps it is religious faith or precritical faith that is displaced, whereas in "Religion, Atheism, and Faith" Ricoeur is referring to postcritical faith.

70. Ibid., pp. 417, 421. For the hope of resurrection, see p. 420.

71. Ibid., p. 415.

72. Ibid., pp. 441, 442.

73. Ibid., p. 445.

74. Ibid., pp. 447, 455, 458-459.

75. Ibid., pp. 409–411.

76. Ibid., pp. 374–375, 410–411.

77. For Ricoeur on Kant and Hegel, see ibid., pp. 412–414; for philosophy and tradition, p. 403 and for the pathology of hope, pp. 418–423.

78. Paul Tillich, *My Search for Absolutes* (New York: Simon and Schuster, 1967), p. 82.

79. Paul Tillich, *The Interpretation of History*, trans. by N. A. Rasetzki and Elsa L. Talmey (New York: Charles Scribner's Sons, 1936), pp. 221–224 and *The Protestant Era*, trans. by James Luther Adams (Chicago: The University of Chicago Press, 1948), p. 76.

80. Paul Tillich, *The System of the Sciences*, pp. 154–155, 183.

81. In his earliest writings Tillich spoke of the unconditional element in culture as the Import which was the ground and abyss of the Form of the act of meaning. This dialectic of Import and Form is similar to the distinction between the unconditional element in the act of meaning and the object or aim of the act of meaning. This gives rise to the distinction between autonomy and theonomy. What the later discussion adds is the notion of

the interaction between subject and object in the cultural acts. Cp. "The Philosophy of Religion," pp. 56–62 and "On the Idea of a Theology of Culture," pp. 163–168, in Paul Tillich, *What is Religion?*, trans. by James Luther Adams *et al.* (New York: Harper & Row, Publishers), 1969.

82. Tillich sometimes uses a different division of the practical into law (*das Recht*) and community (*die Gemeinschaft*), based on a distinction between form and content (*formbestimmte und gehaltbestimmte Funktions*) or between the organizational and organic functions (*The Systems of the Sciences*, p. 158; *Systematic Theology*, I, pp. 72, 92). Since in his early *On the Idea of a Theology of Culture*, the community of love and the state are both discussed after individual ethics, and since in *Systematic Theology*, Volume III, Tillich discusses law under the communal realm, I take the distinction between the individual and the communal to be more basic, the more so since it is the classification which Tillich uses in his most extended discussion of the Unconditional as ground and aim of the functions of culture. Paul Tillich, *Systematic Theology*, III, (Chicago: The University of Chicago Press), 1963, pp. 262–265; *What is Religion?*, pp. 171–177.

83. Tillich, *Systematic Theology*, III, pp. 64–65, 67.

84. Tillich, *My Search for Absolutes*, pp. 126–127.

85. See Schubert M. Ogden, *The Reality of God and Other Essays* (New York: Harper and Row, Publishers, 1966), p. 140. Cf. pp. 34–43, 123–142; Josiah Royce, *The Religious Aspect of Philosophy: A Critique of the Bases of Conduct and of Faith* (New York: Harper & Brothers, Publishers, 1885), Chapter XI; *The Philosophy of Loyalty* (New York: The Macmillan Company, 1908), pp. 118–119, 313–314; *The Problem of Christianity*, Vol. I (New York: The Macmillan Company, 1913), I:96–106; IV: ii–iv); Charles Hartshorne, *The Logic of Perfection and other Essays In Neo-classical Metaphysics*, (LaSalle, IL: Open Court Publishing Company, 1962), p. 297; *A Natural Theology for Our Time* (LaSalle, IL: Open Court Publishing Co., 1967), pp. 45–46. Bernard J. F. Lonergan, *Insight: A Study of Human Understanding* (New York: Harper & Row, Publishers, 1958), pp. 319–431; Emerich Coreth, *Metaphysics*, trans. by Joseph Donceel (New York: Herder and Herder, 1968), pp. 22–41; Charles E. Winquist, *The Communion of Possibility* (Chico, CA: New Horizons Press, 1975), pp. 33–46. Cf. also Jerome A. Stone, "A Minimal Model of Transcendence," *American Journal of Theology and Philosophy*, Vol. 8, No. 3, (1987), pp. 132–133. For my criticism of Hartshorne and Ogden, see chapter Five.

Chapter Three. The Ethics of Openness

1. Paul Edwards, *The Logic of Moral Discourse* (Glencoe, IL.: The Free Press of Glencoe, 1955), pp. 105–120; Michael Polanyi, *Personal Knowledge:*

Towards a Post-Critical Philosophy (Chicago: The University of Chicago Press, 1958), chs. 8 and 10. An ethical study making "appreciation" a key category has just appeared, too recently to incorporate into this study. See Holmes Rolston, III, *Environmental Ethics: Duties and Values in the Natural World* (Philadelphia: Temple University Press, 1988). For Maguire see Daniel Maguire, *The Moral Choice* (New York: Winston Press, 1979), pp. 72–73. See pp. 71–93. For Sturm, see Douglas Sturm, "Human Rights and Political Possibility: A Religious Inquiry," *Criterion*, Vol. 23, No. 1 (Winter 1989), pp. 2–8.

2. Bernard Gert, *The Moral Rules: A New Rational Foundation for Morality* (New York: Harper & Row, Publishers, 1973), chap. 3.

3. Polanyi has a similar point. Michael Polanyi, *Personal Knowledge: Towards a Post-Critical Philosophy* (Chicago: The University of Chicago Press, 1958), pp. 49–68; *The Tacit Dimension* (Gloucester, Mass.: Peter Smith, 1983), pp. 3–25.

4. There is a sense, of course, that we have a greater responsibility for those to whom we are especially related. This tension between the local and the cosmopolitan, the particular and the universal in ethics is reflected in Chinese philosophy in the debate between the Confucians, representing the dominance of the proximate, and the Mohists, representing the demand of the universal. While my comments are in the Mohist direction, a full ethical treatment needs to acknowledge the Confucian side of the dialectic.

5. H. Richard Niebuhr, *Radical Monotheism and Western Culture: with Supplementary Essays* (New York: Harper & Brothers, Publishers, 1960), pp. 24–37, 64–77.

6. Ibid., pp. 33–34.

7. Ibid., p. 32.

8. Ibid., pp. 27–28.

9. Ibid., p. 35.

10. Ibid., p. 36.

11. Ibid., p. 37.

12. For my use of this triad, see p. 21 above.

13. Niebuhr, *Radical Monotheism*, pp. 66–67.

14. H. Richard Niebuhr, *The Responsible Self: An Essay in Christian Moral Philosophy* (New York: Harper & Row, Publishers, 1963), p. 85; Niebuhr, *Radical Monotheism*, pp. 66–67. Cp. pp. 95–96.

15. Niebuhr, *Radical Monotheism*, pp. 68–77.

16. Ibid., p. 70. The quotations from Macintosh are taken from Zechariah Chafee, Jr., *Free Speech in the United States* (Cambridge: Harvard University Press, 1941), pp. 368–369.

17. *U.S. v. Macintosh*, 283 U.S. 605, October term, 1930, quoted in *Radical Monotheism*, p. 71n.

18. Niebuhr, *Radical Monotheism*, p. 72.

19. Ibid., p. 77.

20. H. Richard Niebuhr, *The Responsible Self: an Essay in Christian Moral Philosophy* (New York: Harper & Row, Publishers, 1963), pp. 85–87. George Herbert Mead points out that we can go against our community only by setting up a higher sort of community in the name of which we speak, whether it be the voice of reason or the voices of the past and future. George Herbert Mead, *Mind, Self, and Society from the Standpoint of a Social Behaviorist*, ed. by Charles W. Morris (Chicago: The University of Chicago Press, 1934), pp. 167–168.

21. Niebuhr, *Responsible Self*, pp. 86–87.

22. Ibid., pp. 87–88.

23. Mead, *Mind, Self, and Society*, p. 175.

24. H. Richard Niebuhr, "The Ego-alter Dialectic and the Conscience," *The Journal of Philosophy*, XIII (1945), pp. 352–359. Niebuhr also criticized Mead for overlooking the occasional aggressiveness or harshness of the judgment of the community upon the self. Finally, Niebuhr suggested that the self does not exist in relation to generalized others, but in relation to specific Thou's who are members of a group and whose interactions have constancies such that the self can interpret the present and anticipate future actions upon it.

25. Mead, *Mind, Self, and Society*, pp. 167–168.

26. Josiah Royce, *The Philosophy of Loyalty* (New York: The Macmillan Company, 1913), pp. 118–119.

27. Josiah Royce, *The Problem of Christianity*, Vol. I (New York: The Macmillan Company, 1913), pp. 96–106; Lecture IV: ii–lv; Royce, *The Philosophy of Loyalty*, p. 377.

28. Jonathan Edwards, *The Nature of True Virtue* (Ann Arbor: The University of Michigan Press, 1960), p. 3.

29. Edwards, *True Virtue*, pp. 18–22.

30. My notions of appropriation of a tradition have been influenced by Gadamer and Ricoeur. Hans-Georg Gadamer, *Truth and Method*, trans. by Garrett Barden and John Cumming (New York: The Seabury Press, 1975),

pp. 250,261; Hans-Georg Gadamer, *Philosophical Hermeneutics,* trans. and ed. by David E. Linge (Berkeley: University of California Press, 1976), Paul Ricoeur, *The Symbolism of Evil,* trans. by Emerson Buchanan (Boston: Beacon Press, 1967), pp. 347–357; *The Conflict of Interpretations: Essays in Hermeneutics,* ed. by Don Ihde (Evanston: Northwestern University Press, 1974), pp. 280–334, 340–345, 481–497.

31. *A Sourcebook in Indian Philosophy,* ed. by Sarvepalli Radhakrishnan and Charles A. Moore (Princeton: Princeton University Press, 1957), p. 578.

32. John S. Mbiti, *African Religions and Philosophy* (Garden City: Doubleday & Company, Inc., 1970); John V. Taylor, *The Primal Vision: Christian Presence Amid African Religion* (London: SCM Press, Ltd., 1963), pp. 93–96, 99–106, 108. Jerome A. Stone, "A View of African Culture," in *AITIA: Philosophy-Humanities Magazine,* SUNY, Farmingdale, N.Y., 1982.

33. Fung Yu-Lan, *A Short History of Chinese Philosophy,* ed. by Derk Bodde (New York: The Macmillan Company, 1948), pp. 53–55; Yi-Pao Mei, *Motse: The Neglected Rival of Confucius,* Chap. V (London: Arthur Probsthain, 1934); Motse, *The Ethical and Political Works of Motse,* trans. by Yi-Pao Mei, (London: Arthur Probsthain, 1929), chaps. xiv–xvi; Chan, Wing-Tsit, *Chu Hsi: New Studies* (Honolulu: University of Hawaii Press, 1989), pp. 282, 297–300; Homer H. Dubs, "The Development of Altruism in Confucianism," *Philosophy East and West,* Vol. I, 1951, pp. 48–55; T'oegye, Yi, *To Become a Sage: The Ten Diagrams on Sage Learning,* chap. 2, "Diagram of the Western Inscription," (New York: Columbia University Press, 1988).

34. Immanuel Kant, *Religion within the Limits of Reason Alone,* trans. by Theodore M. Greene and Hoyt H. Hudson (New York: Harper & Brothers, 1934); G. W. F. Hegel, *Lectures on the Philosophy of Religion,* Peter C. Hodgson, ed., (Berkeley: University of California Press, 1988); Friedrich W. J. Schelling, *Philosophie der Offenbarung, Schellings Werke,* 6er Band, hrsg. von Manfred Schröter (München: C. H. Beck'sche Verlagsbuchhandlung, 1927).

35. Josiah Royce, *The Problem of Christianity,* Vol. II (New York: The Macmillan Company, 1914); Wieman, *The Source of Human Good,* pp. 39–44; Henry Nelson Wieman, *Science Serving Faith,* ed. by Creighton Peden and Charles Willig (Atlanta: Scholars Press, 1987).

36. Alfred North Whitehead, *Process and Reality: an Essay in Cosmology,* corrected edition, ed. by David Ray Griffin and Donald W. Sherburne (New York: The Free Press, 1978). See *inter alia,* pp. 47, 211.

37. Paul Ricoeur, *Essays in Biblical Interpretation,* ed. by Lewis S. Mudge (Philadelphia: Fortress Press, 1980); *Interpretation Theory: Discourse and the Surplus of Meaning* (Fort Worth: The Texas Christian

University Press, 1976); *The Conflict of Intrepretations: Essays in Hermeneutics;* "Paul Ricoeur on Biblical Hermeneutics", *Semeia* Vol. 4, 1975; *The Symbolism of Evil.*

38. Gabriel Marcel, *Man Against Mass Society,* trans. by G. S. Fraser (Chicago: Henry Regnery Company, 1962), pp. 193–210, 249–255; Martin Heidegger, *Being and Time,* trans. by John Macquarrie and Edward Robinson (New York: Harper & Brothers, 1962), pp. 435–437.

39. Michael Polanyi, *Science, Faith and Society* (Chicago: University of Chicago Press, 1964), pp. 56–57.

40. Gadamer, *Truth and Method,* pp. 250, 261–262; William J. Hynes, *Shirely Jackson Case and the Chicago School: The Socio-historical Method* (Chicago: Scholars Press, 1981), pp. 57–86.

41. Royce, *Philosophy of Loyalty,* pp. 124–145.

42. See John Dewey, *Human Nature and Conduct* (Madison: United States Armed Forces Institute, 1944), pp. 210–228; *Reconstruction in Philosophy,* 2nd ed. (Boston: Beacon Press, 1948), pp. 210–211.

43. Tom L. Beauchamp and James F. Childress, *Principles of Biomedical Ethics,* 2nd ed. (New York: Oxford University Press, 1983), pp. 164–165, 322–324.

44. Douglas John Hall, *Lighten Our Darkness: Towards an Indigenous Theology of the Cross* (Philadelphia: The Westminster Press, 1976), pp. 43–59.

45. Paul Tillich, *The Courage to Be,* pp. 155–190; Paul Tillich, *Systematic Theology,* Vol. I, pp. 192–201.

46. Herbert Marcuse, *One Dimensional Man: Studies in the Ideology of Advanced Industrial Society* (Boston: Beacon Press, 1967), pp. 123–143.

47. Eric Hoffer, *The True Believer* (New York: Harper & Row, Publishers, 1966).

48. Gilkey, *Naming the Whirlwind,* pp. 305–414.

49. Ronald H. Stone, *Paul Tillich's Radical Social Thought* (Atlanta: John Knox Press, 1980); *Reinhold Niebuhr: Prophet to Politicians* (Lanham: University Press of America, 1981).

50. Meland, *Faith and Culture,* p. 179.

51. Ibid.

52. Marcuse, *One Dimensional Man,* pp. 123–143.

53. Cornel West, *Prophesy Deliverance: An Afro-American Revolutionary Christianity* (Philadelphia: The Westminster Press, 1982), pp. 134–137.

54. John Rawls, *A Theory of Justice* (Cambridge: Harvard University Press, 1971), pp. 274–280.

55. I have been helped in my understanding of liberation especially by four books: Lerone Bennett, Jr., *Confrontation Black and White* (Baltimore: Penguin Books, Inc., 1965); William E. B. DuBois, *The Autobiography of W. E. B. DuBois: A Soliloquy on Viewing My Life from the Last Decade of Its First Century* (New York: International Publishers Co., Inc., 1968); Beverly Wildung Harrison, *Making the Connections: Essays in Feminist Social Ethics* (New York: Harper & Row, 1985); Albert Memmi, *The Colonizer and the Colonized* (Boston: Beacon Press, 1967).

Chapter Four. A Generous Empiricism

1. William Dean, *American Religious Empiricism* (Albany: State University of New York Press, 1986); William Dean, *History Making History: The New Historicism in American Religious Thought* (Albany: State University of New York Press, 1988); Nancy Frankenberry, *Religion and Radical Empiricism* (Albany: State University of New York Press, 1987).

2. Richard J. Bernstein, *Beyond Objectivism and Relativism: Science, Hermeneutics, and Praxis* (Philadelphia: University of Pennsylvania Press, 1983).

3. Dean, *American Religious Empiricism*, p. 83. I have not had a chance to digest James Gustafson's notion of "moral discernment." A study of this concept will undoubtedly be very fruitful for the moral implications of radical empiricism. See James M. Gustafson, *Ethics from a Theocentric Perspective*, Vol. I, Chap. 7 (Chicago: The University of Chicago Press, 1981).

4. Vergilius Ferm, "Varieties of Naturalism," in Vergilius Ferm, ed., *History of Philosophical Systems* (Paterson: Littlefield, Adams & Co., 1965), p. 430; Arthur C. Danto, "Naturalism" in Paul Edwards, ed., *The Encyclopedia of Philosophy*, Vol. V (New York: The Macmillan Publishing Co., Inc., 1967), p. 449.

5. Larry R. Churchill, "Reviving a Distinctive Medical Ethic," *Hastings Center Report*, Vol. 19, No. 3 (May, June 1989), pp. 28–34.

6. See note one. Unfortunately I have not had a chance to dialogue seriously with two very rich recent publications which I have found stimulating and helpful, David Lee Miller's *Philosophy of Creativity* and Marvin Shaw's *The Paradox of Intention*. See David Lee Miller, *Philosophy of Creativity* (New York: Peter Lang Publishing, Inc., 1989); Marvin C. Shaw, *The Paradox of Intention: Reaching the Goal by Giving Up the Attempt to Reach It* (Atlanta: Scholars Press, 1988).

7. Pete A. Y. Gunter, ed., *Bergson and the Evolution of Physics,* (Knoxville: The University of Tennessee Press, 1969), p. 23. For a treatment of Bergson which is similar to mine in treating his "intuition" as a penetrating and open discernment, see T. E. Hulme, *Speculations: Essays on Humanism and the Philosophy of Art,* 2nd ed., ed. by Herbert Read (London: Routledge & Kegan Paul, 1936), pp. 149–160, 166.

8. Perhaps I overstated this dichotomy. Čapek claims that in *Matter and Memory* the "untenable dualism of the temporal mind and timeless matter was given up, since becoming was reinstated into the physical realm." Gunter seems to support this interpretation. Milič Čapek, *Bergson and Modern Physics: A Reinterpretation and Re-evaluation* (Dordrecht: D. Reidel Publishing Company, 1971), p. 91; Pete A. Y. Gunter, "The Heuristic Force of Creative Evolution," *Southwestern Journal of Philosophy,* Vol. I, No. 3 (Fall 1970), p. 112.

9. Henri Bergson, *Creative Evolution,* trans. by Arthur Mitchell (New York: Henry Holt and Company, 1911), p. 176.

10. Henri Bergson, *The Creative Mind,* trans. by M. L. Andison (New York: Philosophical Library, Inc., 1946), p. 77.

11. Pete A. Y. Gunter, "Bergson's Philosophical Method and its Application to the Sciences," *The Southern Journal of Philosophy,* Vol. XVI, No. 3, (1978), pp. 169, 172. See Gunter, *Bergson and the Evolution of Physics,* pp. 19–20, 25–42 for Gunter's challenge to conventional interpretations of Bergson.

12. Bergson, *The Creative Mind,* pp. 147–148; Gunter, *Bergson and the Evolution of Physics,* pp. 26–27.

13. Čapek, *Bergson and Modern Physics,* p. 87.

14. Mary Christine Morkovsky, "Crystallized Creativity—Bergson's View of Customs," *Humanitas,* Vol. 7, No. 1 (Spring 1971), p. 41; Gunter, "Bergson's Philosophical Method and its Application to the Sciences," p. 175.

15. Gerald Birney Smith, "Is Theism Essential to Religion?," *The Journal of Religion,* Vol. V, No. 4, (1925), pp. 356–377; see also Gerald B. Smith, "The Nature of Science and of Religion and their Interrelation," *Religious Education,* Vol. 23 (1927), pp. 304–310.

16. Bernard E. Meland, "Can Empirical Theology Learn Something from Phenomenology?," in *The Future of Empirical Theology,* ed. by Bernard E. Meland (Chicago: The University of Chicago Press, 1969), p. 292. Cp. Frankenberry, *Religion and Radical Empiricism,* pp. 130–133. For recently published treatments of appreciative awareness by Meland, see his *Essays in Constructive Theology: A Process Perspective,* ed. by Perry LeFevre (Chicago: Exploration Press, 1988), pp. 43, 73.

17. Bernard E. Meland, *Faith and Culture* (London: George Allen and Unwin, Ltd., 1955), p. 117.

18. Bernard E. Meland, *Higher Education and the Human Spirit* (Chicago: The University of Chicago Press, 1953), p. 63. Cp. Meland, *Faith and Culture*, pp. 115, 118–119.

19. Meland, *Higher Education and the Human Spirit*, p. 62.

20. Bernard Meland, "The Structure of Christian Faith," *Religion in Life*, Vol. XXXVII, No. 4 (Winter 1968), pp. 560–561.

21. Meland, *Higher Education and the Human Spirit*, pp. 48–49.

22. Ibid., p. 106.

23. Ibid., p. 54.

24. Ibid., pp. 67–68.

25. Bernard E. Meland, *Realities of Faith, p. 210; Faith and Culture*, pp. 43, 108; cp. "Interpreting the Christian Faith within a Philosophical Framework," *Essays in Constructive Theology*; Bernard E. Meland, "The New Realism in Religious Inquiry," *Encounter*, Vol. 31, No. 4 (Autumn 1970), p. 321; "Can Empirical Theology Learn Something from Phenomenology?," p. 303.

26. Meland, *Faith and Culture*, pp. 115, 162.

27. Meland, *Faith and Culture*, p. 129. Cp. p. 92.

28. Meland, *Higher Education and the Human Spirit*, pp. 64, 65.

29. Meland, *Faith and Culture*, p. 120.

30. Meland, *Higher Education and the Human Spirit*, p. 69, summarizing the discussion starting on p. 63.

31. Ibid., pp. 18–19.

32. Meland, *Faith and Culture*, pp. 115–117.

33. Meland, *Higher Education and the Human Spirit*, pp. 62, 63, 77, 50. Cp. p. 71.

34. Ibid., pp. 62, 72. Cp. pp. 54, 78; "Can Empirical Theology Learn Something from Phenomenology?," p. 301.

35. Meland, *Higher Education and the Human Spirit*, pp. 71–72.

36. Ibid., pp. 64, 73–75.

37. Ibid., pp. 75, 72.

38. Meland, *Faith and Culture*, p. 117.

39. Meland, *Higher Education and the Human Spirit,* p. 76.

40. Ibid., p. 16; Meland refers to the role of Bergson and James and also of cultural anthropology and the history of religions in developing his own sensitivity. Bernard E. Meland, "Interpreting the Christian Faith within a Philosophical Framework," *The Journal of Religion,* XXXIII, No. 2 (April 1953), pp. 89–90. Bergson and James both spoke of the possibility of increasing and training sensitivity. Bergson, *Creative Mind,* chapter 5; Meland, *Higher Education and the Human Spirit,* p. 16.

41. Meland, *Higher Education and the Human Spirit,* pp. 14, 79, 81–83.

42. Ibid., pp. 76, 78. For Meland's appreciation of Merleau-Ponty, see "Can Empirical Theology Learn Something from Phenomenology?," esp. pp. 299–303. Meland is very appreciative of Dorothy Emmet's distinction between the "accusative" and the "adverbial" modes of sensation or perception, with the adverbial being close to his notion of sensitive awareness. The adverbial mode is "a responsive state of the organism in *rapport* with, or receiving shocks from its environment." I believe that Meland's notion speaks more to the possibility of the nurture and critical discipline of awareness. See Dorothy M. Emmet, *The Nature of Metaphysical Thinking* (London: Macmillan & Co. Ltd., 1949), p. 61. Cp. pp. 42–43, 61–67. It has long puzzled me why Meland did not make use of, or at least discuss, Emmet's chapters on "Analogies in Religious Symbolism" and "Metaphysical Analogies."

43. Frankenberry, *Religion and Radical Empiricism* (Albany: State University of New York Press, 1987), p. ix.

44. Nancy Frankenberry, *Religion and Radical Empiricism,* p. 139. Whether Meland consistently opens the linguistic gap needs further study. I suggest that it explicitly emerges only in his later writings in *Fallible Forms and Symbols,* when he speaks more explicitly of a "primal disparity between language and reality." Bernard E. Meland, *Fallible Forms and Symbols: Discourses on Method for a Theology of Culture* (Philadelphia: Fortress Press, 1976), p. 137. Frankenberry bases her analysis on these passages. (Frankenberry, *Religion and Radical Empiricism,* pp. 136–144). For this entire discussion of the transactional nature of experience, see John Dewey, *inter alia, Democracy and Education: An Introduction to the Philosophy of Education* (New York: The Macmillan Company, 1916), pp. 92, 195–197.

45. Frankenberry, *Religion and Radical Empiricism,* p. 143.

46. William Dean, in *History Making History,* has a helpful interpretation of American historicism. I wish to affirm, as I believe Dean also does, that history is in contact with extra-historical processes, although the contact is mediated through language and tradition. Inquiry into facts can make the historian change her mind and a transactional model can better

account for such a change in mind than the view that all we have all the way down is history. Such a model also lessens the dangers of relativism.

47. For a partial list of a variety of realistic theses in current discussion in philosophy of science, see Jarrett Leplin, (ed.), *Scientific Realism* (Berkeley: University of California Press, 1984), pp. 1–2.

48. For Dewey's "transactional realism" see John Dewey, *Experience and Nature, The Later Works*, Vol. 1 (Carbondale: Southern Illinois University Press, 1988), pp. 198–199. Helpful discussions are found in Raymond D. Boisvert, *Dewey's Metaphysics* (New York: Fordham University Press, 1988), pp. 73–76, 81–87 and R. W. Sleeper, *The Necessity of Pragmatism: John Dewey's Conception of Philosophy* (New Haven: Yale University Press, 1986), pp. 23, 69–70, 91–92. See also John Herman Randall, Jr., *Nature and Historical Experience: Essays in Naturalism and in the Theory of History* (New York: Columbia University Press, 1958), pp. 278–285.

49. John Dewey, *Essays in Experimental Logic, Middle Works,* Vol. X (Carbondale: Southern Illinois University Press, 1980), p. 338.

50. Ibid., pp. 340–341.

51. Ibid., p. 329.

52. Ibid., p. 360.

53. Tom Alexander, *John Dewey's Theory of Art, Experience and Nature,* p. 109.

54. The realism developed here is quite different from the realism in philosophy of science of Hilary Putnam, Ernan McMullin, and Jarrett Leplin. The realism spoken of in anticipatory realism, especially in religious inquiry, is quite different from the "scientific realism" of these writers. See the collection of papers in Jarrett Leplin, ed., *Scientific Realism.* However, the use of the term "realism" suggests a reference to objective realities which I wish to affirm, however minimally, cautiously, and by anticipation.

55. For Rorty's discussion of the Galileo-Bellarmine dispute, see Richard Rorty, *Philosophy and the Mirror of Nature* (Princeton: Princeton University Press, 1979), pp. 328–331.

56. Development of the position sketched here would include study of critical realism and metaphor. Ernan McMullin, Paul Ricoeur, and Wenzel van Huyssteen are currently engaging my attention. (Ernan McMullin, "A Case for Scientific Realism," in Jarrett Leplin, ed., *Scientific Realism;* Paul Ricoeur, *The Rule of Metaphor: Multidisciplinary Studies of the Creation of Meaning in Language,* trans. by Robert Czerny et al. (Toronto: University of Toronto Press, 1977); Wenzel van Huyssteen, *Theology and the Justification*

of Faith: Constructing Theories in Systematic Theology, trans. H. F. Snijders (Grand Rapids: William B. Eerdmans Publishing Company, 1989, ch. 8).

57. Dean, *American Religious Empiricism,* pp. 12–14.

58. Richard Rorty, *Consequences of Pragmatism* (Minneapolis: University of Minnesota Press, 1982), p. xlii.

59. Wayne Proudfoot, *Religious Experience* (Berkeley: University of California Press, 1987), p. 154.

60. Ibid., p. 148.

61. Ibid., pp. 102, 222.

62. George A. Lindbeck, *The Nature of Doctrine: Religion and Theology in a Postliberal Age* (Philadelphia: The Westminster Press, 1984), p. 32. The phrase in single quotation marks is from William Christian.

63. George A. Lindbeck, *The Nature of Doctrine,* p. 33.

64. Ibid., p. 30.

65. Ibid., pp. 33–34.

66. Ibid., pp. 36–37.

67. Ibid., pp. 68–69.

68. Ibid., pp. 130–132.

69. Ibid., pp. 106, 131.

70. H. Richard Niebuhr, *The Responsible Self: An Essay in Christian Moral Philosophy* (New York: Harper & Row, Publishers, 1963), pp. 101–107, 117–118; Stephen Toulmin et al., *An Introduction to Reasoning* (New York: Macmillan Publishing Co., Inc., 1979), pp. 265–284; Michael Polanyi, *Personal Knowledge: Towards a Post-Critical Philosophy* (Chicago: The University of Chicago Press, 1958), pp. 49–131; *Science and Faith and Society* (Chicago: The University of Chicago Press, 1964), pp. 85–89; *The Tacit Dimension* (Gloucester, Mass.: Peter Smith, 1983), pp. 1–26.

71. Charles Harvey Arnold, *Near the Edge of Battle: A Short History of the Divinity School and the "Chicago School of Theology" 1866–1966* (Chicago: The Divinity School Association, 1966); Larry E. Axel, "Bernard Meland and the American Theological Tradition," in *Religion and Philosophy in the United States of America,* Vol. I (Essen: Die Blaue Eule, 1987), pp. 13–30; Larry Axel, "The 'Chicago School' of Theology and Henry Nelson Wieman," *Encounter,* Vol. 40 (Fall 1979), pp. 341–358; Larry Axel, "A New Turn in Religious Inquiry: Wieman, Creative Interchange and the Social Theologians," in John A. Broyer and William S. Minor, eds., *Creative Interchange* (Carbondale: Southern Illinois University Press, 1982), pp. 35–46;

Larry E. Axel, "Shailer Mathews and the Theology of Modernism: A Note to C. Peden's Essay" *URAM* 6:52–60, *Ultimate Reality and Meaning,* Vol. 8 (1985), pp. 299–303; William Dean, *American Religious Empiricism* (Albany: State University of New York Press, 1986), pp. 67–86; *History Making History: The New Historicism in American Religious Thought* (Albany: State University of New York Press, 1988), pp. 45–74, 111–122; Bernard E. Meland, "The Empirical Tradition in Theology at Chicago," in *The Future of Empirical Theology,* ed. by Bernard E. Meland (Chicago: The University of Chicago Press, 1969), pp. 1–62; "The New Realism in Religious Inquiry," *Encounter,* Vol. 31, No. 4 (Autumn 1970), pp. 311–324; *The Realities of Faith,* pp. 111–130; Henry Nelson Wieman and Bernard Eugene Meland, *American Philosophies of Religion* (Chicago: Willett, Clark & Company, 1936), pp. 272–308; Randolph Crump Miller, *The American Spirit in Theology* (Philadelphia: United Church Press, 1974), pp. 59–100; Creighton Peden, *The Chicago School: Voices in Liberal Religious Thought* (Bristol, Indiana: Wyndham Hall Press, Inc., 1987); Edgar A. Towne, "God and the Chicago School in the Theology of Bernard E. Meland," *American Journal of Theology and Philosophy,* Vol. 10, No. 1, (January 1989), pp. 3–20.

72. Susan Thistlethwaite, the church historian at Chicago Theological Seminary, in working with abused women, has struggled in a very personal way with the problem of how a white, middle-class, professional woman can relate to women of other ethnic groups and other income and occupational strata. In commenting on this to a meeting sponsored by the *American Journal of Theology and Philosophy* at a recent meeting of the American Academy of Religion, she has stated that women must realize that most of them stand with one foot among the powerful and one foot among the powerless. To do otherwise is to pretend a neutrality of interest and perception which is not only naive but dangerous. Her reflections were helpful to me and I am extending them, as I believe she would, to include all persons.

73. Hans-Georg Gadamer, *Philosophical Hermeneutics,* trans. and ed. by David E. Linge (Berkeley: University of California Press, 1976), pp. 3, 29, 62.

74. For Linge, see ibid. The translation of *Warheit und Methode,* edited by Garrett Barden and John Cumming, uses the term "prejudice." See Hans-Georg Gadamer, *Truth and Method* (New York: The Seabury Press, 1975), pp. 235–274.

75. Gadamer, *Truth and Method,* p. 244; *Philosophical Hermeneutics,* p. 9.

76. Gadamer, *Truth and Method,* p. 246.

77. Ibid., p. 263.

78. Ibid., pp. 264–265.

79. Ibid., p. 265.

80. Ibid., p. 266. For a similar point see Gunnar Myrdal, *An American Dilemma: The Negro Problem and American Democracy* (New York: Harper and Row, Publishers, 1962), pp. 1035–1064.

81. Gadamer, *Philosophical Hermeneutics,* p. 92. In his *Validity in Interpretation,* E. D. Hirsch criticizes Gadamer for providing no norm or criterion of validity in interpretation. But Gadamer is not as skeptical as Hirsch intimates. For Gadamer there are legitimate pre-judgments and it is the task of critical reason to separate them from illegitimate prejudices. It is a never-ending task, for the pre-judgments can be questioned, when brought to awareness, by the continued process of challenging them with other understandings. When understanding is seen as completable in principle, which Hirsch seems to do while Gadamer does not, then Hirsch's defense of such norms of validity in interpretation becomes urgent. But the solution to the Cartesian anxiety as to whether our present understanding will someday be reversed is not to be found in norms but in the courage to continue questioning. See E. D. Hirsch, Jr., *Validity in Interpretation* (New Haven: Yale University Press), pp. 46, 153, 245–264.

82. Gadamer, *Truth and Method,* pp. 492–493. William Dean sees Gadamer as seeking a method for guaranteeing truth in the human sciences. A support for Dean's interpretation is found in the last sentence of Gadamer's *Truth and Method,* affirming that "the discipline of questioning and research . . . guarantees truth" (Gadamer, *Truth and Method,* p. 447). However, this difficult passage may need to be construed in the context of the whole book. I take it that the infinity of questioning softens the meaning of "guarantees" to something like my anticipatory realism. (William Dean, *History Making History,* p. 27.)

83. Gadamer, *Truth and Method,* p. 250.

84. Ibid., pp. 250, 261.

85. Ibid., p. 262.

86. Ibid., pp. 267–268.

87. Ibid., p. 273.

88. Gadamer, *Philosophical Hermeneutics,* pp. 10, 94.

89. Henry Nelson Wieman, *Science Serving Faith,* ed. by Creighton Peden and Charles Willig (Atlanta: Scholars Press, 1987), p. 34.

90. Henry Nelson Wieman, *The Source of Human Good* (Carbondale: Southern Illinois University Press, 1946), p. 211.

91. Henry Nelson Wieman, *Seeking a Faith for a New Age,* ed. by Cedric L. Hepler (Metuchen, N.J.: The Scarecrow Press, Inc., 1975), p. 273.

92. Henry Nelson Wieman, *Religious Inquiry: Some Explorations* (Boston: Beacon Press, 1968), p. 30. Cp. p. 32.

93. Ibid., pp. 92–94.

94. Wieman, *Science Serving Faith*, p. 61.

95. Wieman, *Seeking a Faith for a New Age*, pp. 288–289. Charley Hardwick has brought out another dimension of Wieman's empiricism. Hardwick points out that for Wieman the knowledge of God occurs only in faith. This is correct. I have been concentrating on Wieman's theory of religious inquiry. Wieman does talk as if faith or openness is something which is essential to religious inquiry, but more of something preliminary to the specification and testing of the hypotheses. Hardwick's article would round out my discussion. Charley D. Hardwick, " 'Faith' in a Naturalistic Theology: Henry Nelson Wieman and American Radical Empiricism," in Peter Freese, ed., *Religion and Philosophy in the United States of America*, Vol. I, (Essen: Verlag Die Blaue Eule, 1987), p. 381.

96. Bernard E. Meland, *Faith and Culture* (London: George Allen and Unwin, Ltd., 1955), p. 43.

97. Bernard E. Meland, *The Realities of Faith: The Revolution in Cultural Forms* (New York: Oxford University Press, 1962), p. 210. For Meland on the rootedness of inquiry, see also his *Essays in Constructive Theology: A Process Perspective*, pp. 28, 48, 122–123.

98. Meland, *Faith and Culture*, p. 44, 95.

99. Ibid., pp. 84–85. For further discussion of the question of "the capacity for adequately apprehending" the objective realities which transcend us, see Bernard E. Meland, *Essays in Constructive Theology: A Process Perspective*, p. 86.

100. Meland, *Realities of Faith*, p. 93.

101. Meland, *Faith and Culture*, p. 187.

102. Meland, *Realities of Faith*, pp. 208–209.

103. Ibid., p. 223; Meland, *Faith and Culture*, pp. 6–7. For a helpful perspective on the rootedness of human thought, see Albert Memmi, *The Colonizer and the Colonized*, trans. by Howard Greenfeld (Boston: Beacon Press, 1967).

104. Meyer H. Abrams, *The Mirror and the Lamp: Romantic Theory and the Critical Tradition* (Oxford: Oxford University Press, 1953).

105. Friedrich Schleiermacher, *The Christian Faith*, trans. by H. R. Mackintosh and J. S. Stewart (Edinburgh: T. & T. Clark, 1928), pp. 7, 118.

106. Langdon Gilkey, *Naming the Whirlwind: The Renewal of God-Language* (Indianapolis: The Bobbs-Merrill Company, Inc., 1969), pp. 415–470; Langdon Gilkey, *Religion and the Scientific Future: Reflections on Myth, Science, and Theology* (New York: Harper & Row, Publishers), pp. 101–136; Sally McFague, *Models of God: Theology for an Ecological, Nuclear Age* (Philadelphia: Fortress Press, 1987); Paul Ricoeur, *The Conflict of Interpretations*, pp. 269–499; Paul Ricoeur, *Du Texte à l'action: Essais d'hermeneutique, II* (Paris: Editions du Seuil, 1986); Paul Ricoeur, *Essays on Biblical Interpretation;* Paul Ricoeur, *Hermeneutics in the Human Sciences: Essays on Language, Action, and Interpretation,* ed. and trans. by John B. Thompson (Cambridge: Cambridge University Press, 1981), pp. 131–195; Paul Ricoeur, *Interpretation Theory,* pp. 45–70; Paul Ricoeur, *The Philosophy of Paul Ricoeur: An Anthology of His Work,* ed. by Charles E. Reagan and David Stewart (Boston: Beacon Press, 1978), pp. 36–58, 134–148, 223–246; Paul Ricoeur, *Semeia* 4, pp. 75–145; Paul Ricoeur, *The Symbolism of Evil,* pp. 347–357; Wentzel van Huyssteen, *Theology and the Justification of Faith,* pp. 132–197; Janet Martin Soskice, *Metaphor and Religious Language* (Oxford: Clarendon Press, 1985).

107. Origen, *De Principiis,* iv, ii, 4; John Calvin, *Comm. Rom.* 1:19, *Calvini Opera* XLIX, 23 c; *Comm. 1 Cor., Calvini Opera* XLIX, 337d; Edward A. Dowey, Jr., *The Knowledge of God in Calvin's Theology* (New York: Columbia University Press, 1952), pp. 3–17; Wilhelm Pauck, "Introduction," *Luther: Lectures on Romans* (Philadelphia: The Westminster Press, 1961), pp. xxiv–xxxiv.

108. See especially Gilkey, *Religion and the Scientific Future* Chap. II–IV; Langdon Gilkey, *Naming the Whirlwind,* Part II.

109. Henry Nelson Wieman, *Science Serving Faith,* pp. 99–100, 190; Henry Nelson Wieman, *Religious Inquiry: Some Explorations* (Boston: Beacon Press, 1968), p. 30, 32.

110. John Dewey, "Philosophy and Civilization" in *Art as Experience* (New York: G. P. Putnam's Sons, 1958); Langdon Gilkey, *Naming the Whirlwind,* pp. 305–306.

111. Wieman, *Science Serving Faith,* pp. 143–152.

112. William Ernest Hocking, *The Meaning of God in Human Experience: A Philosophic Study of Religion* (New Haven: Yale University Press, 1912), pp. 405–427; Bernard Meland, *Faith and Culture,* pp. 93–94.

Chapter Five. A Dialogue with Alternative Visions

1. It would seem that the three modalities are necessity, possibility, and impossibility. However, the term "possibility" is ambiguous. It can be

used in an *inclusive* sense to include necessity. This is the way the term is normally used in modal logic, when the possibility operator '◇p' is defined as '~□~p'. It can be used in an *exclusive* sense to exclude necessity. In this sense it is equivalent (in many contexts) to 'contingent'. This is Hartshorne's frequent usage. See Charles Hartshorne, *The Logic of Perfection and Other Essays in Neoclassical Metaphysics* (LaSalle, Ill.: Open Court Publishing Company, 1962), *inter alia*, pp. 56, 103–104. I shall be using "possibility" in the exclusive sense of "it is possible that 'p' and it is possible that not 'p'," symbolized as "◇A • ◇~A."

2. Ibid., p. 56.

3. Ibid., p. 103.

4. Ibid., pp. 65, 103–104.

5. Ibid., pp. 95–96.

6. John Hick, *Arguments for the Existence of God* (New York: The Seabury Press, 1971), p. 92.

7. Hartshorne, *The Logic of Perfection,* pp. 68, 93.

8. Ibid., pp. 68–69.

9. Charles Hartshorne, *A Natural Theology for Our Time* (LaSalle, Ill., Open Court Publishing Company, 1967), pp. 85–86.

10. Hartshorne, *The Logic of Perfection,* p. 39.

11. Ibid., pp. 38–39.

12. Charles Hartshorne, *The Divine Relativity: A Social Concept of God* (New Haven: Yale University Press, 1948), pp. 32–33, 87.

13. Hartshorne, *A Natural Theology,* pp. 49, 53.

14. Ibid., p. 50.

15. Ibid., p. 54.

16. Ibid., p. 57. For Hartshorne's discussion of moving from dichotomies to trichotomies, see Charles Hartshorne, *Creative Synthesis and Philosophic Method* (LaSalle: The Open Court Publishing Co., 1970), pp. 99–101.

17. Hartshorne, *A Natural Theology,* p. 45.

18. Ibid., p. 46.

19. Schubert Ogden, *The Reality of God and Other Essays* (New York: Harper & Row, Publishers, 1966), pp. 33–34.

20. Ibid., p. 141.

21. Alan Gewirth, *Reason in Morality* (Chicago: The University of Chicago Press, 1978), pp. 171, 198.

22. Ogden, *The Reality of God,* pp. 140, 142.

23. Ibid., p. 33.

24. Ibid., p. 35.

25. Ibid., p. 33.

26. Ibid., pp. 41–42.

27. Albert Camus, *The Myth of Sisyphus and Other Essays,* trans. by Justin O'Brien (New York: Random House, Inc., 1955), p. 16.

28. Much of this treatment of Gilkey has appeared in my "What Religious Naturalism Can Learn from Langdon Gilkey: Uncovering the Dimension of Ultimacy," in *God, Values, and Empiricism,* ed. by Creighton Peden and Larry E. Axel (Macon: Mercer University Press, 1990).

29. This list sounds provincially Protestant. *Mea culpa!*

30. Langdon Gilkey, *Naming the Whirlwind: The Renewal of God-language* (Indianapolis: The Bobbs-Merrill Company, 1969), pt. 2; *Religion and the Scientific Future: Reflections on Myth, Science and Theology* (New York: Harper & Row, Publishers, 1970), chs. 2–4. For brevity I am omitting Gilkey's brief discussion of temporality; also his very rich treatment of historicity in *Reaping the Whirlwind: A Christian Interpretation of History* (New York: The Seabury Press, 1976), esp. chapter 2. We do not have the space to elaborate Gilkey's use of Augustine, Heidegger, Kuhn, Lonergan, Polanyi, Rahner, Toulmin, and, above all, Tillich. See esp. Gilkey's *Gilkey on Tillich* (Los Angeles: Crossroads Press, 1990). For a segment of my own naturalistic critical interpretation of Tillich's notion of *agape* as a moral norm, see my "A Tillichian Contribution to Contemporary Moral Philosophy," in *Being and Doing: Paul Tillich as Ethicist,* ed. John J. Carey (Macon, GA: Mercer University Press, 1987).

31. See Gilkey's reference to Reinhold Niebuhr in *Naming the Whirlwind,* p. 321n.

32. See Martin Heidegger, *Being and Time,* pp. 182–195.

33. Gilkey, *Naming the Whirlwind,* p. 409.

34. Gilkey, *Religion and the Scientific Future,* pp. 48–49.

35. Ibid., p. 57.

36. Ibid., p. 58.

37. Ibid., pp. 60–62.

38. Gilkey, *Naming the Whirlwind*, p. 306.

39. Langdon Gilkey, *Reaping the Whirlwind: A Christian Interpretation of History* (New York: The Seabury Press, 1976), chapter 12. For Gilkey's response to my own position, see his reply to my "The Viability of Religious Naturalism," forthcoming in the *American Journal of Theology and Philosophy*.

40. Camus, *The Myth of Sisyphus*, pp. 13, 16, 27, 45–46.

41. Oliver W. Holmes, Jr., *Collected Legal Papers*, p. 310.

42. Albert Camus, *The Stranger*. For the affirmation of meaning in a meaningless situation, which I take to be the limiting case of a one-sided transaction, see Viktor Frankl, *Man's Search for Meaning: An Introduction to Logotherapy*, trans. by Ilse Lasch (New York: Simon and Schuster, 1962).

43. Albert Camus, *The Rebel: An Essay on Man in Revolt*, trans. by Anthony Bower (New York: Random House, 1956), pp. 3–22, 279–306.

44. Albert Camus, *The Plague*, trans. by Stuart Gilbert (New York: Random House, 1948).

45. *Humanist Manifestos I and II* (Buffalo: Prometheus Books, 1973).

46. Ibid., p. 7.

47. For helpful treatments of humanism, see: Paul Beattie, "Humanism: Secular or Religious," *Free Inquiry*, Vol. I (Winter 1980–1981), pp. 11–13; Jerome D. Frank, "Nature and Functions of Belief Systems: Humanism and Transcendental Religion," *American Psychologist* (July 1977), pp. 555–559; Robert J. Hutcheon, *Humanism in Religion Examined* (no date or publisher, secured through the library of Meadville Theological School); Cassius J. Keyser, "Humanism and Pseudo-Humanism," *The Hibbert Journal*, 29 (Jan. 1931), pp. 227–238; William P. King, ed., *Humanism: Another Battle Line*, containing "The Vicissitudes of a Noble Word" by Hough, "Contemporary Humanism," by Douglas Clyde Macintosh, "Can We Have Religion without God," by Shailer Mathews (Nashville: Cokesbury Press, 1931); Paul Kurtz, ed., *The Humanist Alternative: Some Definitions of Humanism* (Buffalo: Prometheus Books, 1973); Donald H. Meyer, "Secular Transcendence: The American Religious Humanists," *American Quarterly*.

48. *Humanist Manifestos* I and II, p. 9.

49. Ibid., p. 15.

50. Ibid.

51. Ibid., p. 16.

52. Ibid., p. 10.

53. Ibid., p. 14.

54. Ibid.

55. Ibid., pp. 17–18; cp. p. 22.

56. Ibid., pp. 16, 23.

57. Ibid., pp. 8–9, 11–12.

58. Ibid., pp. 17, 18 (emphasis in *Manifestos*).

59. Ibid., p. 19.

60. John Dewey, *The Public and Its Problems* (Chicago: The Swallow Press, Inc., 1927), p. 148; *Democracy and Civilization, Middle Works* Vol. IX, Chap. VII, Sec. 1. For a finely balanced treatment of Dewey's "activism," see Bob Pepperman Taylor, "John Dewey and Environmental Thought," *Environmental Ethics,* Vol. 12, No. 2 (Summer 1990), pp. 175–184.

61. John Dewey, *Human Nature and Conduct* (Madison, WI: US Armed Forces Institute, 1944), pp. 262–263.

62. John Dewey, *A Common Faith* (New Haven: Yale University Press, 1963), p. 42.

63. Ibid., pp. 47–48.

64. Ibid., pp. 52, 54.

65. Ibid., p. 53.

66. Gordon D. Kaufman, *An Essay on Theological Method,* rev. ed. (Missoula, MT: Scholars Press, 1979), pp. 11, 13.

67. Gordon D. Kaufman, *The Theological Imagination: Constructing the Concept of God* (Philadelphia: The Westminster Press, 1981), p. 22.

68. Kaufman, *Essay on Theological Method,* pp. 11, 13.

69. Kaufman, *Theological Imagination,* p. 52.

70. Ibid., pp. 50, 41.

71. Ibid., p. 50. For amplification of my critique of Kaufman, see my contribution to *New Essays in Religious Naturalism,* Larry Axel and Creighton Peden, Eds. (Macon, GA: Mercer University Press, forthcoming).

72. Mark C. Taylor, "Toward an Ontology of Relativism" and "Interpreting Interpretation," in *Deconstructing Theology* (New York and Chico, CA: The Crossroad Publishing Company & Scholars Press, 1982), pp. 45–85.

73. Mark C. Taylor, *Erring: A Postmodern A/theology* (Chicago: The University of Chicago Press, 1984), p. 7.

74. Ibid., p. 103.

75. Ibid., p. 106. The quotation is from Jacques Derrida, *Dissemination*, trans. by B. Johnson (Chicago: The University of Chicago Press, 1981), p. 77.

76. Taylor, *Erring*, pp. 108–109.

77. Ibid., pp. 19–33, 97–120.

78. After his survey of some recent movements in Hebrew Bible interpretation, Dean points out, with approval, that the historicism of these movements includes the affirmations that the past signified contributes to and places limits on the present interpretation and its viability. Thus subjectivistic and relativistic nihilism are denied. I take this to be a major point in Dean's departure from deconstruction. It is a point which Dean needs to emphasize. William Dean, *History Making History*, p. 42.

79. Taylor, *Erring*, pp. 34–51, 121–148.

80. George Herbert Mead, *Mind, Self and Society from the Standpoint of a Social Behaviorist*, ed. by Charles W. Morris (Chicago: The University of Chicago Press, 1934); George Herbert Mead, *Selected Writings*, ed. by Andrew J. Reck, chaps. VII–XII (Indianapolis: The Bobbs-Merrill Company, Inc., 1964); Robert C. Neville, *Recovery of the Measure: Interpretation and Nature* (Albany: State University of New York Press, 1989).

81. Taylor, *Erring*, pp. 52–73, 149–169.

82. William Dean, *American Religious Empiricism*, pp. 56–63, 67–71; Shirley Jackson Case, *The Christian Philosophy of History* (Chicago: The University of Chicago Press, 1943), especially the last chapter; Case, "The Religious Meaning of the Past," *The Journal of Religion*, IV, 1924, pp. 576–591; Case, "Whither Historicism in Theology?," *The Process of Religions: Essays in Honor of Dean Shailer Mathews*, ed. by M. H. Krumbine (New York: The Macmillan Co., 1933), pp. 52–71; William J. Hynes, *Shirley Jackson Case and the Chicago School* (Chico, CA: Scholars Press, 1981).

83. Taylor, *Erring*, p. 151.

84. William Dean, *American Religious Empiricism*, p. 41; William Dean, *History Making History*, pp. 7, 42, 131; John Dewey, *Logic: The Theory of Inquiry, The Later Works*, XII, *1938*, Chapter VI, "The Common Pattern of Inquiry," Ed. by Kathleen Poulos (Carbondale & Edwardsville: Southern Illinois University Press, 1986); Nancy Frankenberry, *Religion and Radical Empiricism*, pp. 187–192.

85. Taylor, *Erring*, p. 151.

86. Ibid., p. 176. The quotation is from Friedrich Nietzsche, *The Will To Power*, trans. by Walter Kaufmann (New York: Random House, 1966), p. 317.

87. Sri Aurobindo, *Arya* (New York: The Greystone Press, 1949), pp. 764–765; in Sarvepalli Radhakrishnan and Charles A. Moore, *A Sourcebook in Indian Philosophy* (Princeton: Princeton University Press, 1957), pp. 578–579.

88. Taylor, *Erring,* p. 156.

89. Ibid., p. 147.

90. William Dean has a different analysis and evaluation of Taylor. Dean sees, correctly I believe, that Taylor has the potential for a process-relational naturalistic theism. Dean's main point is that Taylor never moves from his methodological stance of deconstruction to develop his implicit naturalism. As Dean sees it, Taylor remains at "the level of a deconstructive negativity . . . that by itself is not ineluctably theological." Instead of pushing "through to a positive notion of God," Taylor "dissolves his notion of God into pure methodology. . . . What is the theologian to do, but . . . to talk simply about the method of erring itself?" (William Dean, *History Making History,* p. 136). Although Dean's analysis of Taylor's problem focuses on his methodologism (or anti-methodologism), I am in essential agreement with the thrust of Dean's comments.

INDEX

Absolute: achievement, 39; criticism of, 47; false, 188; yearning for, 187

Absurdity, 192–196; ambiguity in, 180; Camus, Albert, 180–181; positivistic, 178

Acceptance: community of, 184; need for, 184

Accusation, 74–76

Agape, 80, 98, 100

Agnosticism, ix, 32

Agreement: definitional, 151; observational, 151

Alexander, Samuel, 49, 50, 209, 212

Alienation, 3, 4, 5, 192; and despair, 215

Allah, 23, 102

Ambiguity, ix; in absurdity, 180; divine, 20, 64; of freedom, 182

Ames, Edward, 42, 52–54, 55, 143

Anselm, 11

Anthropocentrism, 151

Anthropology, philosophical, 74

Anthropomorphism, 53, 57, 58

Antitheism, xi, 54, 55, 56

Anxiety: Cartesian, 111, 241n81; of finitude, 36

Apathy, 107, 109; protective, 108

Apocalypticism, 22

Appreciation: aesthetic, 125; sensitive, 83

Aquinas, 11

Arguments, cosmological, 29

Aristotle, 26, 103; rational consciousness, 122

Atheism, 74

A/theology, 210–214; deconstructive, 211

Augustine, 11, 107, 181, 210

Aurobindo, Sri, 101, 214

Authority: political, 54; religious, 9, 30

Autonomy, 219n2; in healing, 184; respect for, 86; ultimacy in, 183–184; vs. theonomy, 228n81

Awareness: aesthetic, 125; appreciative, 58, 89, 112. See also Discernment, sensitive; of ultimacy, 160

Bacon, Francis, 145

Baha' u'llah, 9

Barbour, Ian, 118, 159

Barth, Karl, 70, 150

Beauty: in esthetic realm, 79; pursuit, 72

Being: benevolence to, 96–97; courage in, 106; existence, 170; experience, 183; limited significance, 205; necessary, 29, 76; necessity of a Perfect, 172, 173; power of, 78; supreme, 57; universal community of, 96; value of, x; without bias, 149

Belief: in equality, 93; justifying, 30; religious, 24

Bergson, Henri, 49, 50, 158; concept of intuition, 116–117; radical empiricism, 6, 112, 115–118

Bernstein, Richard, 111

Beyond Objectivism and Relativism (Bernstein), 111

Bhagavad Gita, 102, 214

251

sity, 170–178; criticism, 181; Modal
Arguments, 28; pursuit of meaning, 82
Healing: autonomy in, 184; in defeat,
34; resources, 18, 20, 77, 113
Hegel, Georg, 49, 77, 103, 157, 210, 213;
organicism, 73
Heidegger, Martin, 103
Henotheism, 88, 91, 92, 93, 96; natural-
istic, 89
Hick, John, 173, 175
Hinduism: triadic schema, 23; view of
ahimsa, 101
History Making History (Dean), 212
Holmes, Oliver Wendell, Jr., 105, 193
Honesty, intellectual, 32
Hope, 67, 179–180; Biblical symbols,
76; faith displaced by, 228n69; pa-
thology, 77; realism of, 130; thinking
according to, 74, 75
Horizons, of ultimacy, 182
Hughes, Chief Justice Charles Evans, 92
Humanism, ix, xi, 73, 89, 196–202,
246n47; criticism, 56; religious, 6;
secular, 9, 101
Humanist Manifestos, 196–202
Hume, David, 6, 41–42; on attributes
of Deity, 41; on revelation, 70; skepti-
cism, 72
Hypocrisy, 91
Hypotheses: emergence, 149; testing,
112, 149

Ideal: ambiguous, 17; causing estrangement, 213; challenging, 11, 12, 16, 17,
83, 112, 203; continually transcendent, 32; contrasting, 25; ethical,
198; fanatical, 17; God as standard,
53; non-moral, 72; proximate, 188;
reconstruction, 203; unattainable,
203; unity, 105, 205–207
Idealism, personalistic, 63–64
Ideal Transcendent, 17
Idolatry, 182, 190; absolute, 184; avoiding, 215; in monotheism, 15; myth
in, 183
Ihde, Don, 228n69
Imagination, 205; idealizing existence,
206; metaphysical, 32; mythological,
32; projection of God in, 73, 207–210;
role, 50

Immanence: transcendent elements,
60, 112
Immortality, 72; postulated, 75
Impossibility, 171, 243n1; existential, 172
Infinite, search for, 188
Infinity, 67
Inhumanity, 184
Inquiry: cognitive, 160, 182, 185, 191; in
creativity, 161; critical, 124; empirical, 58, 111, 142–156, 149–153; historical rootedness, 99, 111, 154, 155;
language, 20, 111, 118, 152, 157–167;
myth in, 154; objects, 131; principles,
150; process, 131; rational, 82, 125;
reflective, 38, 81; religious, 71, 149,
151, 152, 153, 238n54, 242n95; role of
experience, 139; scientific, 114, 185,
204; socio-historical, 167; theoretical,
82; unconditional basis, 82
Instrumentalism, 132
Intellectualization, 51
Intelligence, 69; critical, ix; finiteness,
203; limited function, 117; self-
delusion in, 203, 204; vs. intuition, 118
Intelligible Religion (Phenix), 66
Intent: partial, 90; pseudo-universal,
88; universal, 87–90, 94, 95
Interaction: creative, 152; localized,
176; personal, 183; selves, 57; univer-
sal, 176
Intervention, positive lack of, 134
Introduction to Metaphysics
(Bergson), 115
Intuition, 116; form of reflection, 117;
testing, 116; vs. intelligence, 116, 118
Irrationalism, 114, 116, 117, 118, 141,
192; experience of, 66
Isolation, 184
"Is Theism Essential to Religion?"
(Smith, G.), 54, 118

James, William, 25, 41, 42, 45–48, 49,
50, 51, 71, 115, 222n22; alternative
schemas, 26; radical empiricism, 6;
on structure of religion, 24
Jesus, 99–100, 102, 107
Joy: in community, 183; in existence,
190; experiences of, 34–35